ENDORSEMENTS

"One of the traditions of the Air Force Academy is a program called the Legacy Class Program wherein the newest class is paired with the class that graduated 50 years before them. This pairing begins with the arrival of the new class and grows through the four years until graduation and beyond. Since the inception of the program this pairing has taken several different forms and resulted in many lasting relationships. The Class of 1973 has taken the program to a new level with the assimilation and publication of a book "Becoming Leaders of Character: Conversations with the U.S. Air Force Academy Class of 1973."

The stories in the book reflect the make-up and accomplishments of the Class of 1973...self-described as the "Illustrious Class of 1973." In several ways it was a watershed class...the members entered in 1969, came from the society of the 60's with the anti-war movements and protests. It was the first Academy class to not participate in the Vietnam War... their wars would come later in their careers.

This book is important for a couple of reasons, but primarily because it focuses on the sole purpose of the Academy...to produce leaders of character. The book is a compendium of stories told by members of the Class of '73 as they look back on the fifty years since their graduation. The reflections actually start with their arrival at the Academy and introduction to cadet life. They describe role played by living under the Honor Code and learning how the Core Values became the path to developing leaders of character. Through the stories the importance of the Core Values in developing a moral compass to guide them on the path to becoming leaders of character is shown.

Included are first person accounts from those who rose to highest leadership positions within the Air Force and public and private life. A Chief of Staff of the Air Force, numerous flag officers, CEOs, the Hero on the Hudson and those who left the military and public life to pursue other interests provide their personal perspectives on what went into their becoming leaders of character. When the stories are told and one reflects on what it takes to be recognized and respected as a leader it boils down to three ingredients: Courage, Competency, and Character. The courage to do what is right, the competency to meet the requirements of the task at hand and the character to embrace the core values of Integrity, Service Before Self and Excellence.

The class of '73 has dedicated this book to the Class of 2023, to prospective cadets, to the families of the members of the Class of 73 and to those aspiring to leadership in their organizations and communities. This book should be part of any professional reading program."

GENERAL RONALD FOGLEMAN
United States Air Force Academy (USAFA) Class of 1963,
former history professor, and first USAFA graduate to
serve as the 15th Chief of Staff, United States Air Force:

"It has been several generations since we have so desperately needed a book like the Class of 1973's *Becoming Leaders of Character*. The rate and complexity of change remains in a cycle of constant acceleration. To meet the challenges of our evolving world, we need leaders prepared to adapt and succeed in conditions with limited historical parallels. The return of great power competition, emergence of new technologies like artificial intelligence on the battlefield, and generational conceptions of service are all converging to create profoundly complex environments in which to lead. We must win but must do so with character and within frameworks based on ethics and honor. This book will serve as an exceptional guide for those willing to accept the challenges of this critical time for our country, and the world."

MAJOR GENERAL (VSM) MARK ANARUMO, PH.D.
President, Norwich University, former Director and Permanent Professor for the USAFA Center for Character and Leadership Development

"The legendary Brigadier General George A. Lincoln USA (Ret) famously said of his alma mater (USMA 1929) *"The engraving on monuments of stone and bronze does not mark achievement. Only the engraving on the character and competence of our cadets and our young officers counts toward the fulfillment of our mission."* Nearly 100 years later, amongst USAFA's static displays, and monuments of marble, bronze and glass, this guiding principle is even more crucial for our Academy as so brilliantly expressed in the Class of *1973's Becoming Leaders of Character."*

BRIGADIER GENERAL DANA BORN
United States Air Force, Retired; USAFA Dean #9, 2004-2013; Class of 1983; Chair, Senior Executive Fellows (SEF) Program Faculty; Advisor, Black Family Graduate Fellows; Lecturer in Public Policy, HARVARD Kennedy School of Government

Becoming Leaders of Character: Conversations with the U.S. Air Force
Academy Class of 1973

Copyright 2022 © by Michael L. Mosier
(Alliance Publishing and Media, LLC)

Printed in the United States of America

10 9 8 7 6 5 4 3 2 1

ISBN-13: 978-1-7320596-8-9(Paper Back)

ISBN-13: 978-1-7320596-9-6 (eBook)

Published by Alliance Publishing and Media, LLC

Bulk orders of this book may be obtained by contacting Alliance
Publishing and Media, LLC at: www.alliancepressmedia.net.

Alliance Publishing and Media, LLC
409-234-3949
admin@alliancepressmedia.net

DEDICATION

To the Class of 2023, with the expectation that the Core Values will continue to guide you on your journey toward becoming leaders of character.

To prospective cadets, that our experiences may inspire you to join the tradition of the Long Blue Line.

To our families, to provide you with a greater understanding of the events that shaped and inspired us.

And to those aspiring to leadership in their organizations and communities. Your service will make our Nation stronger.

TABLE OF CONTENTS

Foreword.. xi
Preface... xv
Introduction xvii

PART I: BECOMING THE CLASS OF 1973.....................1
   1. The Journey Begins 3
   2. Formative Years At The Academy........................... 20

PART II: BECOMING LEADERS OF CHARACTER 83
   3. Our Early Careers 85
   4. The Core Values: A Watershed Moment............................ 103

PART III: APPLYING THE CORE VALUES 111
   5. Integrity First.. 113
   6. Service Before Self 132
   7. Excellence In All We Do 141

**PART IV: LEADERS OF CHARACTER FROM AN INSTITUTIONAL
PERSPECTIVE 153**
   8. An Air Force Chief Of Staff's Perspective.................... 155
   9. A Superintendent's Perspective 163
   10. A Majcom Commander's Perspective 169
   11. An Air And Space Forces Association
       President's Perspective.. 180
   12. A Joint Agency Perspective................................. 189
   13. The Adjutant General's Perspective 195

PART V: LEADERS OF CHARACTER IN MOMENTS OF CRISIS........209

14. Desert Storm And Secret Squirrel....................................211
15. Crisis At The Edge Of Space 217
16. Peering Behind The Iron Curtain 226
17. Rescue From The Frigid Waters 236
18. From Fighter Pilot To Infantry Platoon Sergeant 243
19. Professional Competence And The Unexpected............... 252

PART VI: A LIFETIME OF SERVICE 261

20. From The Academy To The Boardroom 263
21. The Road To Senior Executive Service............................. 269
22. From Air Force Officer To Catholic Priest 283
23. Relationships Matter.. 289
24. Medicine And Leadership 301
25. Choosing The Harder Right 306
26. Community Leadership 315
27. Investing In Character... 324
28. Character In The Courtroom 334
29. Leadership In Public Education..................................... 342
30. Remember Your Roots 354

PART VII: UPON REFLECTION 363

Conclusion 397

APPENDICES

Appendix A: Taking Responsibility:
    A Message To Cadets In Retrospect............................ 399
Appendix B: The Honor Code And The Class Of 1973 407
Appendix C: A Short History Of
    The United States Air Force Academy 415
Appendix D: "Bring Me Men" News Article
    By Rocky Mountain News, June 1964 418

Acknowledgments 421

FOREWORD

Early on the morning of June 23, 1969, my parents dropped me off at the Base of the Ramp at the Air Force Academy and bid me a final farewell. I eagerly bounded up the Ramp to join my future classmates— as young and naive as we all were—as a member of the future "Illustrious" Class of 1973.

We weren't an "illustrious" class in those days—far from it. We still faced a long, hard summer before being accepted as cadets. And it would be another four years of grueling academics, intense military training, and physical challenges before we received our commissions as second lieutenants in the world's greatest Air Force. Even then we couldn't consider our class "illustrious." We were just beginning the journey toward becoming leaders of character in the active-duty U.S. Air Force. There were hard lessons to learn, scar tissue to build up, and a broader perspective to gain—things that only come with time. More than 50 years later, I can now say that our class is often referred to as "The Illustrious Class of 1973." I credit that not just to longevity, but to the values we learned at the Academy, our collective hard work and dedicated service, and a determined effort to live honorable lives, both in and out of the Air Force.

One thing we've learned over the years—and what you'll see reflected in the stories and vignettes in this book—is that career satisfaction goes beyond attaining rank or position. Instead, satisfaction is derived from helping others and serving something bigger than yourself. The reality is that one doesn't have to be an Academy graduate or a career officer to serve our great country; in fact, many of our classmates left the Air Force after fulfilling their initial commitment. As you'll read in this book, service opportunities abound in America in all walks of life. And, just as in the Air Force and the Space Force, our Nation's professions and institutions have a desperate need for honorable, selfless, and principled leadership—leadership that builds and sustains our society. Perhaps most significantly, the Core Values you'll read about here are essential elements of that principled leadership and are therefore relevant to anyone who picks up this book.

To the Class of 2023: when you raised your right hands and took the oath of office, you made a deliberate decision to become defenders of our great Nation. It doesn't matter what part of the country you came from, how much money you have or don't have, what sex or race you are, or what your parents did or did not do. Your fellow citizens depend on your willingness to defend this Nation against all enemies foreign or domestic, and to support and defend our great Constitution. It won't be an easy life. As at the Academy, your time in the Air Force and Space Force will be marked by difficult training and demanding education. You'll end up moving many times, sometimes to dangerous parts of the world. There will be times when you'll be tired, scared, uncomfortable, and missing your family back home. But know this: you'll be serving a noble cause alongside other great Americans. While you'll be forced out of your comfort zone time and time again, as a defender you'll never stop growing as a human being and as a leader. You'll get to do things that you've not dreamed of, because our great military lets ordinary people do extraordinary things.

Fifty years have passed since my classmates and I eagerly took those first steps from the Base of the Ramp to lives of service. *Becoming Leaders of Character* chronicles our journey along the way. It's an important story, not because we did everything perfectly, but because of our continuing determination and commitment to lead honorable lives.

It's our hope that these examples will inspire others as we pass the sword to a new generation.

Stephen R. Lorenz
General, USAF (Ret.)

PREFACE

Writing is in our blood.

During our four years at the Air Force Academy, we slaved over too many papers to count—some written over a period of days and weeks, and some the night before the paper was due (hence the cynical cadet mantra, "If the deadline weren't soon enough, it wouldn't be the deadline"). Once we graduated, our Air Force writing took the form of countless staff studies, detailed analyses, and position papers. But what you'll see in these pages is different. What you'll see here is not so much objective and quantitative analysis; it's more the result of backward glances, thoughtful introspection, and even emotion.

Several years ago, our class officers began to consider what we might be able to leave to our legacy Class of 2023—those graduating exactly 50 years after us—that would be meaningful to them as they began their careers of service. A congratulatory party? Hearty handshakes and best wishes? Gold second lieutenant bars? After a great deal of consideration, our class decided to offer lessons learned during our years of service, both in and out of the Air Force. This was the genesis for *Becoming Leaders of Character*. We're under no illusions here; we don't presume to have all the answers, nor have we necessarily made the best decisions in all circumstances. But, in the end, the true value of lessons learned is in that realization.

What age takes away in physical strength, it generously replaces with hard-earned perspective. *Becoming Leaders of Character* is our attempt to pass that perspective along, and we sincerely hope it resonates—not only with our legacy class, but with whomever might aspire to lead.

INTRODUCTION

As our legacy Class of 2023 approaches graduation and their new lives as Air Force and Space Force officers, there's a great deal of excitement and anticipation. But, while the new graduates have all imagined what lies ahead, the future and their role in it remains largely unknown. On the other hand, for the Class of 1973, the story of our professional lives has been largely written.

It's a legitimate question to ask: "Why is it important to know what the Class of 1973's experience has been?" After all, nearly all aspects of the Academy experience have greatly evolved between 1973 and 2023—from academics to technology to military training. Even more fundamentally, our class was all male, and we lacked the more diverse demographic that characterizes the Air Force Academy Class of 2023. Furthermore, there are significant differences between daily life in the Academy of 1973 and the Academy of 2023. We marched to the parade field down the "Bring Me Men" Ramp. Sijan Hall was called the "New Dorm." There was no Center for Character and Leadership Development with the spectacular glass spire pointing toward the North Star. We didn't have to deal with the challenges and hardships of a global pandemic—no social and emotional isolation, quarantines, Zoom classes, or uncertain futures. But the relevance of our experience lies in the common experiences that all Academy graduates share. We all walked onto the Terrazzo with some degree of apprehension, not really knowing what to expect. We suffered through the trials and tribulations of the fourth-class system. We spent four years under continual pressure, operating on little sleep. We pulled "all-nighters," writing last-minute papers and cramming for finals. We all faced challenges with new and unfamiliar responsibilities. And, through it all, we experienced the highs and lows of youth.

This book is organized around the three Core Values that define service in the Air and Space Forces: Integrity First, Service Before Self, and Excellence in All We Do. *Becoming Leaders of Character* uses a story-telling methodology to impart hard-earned lessons accumulated over many years of service; the stories presented here are intended to provide texture and nuance to what might otherwise be a collection of dry biographies. But this is not a "how-to" book on leadership; rather, it's about our experiences, both good and bad.

Some stories you'll read were contributed by well-known classmates, like former Air Force Chief of Staff General Nort Schwartz and Captain Sully Sullenberger of "Miracle on the Hudson" fame. Others were submitted by lesser-known classmates, but with equally powerful messages: you'll learn how character and leadership were tested in a perilous rescue of helpless survivors of a burning ship in the Gulf of Alaska, a series of dangerous Cold War missions in East Germany, and a complex effort to rescue an Afghani family from the hands of the Taliban following the withdrawal from Afghanistan. You'll even be asked to consider how you'd respond to a moral dilemma at the top of Mount Everest. Taken together, each story provides critical insight into leadership under the most difficult circumstances.

It's important to note that becoming a leader of character doesn't follow a linear path—it typically has twists and turns, with the occasional stumble along the way. Some of life's most enduring lessons are generated by failure, as much as by success. While *Becoming Leaders of Character* doesn't chronicle all our failures, those failures have inevitably contributed to the successes we've enjoyed. It's also important to remember that character isn't defined by how we fall, but rather by how we get up. As we discovered over the years, misfortune and failure—or, more important, how one deals with misfortune and failure—play a significant role in the continuing education of a leader of character.

This book is the result of a great deal of introspection. As a class, we have the advantage of being able to look back and see how our formative years at the Academy molded our character and guided us on our journey through life, during our time in the Air Force and in follow-on careers. This book is the compilation of history, introspection, and consideration of what was and what could have been.

To the legacy Class of 2023: While the times and circumstances that have shaped our journey may differ from yours, we will all stand together as you take your place in the Long Blue Line.

You're just beginning to write your story.

This is ours.

PART I

BECOMING THE
CLASS OF 1973

We came to Colorado's Front Range from all parts of the country to start our new lives as cadets at the United States Air Force Academy. Some of us were brought to the Base of the Ramp by anxious and proud parents; others were dropped off by well-wishing friends. Some of us were delivered by large silver-and-blue buses with "United States Air Force Academy" emblazoned on the sides. But, regardless of how we arrived, we were all transfixed by the large, awe-inspiring commandment in silver letters on the wide arch above the Ramp: "Bring Me Men."[1]

As we climbed the Ramp, suitcases in hand, we left the past behind and took our first tentative steps into a new world. At the top of the Ramp, the gleaming silver-and-glass buildings, broad, marble-striped

---

1 | "Bring me men to match my mountains. Bring me men to match my plains. Men with empires in their purpose. And new eras in their brains." *Bring Me Men to Match My Mountains*, Sam Walter Foss. See Appendix D, *Rocky Mountain News* article from June 1964.

Terrazzo, and spectacular Chapel with its 17 aluminum spires pointing toward the heavens lay before us, all nestled against steep forested green mountains and deep blue Colorado sky.

We didn't know what our futures would bring, but there was one thing we knew for sure:

This was our destiny.

1

THE JOURNEY BEGINS

You could have heard a pin drop.

After three days of long lines, shots in arms, uniform issue, short buzz haircuts, never-ending forms, and a mind-numbing battery of placement exams, we finally gathered in one place as a class. Herded into Arnold Hall Theater by stern-looking upperclassmen in light blue short-sleeved shirts, black-and-silver shoulder boards, wheel caps, and white gloves, we quietly sat in orderly rows, each lost in his own thoughts. The silence was ominous. We wondered: What next? Am I ready for this?

The heavy silence was broken as a tall man strode onto the center of the stage. He was an imposing figure: blue-green flight suit, sleeves rolled up to mid-forearm. Craggy face, square jaw, thick, rakish moustache, erect muscular frame. He walked back and forth with a deliberate pace, arms crossed, eyes studying our young faces intently. Then he stopped, put his hands on his hips, staring at us, as if daring us to move. Finally, he spoke.

"How many of you graduated in the top ten percent of your high school class?" he demanded in a gravelly voice.

Hands confidently shot up throughout the auditorium.

"How many of you were members of the National Honor Society?"

Again, hands raised high.

The staccato-like questions continued: "How many of you lettered in three or more sports? How many of you were class president? How many class valedictorians?"

With each new question, the show of hands throughout the auditorium remained impressive. Finally, he paused, his intense stare moving from face to face.

"Well, good for you," he growled. "But just look around. You may have been a big deal in your hometown, but here, you're just a face in the crowd. You're all starting from zero. If you're going to survive, you're going to have to prove yourself."

He paused again. "Look to your left. Now look to your right. One of the three of you won't make it to graduation."

He let that sink in. Then he continued, his tone softening a bit. "Okay, let me give you some advice. This next four years will be like trying to eat an elephant."

(Elephant? What?)

"Know how you eat an elephant?" He searched the confused faces. "I'll tell you: one bite at a time. Okay," he concluded, "now get to work." He turned on his heel and abruptly strode off the stage, leaving us in stunned silence.

That was our introduction to Brigadier General Robin Olds: legendary fighter pilot from two wars. Triple ace. Four MiG kills in Vietnam. And, most recently, commander of the 8th Tactical Fighter Wing, stationed at Ubon Royal Thai Air Force Base.

He was also the commandant at the United States Air Force Academy.

THE WINDS OF CHANGE

It would be difficult, if not impossible, to accurately describe the Class of 1973 without over-generalizing. To varying degrees, we reflected the complex and changing social fabric of late-1960s America, displaying equal measures of confidence and self-doubt, courage and uncertainty, idealism and cynicism. We came from varying backgrounds—some from Air Force families, some with no previous exposure to the military. Many of us came from big cities, others from the rural countryside. But, despite our individual differences, we all shared one common characteristic: we were young and passionate. And we believed in the ideals the Academy represented.

As a generation, we baby boomers were experiencing an awakening of social consciousness that demanded action on issues of growing urgency, from civil rights to the threat of nuclear war. The "generation gap," a term used to describe the growing divide between us and our WWII generation parents, was largely the result of a tectonic shift in the social, political, and cultural landscape of the 1960s. Two verses from Bob Dylan's 1964 song, "The Times They Are a Changin,'" illustrate the mood of the times:

> Come gather 'round people
> Wherever you roam
> And admit that the waters
> Around you have grown
> And accept it that soon
> You'll be drenched to the bone
> If your time to you is worth savin'
> And you better start swimmin'
> Or you'll sink like a stone
> For the times they are a-changin'

Come mothers and fathers
Throughout the land
And don't criticize
What you can't understand
Your sons and your daughters
Are beyond your command
Your old road is rapidly agin'
Please get out of the new one
If you can't lend your hand
For the times they are a-changin'[2]

VIETNAM

Of all the issues that bred social conflict in our Nation, the war in Vietnam was among the most divisive. Our parents' generation had won an unconditional surrender over fascism by mobilizing a united and determined American society. There was a universal recognition that Nazi Germany and Imperial Japan were a threat to the very existence of Western civilization. However, while the motivation and outcome of WWII were very clear, the objectives and outcome of the Korean War were arguably less well-defined. In the 1950s, monolithic Communism had replaced fascism as the principal threat to U.S. vital national interests. The American way of war remained total war. It was from this perspective that the United States began a build-up of U.S. advisers to Vietnam in May 1963 to prevent a military takeover of the South by the Communist North.[3]

To many in our generation, it was difficult to view the war in southeast Asia as a direct threat to the American way of life. The escalating

2 | Dylan, Bob. "The Times, They Are a-Changin'. https://www.bobdylan.com. Retrieved May 5, 2021

3 | "Military Advisors in Vietnam: 1963." John F. Kennedy Presidential Library website accessed May 5, 2021.

conflict, optimistically described by senior military and political leadership as "limited" and "winnable," exacerbated the divide between the baby boomers and our parents' generation.

Despite confident assurances from military and civilian leaders in the Johnson administration that the war was a limited one, troop levels continued to climb, and the public watched American deaths mount—16,899 in 1968 alone[4] Student activist groups responded with violent protests across the country. For the most part, the older generation watched the growing storm with equal measures of confusion and concern.

THIS IS THE SPRING WE CAN END THE WAR!
national emergency demonstration

denver april 29
assemble 12 noon
bandshell
city park

ST⊘P THE
BOMBING
U.S. OUT OF SOUTH
EAST ASIA NOW

Still, the administration projected unfailing optimism. On November 21, 1967, General William Westmoreland, commander of Military Assistance Command, Vietnam, told the National Press Club that he was "absolutely certain that, whereas in 1965 the enemy was winning, today he is certainly losing" and that "We have reached an important point when the end begins to come into view."[5] Two months later, the North Vietnamese launched the Tet Offensive.

South Vietnamese and American troops were caught off guard by 70,000 Communist troops who, in January 1968, struck more than 100 towns and cities with swift and stunning ferocity.

4 | National Archives and Records Administration, https://www.archives.gov/research/military/vietnam-war/casualty-statistics. Accessed May 3, 2021.

5 | Reading Copy of General Westmoreland's National Press Club Address; 11/1967; Lyndon Baines Johnson Library, Austin, TX. [Online Version, https://www.docsteach.org/documents/document/westmoreland-press-club, May 3, 2021]

*A second wave of fighting took place in late April,
and a third in August. Although the enemy suffered devastating casualties and their attempt to
spark a general uprising completely failed, many
Americans concluded the U.S. and its allies had
suffered a massive defeat.*[6]

The Tet Offensive was a watershed moment as public opinion, widely
skeptical of the administration's unfailingly optimistic outlook in the
face of growing troop deployments and mounting casualties, began to
irreversibly turn against the war. Adding to a growing public outrage, in
March 1968, an internal Department of Defense document was leaked
to the *New York Times*, outlining Gen. Westmoreland's request for an
additional 205,000 troops, which would bring the number of troops in
Vietnam to 510,000. Public sentiment was quick to react, leading to the
widespread belief among Americans that "the war was stalemated, and
the Johnson administration had lied to them."[7]

From a military perspective, the war in Vietnam cast a shadow over
all our lives; however, the nature and extent of that influence was a function of the communities in which we lived and the households in which
we were raised. Rocky Avvento observed the changing times from his
hometown of Brooklyn, New York. He recalled the cultural upheaval
during those years, as well as the negative perception of the military
among many of our peers.

*In the summer of 1969, America was in a very dark place,
in the middle of the Vietnam War. In fact, the war reached
its peak in the 1968-1969 timeframe. In addition to that,
the country was undergoing radical change from the early*

6 | National Archives Education Division, https://www.docsteach.org/documents/
document/westmoreland-press-club. Accessed May 3, 2021.

7 | Ibid

sixties. Drug use picked up dramatically, the concept of the nuclear family was changing, and many of our contemporaries were adopting different moral standards. Conflict was everywhere, with the anti-government, anti-war movement on one side and what was viewed as a patriotic movement on the other. In that aspect, I guess it wasn't too much different than what we see today, but it had a much bigger impact on us as the entering class in June 1969. Given the backdrop of the war in Vietnam, the

Rocky Avvento
CS-02

military was not looked upon by our contemporaries as a very honorable profession to be in.[8]

Those who came from small towns and more distant rural areas, on the other hand, were often more insulated and less impacted by the raging political and social debate than those who came from larger, more urban areas. Rowe Stayton was from Quinlan, Texas, a small rural town 40 miles east of Dallas. He remembered his rural community defiantly taking a patriotic stand against what they viewed as a hostile, outside world.

I grew up in a rural farming community in north Texas where the values tend to be more homogenous, and people tend to think alike. Of course, this was at the height of the Vietnam War. President Nixon had just been elected. The riots in Chicago had occurred the year before and cities were literally burning.

Rowe Stayton
CS-36

There was a growing awareness in my town that urgent social issues needed to be addressed, but we remained

8 | Interview with Gennaro J. Avvento, April 20, 2021

*somewhat insulated from what was going on in the cities.
A high school classmate of mine's brother had been killed
in Vietnam, and that was about the extent of my personal
exposure to the war. Of course, like most of our classmates,
I watched the news and knew other things were going on
in the world. But, in the rural community where I grew up,
most people remained somewhat inwardly focused and
took the position that 'you're either for us or against us.'—
there wasn't much middle ground. As a result, I came to
the Academy with what we considered a 'pro-American'
point of view, rather than coming down on the other side
of the debate.*[9]

Whether we came from small town America or big cities, it was hard
to look away as the mounting casualties dominated the evening news.
John Mann, who attended Chattanooga High School in Chattanooga,
Tennessee, was struck by the contradictions between optimistic administration announcements and the tragedies unfolding on the ground in
the rice paddies and jungles of Vietnam.

John Mann
CS-25

*Life in the late '60s in the United States was
tumultuous. The war in Vietnam had escalated
beyond belief. Every night I'd come home from
school in the late '60s and see on TV that another
55 Americans had been killed in the war. And
then I'd hear the President try to reassure us, saying we shouldn't worry, that it was a limited conflict. That always confused me—I didn't think
it was a limited conflict for the 55 people who had been
killed that day.*[10]

9 | Interview with Rowe P. Stayton, March 30, 2021.

10 | Interview with John C. Mann, April 15, 2020.

Bob Munson was living in the suburbs of northern Virginia during those difficult times, close to the epicenter of the political debate. He recalled seeing protests in cities and campuses across America, but particularly on the streets of Washington, DC.

Bob Munson
CS-34

Opposition to the Vietnam War produced tremendous social conflict at the time, and it was felt everywhere and by everyone. Many supported the government, but there was also widespread and bitter disagreement on being in the war. That disagreement played out in cities across the country.

I remember the riots in Chicago during the Democratic National Convention, as well as protests on college campuses across the United States. On a day-to-day basis, the war really didn't affect us in my northern Virginia high school. On the other hand, we were right across the Potomac from Washington, DC. I can remember looking down at the city the night after Martin Luther King was shot, watching fires as riots broke out in the District.

That was the world we lived in when we entered the Academy.[11]

THE CIVIL RIGHTS MOVEMENT

While Vietnam dominated much of the political debate, the civil rights movement had also reached a critical point. Despite legislative gains made through the Civil Rights Acts of 1964, 1965, and 1968, the struggle for equal rights continued. A wave of inner-city protests and riots,

11 | Interview with Robert A. Munson, November 29, 2021.

and the rise of the Black Power movement, reflected a continued frustration with discrimination in jobs, education, housing, and politics. The assassination of Martin Luther King, Jr. in April 1968 and Robert F. Kennedy's assassination two months later delivered twin blows to many Americans' belief in a brighter future.

The civil rights movement was very real to William "T" Thompson, as he still has vivid memories of the tense racial environment in his home in Orangeburg, South Carolina. One of the first African Americans to integrate his all-white high school, "T" went to school with a federal marshal and highway patrol escort for a time. However, despite the integration initiatives, racial tensions increased. On February 8, 1968, students gathered at neighboring South Carolina State University to protest racial segregation at the local bowling alley. The protest turned violent as heavily armed South Carolina Highway Patrol officers fired into the crowd. "T" would never forget the chaotic scene.

"T" Thompson
CS-29

South Carolina State was between Orangeburg High School and my house, so it was normal to cut through the campus as we walked home from after-school activities. I was walking home that night and saw some activity up on the campus. There was a big bonfire out on a central lawn where kids had gathered, and some college kids were making speeches. I was just hanging out there watching what was going on when suddenly things literally exploded. I hit the ground and could hear shots being fired by the police, who had gathered across the street from the students. Looking back, I was lucky I didn't get killed because there were three people dead and 27 seriously injured when it was all over. One of the kids who died was Delano 'Bump' Middleton, a high school

*kid I knew. We played against each other in basketball, so
I knew him very well. I didn't know the two college kids
who were killed.*[12]

While it wasn't widely reported, the Orangeburg Massacre occurred two weeks after the Tet Offensive, two months before Martin Luther King, Jr.'s assassination, and two years before the Kent State University killings. It was also the "first deadly confrontation between university students and law enforcement in United States history."[13]

As 1,406 young men walked up the Ramp on June 23, 1969, we stepped into a world vastly different from that of our generational contemporaries. We had begun our journey as the Class of 1973.

FORGING OUR OWN PATHS

Outside of the Academy grounds, the existing social structure was being buffeted on all sides by fundamental changes, from racial strife and the struggle for civil rights, to the drug and hippie culture, to the sexual revolution. The old rules and social mores no longer seemed relevant. This was in stark contrast to the Academy environment of strict order and predictability. John Muse observed societal change from his vantage point at the Academy.

Coming from Tyler, Texas in the late '60s, I hadn't encountered anti-war or anti-military sentiment at all. All of that changed in the summer of 1969. Major events were shaping our culture, such as the moon landing and Woodstock. Music changed dramatically in the late '60s and early '70s. Long hair was in, and short hair was out. I

John Muse
CS-36

12 | Interview with William L. Thompson, December 2, 2021.

13 | Bass, Jack, "Documenting the Orangeburg Massacre." *Nieman Reports. The Nieman Foundation for Journalism at Harvard University.* Vol 57, No. 3, Fall 2003.

began to experience being part of a group that was completely out of fashion, rather than being part of a popular group. Over the remainder of my time at the Academy, I searched for my own beliefs as I watched many of my contemporaries—to include my own brothers—opt for a pacifist approach and question the values of parents and government leaders.[14]

Kevin McHugh lived in the San Francisco Bay area, the epicenter of the hippie movement. He remembered the reaction of his high school classmates when they heard he would be attending the Academy, as well as the reaction from an upperclassman when he heard where Kevin was from.

Kevin McHugh
CS-09

I graduated from a high school in the San Francisco Bay Area—obviously, a pretty liberal place. When my classmates heard about my appointment, some of the guys I played baseball with— the jocks—laughed at me and said, 'Are you stupid? What were you thinking of?' They couldn't understand what would motivate me to go to the Academy, much less join the military. In fact, I can remember getting a photo in the mail from one of my baseball buddies during Doolie Summer.[15] It was a picture of him and a couple of my other teammates sitting by a cooler, each with a beer in one hand and a joint in the other. Seeing that contrast was painful, given the harsh discipline we were going through that summer, but I just

---

14 | Muse, John R. "What a Leader of Character Looks Like from a Business Investor Perspective." May 5, 2020.

15 | Derived from the Greek word *"doulos"* (slave), the term "doolie" is used at the Academy to describe a first-year student.

*wrote those guys off right away. Fortunately, my close
friends and those I admired—the ones who really meant
a lot to me—remained very supportive of my decision.*

*Oddly enough, I did get some pushback from the other
side once I got to the Academy. I remember an upper classman shouting at me: 'Hey, McHugh, I hear you're from
California. Come on, show me your beads. You gotta have
some hippie beads under that shirt somewhere.' While
you could chalk that up to typical upper classman harassment, I was shocked to hear him say that. I'd never lived
anywhere other than California, and it was the first time
I realized that California didn't have a great reputation
around the rest of the country.[16]*

Steve Rossetti also remembered the stark contrast between the outside civilian world and the strict environment we had chosen.

*Our time at the Academy was especially counter
cultural. We entered at the end of the 1960s,
a tumultuous decade. Things like short hair,
belonging to an institution, discipline, and military service were odious to many and reviled.
While the free-love rock fest at Woodstock happened in the summer of 1969 not far from my
home in upstate New York, we doolies had just
had our hair buzzed off and were in Jack's Valley in BCT.
While our peers were smoking marijuana on Yasgur's
Farm, we were sucking dirt in a low crawl with our M-1s.[17]*

Steve Rossetti
CS-37

16 | Interview with Kevin E. McHugh, April 16, 2021.

17 | Rossetti, Stephen. "From Air Force Officer to Catholic Priest." March 29, 2020.

What distinguished us from our generational peers in those times was our singular focus on military, academic, and athletic excellence in a very demanding and structured environment. That singular focus also enabled us to bypass the idealistic passions of our former high school classmates as they protested the war on campuses across America. But it also separated us from them as well: the United States Air Force Academy of June 1969 was a bastion of patriotism, tradition, and faith in our military leadership.

In contrast to professors in civilian universities, our faculty members and Air Officers Commanding (AOCs) were all military, and many were pilots with previous combat tours in Southeast Asia. Therefore, our exemplars were combat-seasoned officers with an aggressive "fly and fight" orientation. A.J. Ranft remembered being surrounded by a variety of iconic figures.

A.J. Ranft
CS-11

From our perspective, because there was a war going on, there was a purpose to our service. That purpose was very visible all the time, from the Memorial in the Air Gardens to talk about fallen comrades. And, of course, there was Brig. Gen. Robin Olds, our commandant. So, to me, the focus and the reason for us being there was really clear: we're going to go through these four years and then into the Air Force. And then, in some form or another, we're going to serve in the war in Southeast Asia. That attitude was reinforced by the faculty and staff. All of our instructors were officers; there were no civilian instructors. Nearly all AOCs were pilots. When we had military training classes, they often involved gun camera film from some of our instructors. In fact, one of my

economics instructors had a MiG kill in Vietnam. So our
purpose for being at the Academy was very visible.[18]

Regardless of any individual opinions of the political calculations that led to our involvement in Southeast Asia, our class's unified view was that the men who unquestioningly followed our Nation into war should be honored, and deserved our deepest respect. Whether the war in Vietnam was justified or not wasn't the issue—our Nation called, and these warriors responded. But it was a different story outside the Academy's main gate. Rich Comer recalled the massive demonstrations held across the country to protest the war, and our collective reaction at the Academy to one event in particular.

I remember the day of the first Moratorium to End the War in Vietnam, in October 1969. All the civilian colleges were taking a day off. Obviously, we didn't. But that night, we were called into Arnold Hall by the Academy leadership to address the political situation.

Rich Comer
CS-30

*As best I can recall, the superintendent spoke first and said a couple of things that were absolutely forgettable. But then our commandant, Robin Olds, took the stage. I distinctly remember him saying, 'Well, it's a f****ed-up war, men, but it's the only war we've got.' That was the warrior attitude that permeated all we did in those days.[19]*

Regardless of one's political views, we all saw a clear distinction between the politicians who established the policies and the courageous and steadfast warriors tasked to implement them. Kees Rietsema described the shared future that we all saw before us.

---

18 | Interview with Andrew J. Ranft, April 27, 2021.
19 | Interview with Richard L. Comer, April 23, 2021.

*I remember listening to the names of fallen graduates in
that overseas war as they were read from the Staff Tower
as part of the mealtime ritual.*

Kees Rietsema
CS-14

*Recently I read Col. Dick Anderegg's book, Sierra
Hotel, about the decade of flying fighters after
the Vietnam War. Anderegg makes an interesting observation. In the years since the end of the
war in Vietnam, Americans have been locked in
a bitter debate over whether we should have been
there in the first place. Yet, to aviators engaged
in combat, the answer to that question was easy:
the Nation called. To those of us attending the Academy,
the issue was that clear-cut. We would eventually serve
as we were called to do. That is the nature of service, military or otherwise.*[20]

While we started out as a cross-section of American society, the
"bluing process" and the values we learned to embrace on the Terrazzo,
the athletic fields, and in the classroom not only built a common experience, but also set us apart from our contemporaries on civilian
campuses. John Muse remembered how challenging it was to deal with
the cultural dissonance created by the growing anti-war attitudes across
America and the revulsion shown toward those charged with
implementing policy.

*The ugliest chapter of this period of time was the disre-
spect shown our men and women in uniform who did not
make these decisions but served under the civilian leaders that did make them. Additionally, it became fashion-
able to throw out virtually all of the values of the greatest*

20 | Reitsema, Kees W. "What a Leader of Character Looks Like from a Former Cadet
Wing Commander Perspective." Undated.

generation, our parents. For the first time in my life, I found my own inner values instead of following the crowd. This was particularly important given the insults and disrespect that I encountered during those years with short hair and in uniform.[21]

John Muse
CS-36

It's been said that we're all products of our environment. While the environment we may have lived in was one of uncertainty and social chaos in our younger years, that environment changed forever when we stepped onto the Terrazzo on June 23, 1969.

21 | Muse, John R. "What a Leader of Character Looks Like from a Business Perspective." May 5, 2020.

2

FORMATIVE YEARS AT THE ACADEMY

We stood on the Terrazzo after the evening meal, standing shoulder to shoulder in wavy and ragged lines—the best we could manage after three days of in-processing. The First BCT group staff stood in formation in front of us at attention, gleaming sabers flashing in the fading light.

The tranquility of the Colorado evening was suddenly broken by a rhythmic cadence behind us, followed by sharp, sequential commands: *"SQUADRON, HALT! LEFT, FACE!"* Heels clicked in unison as the formations came to a halt behind us. A hush swept over the Terrazzo. Then, suddenly, the ominous silence was broken by a deep, booming voice that echoed across the broad expanse:

GENTLEMEN! MAKE. YOUR. CORRECTIONS!

Without warning, it was as if someone had kicked over a fire ant hill. Our world exploded as a swarming mass of upperclassmen fell out, enveloping us in a torrent of screaming abuse. First BCT—informally known as "First Beast"—had arrived with a vengeance. Eighteen-year-old Mike Edwards recalled that moment as one of total shock.

Mike Edwards
CS-13

Even though we may have talked to other cadets or graduates before we arrived at the Academy, for most of us that moment was totally unexpected—we had no idea what was happening. Of course, our Prep School[22] classmates probably had some idea of what was going on but, from the perspective of a green high school graduate, it was like, 'Oh, my gosh, what is this?' I remember a couple of guys about an inch from my face, screaming at me with spittle flying. To say I was apprehensive was a gross understatement—the shock value was pretty high. But this started the breaking-down process, which was the first necessary step in taking young high school kids and rebuilding them into Air Force Academy cadets.[23]

Even amid the chaos and violence, there were a few humorous moments as the upperclassmen swarmed the Terrazzo, rudely introducing us to the fourth-class system. "T" Thompson chuckled as he looked back on one of those moments.

I recall this pounding, this 'boom, boom, boom' as the cadre marched in behind us. One of our classmates was standing right in front of me in formation. His name was Frank Brienzo, and he was a little Italian guy in my flight.

---

22 | United States Air Force Academy Preparatory School is adjacent to the Air Force Academy, and is a one-year program designed to give select enlisted personnel and civilians a pathway to the Academy through academic, leadership, and physical preparation.

23 | Interview with Howard M. Edwards, May 28, 2021.

"T" Thompson
CS-29

I had been getting some flak from the upperclass-men, but not too bad; people just yelled at me and then moved on. I was standing there with my chin in when an upper classman—a big foot-ball player, as it turned out—came up to Frank, who was casually standing there in a vague sem-blance of attention. The upper classman stuck his hand between Frank's arm and side and screamed, 'SQUEEZE MY HAND, SQUAT!' The upper-classman was trying to get my classmate to stand at rigid attention with his arms pressed tightly against his sides. Well, Frank hesitated for a minute, then reached up and grabbed the upperclassman's hand and started to squeeze it. The upperclassman yelled, 'What are you doing? Are you crazy? LET GO OF MY HAND, SQUAT!' I started laughing. I couldn't help myself; it was so funny. But when I started laughing, I attracted a real crowd.

That's when things ceased to be funny![24]

DOOLIE SUMMER

Basic training, also known as "Doolie Summer," consisted of two one-month periods designed to convert high school graduates into fourth-class, or freshman, cadets. The first period, First Beast, started off in the cadet area. After four weeks of endless marching, calisthenics, running in formation, uniform and room inspections, and a dizzying array of classes, we moved to Jack's Valley for Second Beast. While First Beast concentrated on introducing us to the fundamentals of military life, Second Beast introduced field skills and grueling physical challenges. Adjacent to the cadet area, Jack's Valley was five square miles of untamed

24 | Interview with William L. Thompson, December 2, 2021.

Colorado wilderness. Looking back, Bruce Wright remembered the lasting impact the Jack's Valley experience had on our collective futures.

Bruce Wright
CS-39

After the first few weeks of training on the Terrazzo and the obstacle course, we became less a class of individuals and more a class of teams. The transition to Jack's Valley forced us all to take on challenges that prepared us for being in the business of life and death. We were driven and motivated to overcome some of the toughest demands on our physical courage we had ever faced. And, most important, we learned that we would prevail—or not—based on the trust we built in each other.

Through nights and days, dust and mud, while always carrying a heavy WWII-vintage M-1 rifle, our reliance on each other was real. There was no room for quibbling or adding to the risk of all our element teammates if one of us fell behind. If a flight or element classmate slacked off in word or deed, our upperclassmen ensured the consequences were very visible and lasting. One's reputation could take a hit right then and there, and that hit might last for decades.

We faced seemingly impossible challenges during that time that demanded we either quit the program or endure for one more day. We were constantly evaluated from all sides—there was no place to hide. We were held to high performance standards and selfless and authentic commitment to shared objectives.[25]

25 | Wright, Bruce A. "Every Cadet a Warrior." Undated.

Mike Mosier pointed to one particular experience in Jack's Valley and considered how it helped shape his attitude toward perseverance and overcoming adversity.

Mike Mosier
CS-34

Our element leader was a second classman[26] by the name of Sam Clovis, Class of '71. He was a particularly imposing figure to our bedraggled element of basic cadets: loud, gruff, charismatic, and truly larger than life. But he also taught us one particularly valuable and enduring lesson that we've drawn on throughout our lives: what we see as personal limitations are largely self-imposed. He taught us this hard lesson in a dusty corner of Jack's Valley he called 'Sam's Patch.'

We all came to dread the command from Cadet Clovis: 'You've got three minutes. I want everyone formed up, fatigues, under arms.'[27] Then came that sly grin. 'We're going to take a little trip to Sam's Patch.' That was followed by what seemed like an eternity of running up and down dusty hills in the hot Colorado sun, our 10-pound M-1 rifles held high above our heads, arms shaking. We all gasped for breath, sweat soaking through our once neatly pressed and starched fatigues, arms like rubber, perpetually near the breaking point. It was beyond brutal, but somehow none of us dropped out in Sam's Patch—Clovis wouldn't allow it. He always knew how to push us just

26 | Cadets are referred to according to the number of years remaining until graduation. Freshmen are "fourth classmen," sophomores are "third classmen," juniors are "second classmen," and seniors are "first classmen," also called "firsties."

27 | "Under arms" was the command given for all individuals to carry their assigned rifles.

short of the point of total collapse, and then show us we could come back for more.

Looking back, our Sam's Patch experience was clearly designed to build character and teach us to perform under extreme adversity. Clovis demonstrated to us what we wouldn't otherwise have learned on our own: that, regardless of how hopeless a situation might appear, you can always take one more step toward a solution. Take one more breath. Climb one more hill.

We're all indebted to Sam Clovis for teaching us that fundamental lesson in character because we've all drawn on that experience to overcome challenges throughout our lives.

INTEGRATION INTO THE WING

BCT mercifully concluded on a sunny Colorado morning on the lush green parade field at the Acceptance Parade. While we felt a sense of pride in all we had accomplished that summer, the knowledge that the academic year would be starting was sobering.

As Gen. Olds had pointed out in that fateful first meeting in Arnold Hall, all of us had been high achievers in high school. But now we were in the company of equals. Regardless of how well we had performed alongside our high school peers, that comparison was now irrelevant. The definition of "above average" had drastically changed; we had entered a new and highly competitive environment, one in which our performance would be measured against a far higher standard. The rigors of an engineering-oriented curriculum, extremely heavy class load, and an endless stream of Graded Reviews (exams) and pop quizzes required intense effort and academic discipline from us all, regardless of how high our Grade Point Average (GPA) had been in high school. Looking back, Mike Edwards considered the challenges he faced.

Mike Edwards
CS-13

While I was prepared for the physical activities at the Academy, the academic side was another story. My high school was quite small, so I didn't have the opportunity to take any advanced classes—just basic math, up to trigonometry. I didn't have to work very hard to do well in that environment.

Not surprisingly, my first semester doolie year was a real shock. When our first progress report came out, I ended up with a 1.36 GPA with two immediate consequences. First, although I had made the baseball team, I was immediately cut. Second, I was put on Academic Probation.

I had to meet with an academic counselor, who asked me about my academic background in high school. I guess he wasn't too impressed, because he looked me in the eye and bluntly told me, 'You're never going to graduate.' I was really taken aback. I had dreamed of going to the Academy since sixth grade, and here was an Air Force major telling me I was never going to make it.

As it turned out, his approach was a good one because it made me work harder than I'd ever worked in my life. I managed to pull my GPA up to a 2.0 by the end of the first semester and actually made the Dean's List the next semester. But it was tough going.

Looking back, I learned that perseverance leads to success,

*and that you can accomplish whatever you set out to do
as long as you work really hard.*[28]

One of the other things we learned early on in this tough new environment was the need to keep a sense of humor, and pranks helped us keep our morale high in the most grueling of times. In addition to helping us let off steam in the high-pressure academic and military environment, pranks also built class unity. One of the best-known pranks was brilliantly executed by our classmates and a few upperclassmen in Eighth Squadron. As Denny Merideth described it,

I'm not sure it was really a prank as much as it was an architectural achievement. The challenge was to convert the semi-domed Planetarium into an eight ball. Easy in theory, but hard to execute. The squadron had excellent leadership and a handful of upperclassmen who also deserve credit for their part in planning and execution of the entire project.

Denny Merideth
CS-08

As with all classes at the Academy, times were pretty rough for doolies. We weren't getting much sleep, given the academic load. And, of course, there was no free time during the day. So we all had to work on the project late at night. I remember sneaking through the tunnels that ran under the dorm and down to the Cadet Gym. That's where we fashioned this huge black plastic tarp covering for the Planetarium. It was pretty complex, as it had to be geometrically designed in a circle. And it wasn't something you could just pop up there; otherwise, it would fall. So the challenge was in the design: how big did we need to

28 | Interview with Howard M. Edwards, May 28, 2021.

make it to cover the Planetarium? What size was the por-
tion of the eight ball that had the 'eight' on it? How big
did we need to make the actual 'eight' when we started
painting it? My classmate Bob Knarr opined that 'the
interior radius of the planetarium dome is 25 feet, so
the exterior radius is 30 feet or less; the surface area of a
sphere—4 times pi times radius squared—at a radius of

30 feet, the surface area
of the dome is 1/2 of a
sphere, less than 6,000
sq. ft.' We spent nights
that entire week before
trying to get this thing
done, rolling it up, hid-
ing it in the tunnels, bringing it back out the next night,
continuing to work on it. And then we finally got it put up
late Thursday night. It was truly a thing of beauty.

I think it demonstrated the energy we had as a class under
the leadership of a few dynamic upperclassmen. And it
also showed the kind of teamwork it took to accomplish
a project of that magnitude. It was a harmless prank—
with the possible exception of the poor second classman
who was up there trying to get it across the top of this
huge building, or the building superintendent, who had to
take it down. But the sense of comradery and class spirit
we built by completing a mammoth project like that was
essential.

Even though it was just a prank, it illustrated another crit-
ical thing we learned at the Academy: relationships mat-
ter. And, while relationships are forged over time, rather

than as a result of a single event, strong relationships are essential in making great things happen.[29]

THE HONOR CODE

We sat through a multitude of classes during Doolie Summer, from heritage to military deportment. But the most important classes for our overall character development were those on the Academy's Honor Code: "We will not lie, steal, or cheat, nor tolerate among us anyone who does."

For the most part, there were no surprises, as the Code reflected the values we had been raised with and the concepts were familiar to all. Still, regardless of the environment we had come from, the Code left an indelible impression on all of us. Bill Heely stressed how fundamental it was to life at the Academy.

Bill Heely
CS-38

Of all the things at the Academy we dealt with, the Honor Code was like the North Star. To me, it was inviolate. When you want to teach core values, the Honor Code is where you start.

From my perspective, it was very straightforward. If someone asks you a question, you tell the truth. Everyone knows what stealing is, and I think everybody knows what cheating is, and you just don't do it. Toleration may have been an area where some guys had trouble; fortunately, I can't remember ever knowing about somebody doing something that broke the Honor Code, so I didn't have to make that kind of a tough call. But, even though it would have been tough, I don't see that there would have been any wiggle room for that.[30]

29 | Interview with Denny J. Merideth, August 25, 2021.
30 | Interview with William Heely, January 20, 2022.

Although reflecting the values we were raised with, the Code's iron-clad tenets demanded strict adherence and allowed very little room for forgiveness. Consequently, the slightest deviation had the potential for drastic consequences. A.J. Ranft remembered one incident in particular that illustrated the point.

A.J. Ranft
CS-11

To me—and I think to our class as a whole—the Honor Code was an absolute. During Doolie Summer, we were cut some slack as we learned the ins and outs and the intricacies of the Code. But, when the academic year started, the Honor Code was an absolute. No breaks.

I believe the fourth-class system reinforced that. If you didn't do something you were supposed to, and someone questioned you on it, you had to be truthful in your answer. For instance, if you didn't shine your shoes and you were standing in formation and a third classman came up and asked, 'Hey, did you shine your shoes?' Well, it's simple. You say, 'No, Sir.' You may get some kind of punishment or at least yelled at, but through little things like that you learn you have to be truthful, regardless of the consequences. You're accountable for your actions or inactions. Once you accepted that, if an upperclassman asked you a question and you knew you were going to get punished because of your answer, you answered that way anyway. So, when it came to bigger issues, such as cheating or stealing or tolerating, you will have internalized this sense of honor because you've been practicing it.

We learned early on that there were consequences to dishonorable behavior. In our days at the Academy, the consequence of an honor violation was expulsion. That was just black and white. For instance, one of my very good friends our fourth-class year never came back from dinner one evening. He went to an Honor Court and got separated right on the spot—that was it. We never saw him again.[31]

Because the Code was strictly enforced, there was a presumption that those who adhered to its tenets were absolutely trustworthy. As Bill Heely pointed out, living in such a trusting environment offered a number of practical advantages.

Bill Heely
CS-38

The Honor Code was something that was probably within me, based on my upbringing. So, I found it kind of easy and convenient in that I wouldn't lie, steal, or cheat anyway. Fortunately, I never encountered an aspect of toleration. From that standpoint, I found living with the Honor Code kind of easy. Plus, the Honor Code made things convenient because we could leave the door open and know no one was going to steal anything. We could say something and know we were going to be believed. Our professors could give us tests in such a way that they trusted us not to cheat. In that regard, I found the Honor Code liberating.[32]

"PLAYING THE GAME"

While the "lying, stealing, cheating" aspects of the Honor Code may have been natural extensions of our upbringing, the "toleration" clause was something new to all of us. Furthermore, it tended to run counter

31 | Interview with Andrew J. Ranft, April 27, 2021.

32 | Interview with William Heely, January 20, 2022.

to admonitions from upperclassmen to "take care of your classmate." Further muddying the water was an "us vs. them" mentality that arose, generated in large part by what some people saw as demanding and unyielding AOCs taking punitive action against rebellious cadets. "Playing the game" was the strategy many used to survive.

Ongoing tensions between the dean, who was responsible for our academic development, and the commandant's staff, who oversaw the military component, also contributed to an "us vs. them" mentality. While the competition between academic and military requirements was understandable given the extremely time-constrained environment, it was exacerbated by a new commandant, Brig. Gen. Vandenberg. Gen. Vandenberg had a different approach from his charismatic predecessor, Gen. Olds. A bit of a maverick himself, Olds seemed to identify much more easily with cadet life, priorities, and concerns than his hard-nosed, unyielding successor.

Our Cadet Wing Commander Kees Rietsema found himself squarely in the middle of the resulting struggle between the dean and the new commandant. He remembered the problems he had dealing with the competing philosophies.

Kees Rietsema
CS-14

Gen. Vandenberg saw his role as one that emphasized the traditional role of military leader and representative/teacher of traditional military virtues associated with leadership. It was, in his eyes, a sacred trust that he was there to protect and promote. In his view, cadets like me who did not have a strong military background needed to be brought into the fold and molded according to USAF culture. He also saw his role as very different from that of the dean, who was in charge of a faculty the commandant simply did not regard as equally committed to military rigor and training.

32

From an academic perspective, developing a sense of curiosity and a questioning approach was important; however, it certainly wasn't one of the commandant's priorities. So, as the cadet wing commander, there were times when I felt torn between the two ends of Fairchild Hall…the Department of Political Science, where I was encouraged to engage in academic discourse on one end, and the commandant's office on the other end, where I was expected to 'carry on' without debate. For a young 20-year-old, this was a constant source of tension. While I managed to negotiate the dissonance, I have to admit it did bother me, and I regretted for years that it was never clearly addressed.

In sum, I was caught in the middle of tension between the commandant's office and the dean's office. I can still remember the broad grin on Gen. Vandenberg's face when I told him I was turning down an offer to attend graduate school at Tufts University's Fletcher School, opting instead to attend pilot training. It was as if my decision validated his position vis-a-vis the dean…after all, cadets were there to be warriors, not academic stars. I will never forget his comment to my roommate, Orderia Mitchell, who had decided to attend medical school after graduation from the Academy. Said Gen. Vandenberg, 'Can you imagine that? A perfectly good killer going on to medical school?'

Oderia had other things in mind and, after serving his commitment in the Air Force, he established a successful orthopedic practice in Colorado Springs.[33]

---

33 | Reitsema, Kees W. "What a Leader of Character Looks Like from a Former Cadet Wing Commander Perspective." Undated.

STRUGGLES WITH THE HONOR CODE

During our time at the Academy, we had a Cadet Honor Committee, as well as a less visible Cadet Ethics Committee. While the Ethics Committee could forward alleged offenses to a Commandant's Disciplinary Board for evaluation and action—"six and 120," or six months restrictions and 120 hour-long tours, marching back and forth with a rifle on the tour pad, was the maximum punishment—the Honor Committee had the power to recommend dismissal. So, in practical terms, the Honor Code was viewed by some as an absolute, whereas ethical considerations were secondary, at least with respect to consequences. As a result, the litmus test for evaluating questionable actions tended to be "is this an Honor Code violation?" If so, we didn't take the action. But, if it wasn't an Honor Code violation, some took the attitude that it was simply "playing the game." To that extent, ethics didn't play a role in what was otherwise a binary decision-making process.

This false dichotomy between honor and ethics resulted in practices such as "bed stuffing," designed to mislead anyone in authority into believing an offending cadet was in his bed. As John Mann remembered it, that situation highlighted some of the contradictions in the way honor and ethics were applied to daily life.

John Mann
CS-25

As we went through summer basic training, we would have training about this and that, and every now and then we'd have training about the Honor Code. What does it mean? How does it work? I was pretty excited about that. But when we got down into some of the daily life situations, I thought there were some inconsistencies. For example, the Cadet in Charge of Quarters [commonly referred to as the 'CQ'] would come by after taps and check to see if we were in our rooms and in our beds. And it was considered OK to stuff your bed, to intentionally deceive the CQ that you were there when you weren't. Or, after he came and checked that you were in your bed, you could go down the hall and jump in someone else's bed and pretend to be them. I remember being very confused because that didn't fit with the concept that we won't lie, steal, or cheat, because to me that was an intentional deception.

To take that a step further, I would have expected an honor discussion to specifically address this issue. Why were we were even doing this in the first place? Why weren't we in bed like we were supposed to be? Instead, bed stuffing was considered to be harmless, just 'playing the game.' That was the common phrase you'd hear. But then, if you'd veer into something more clear-cut, something that was clearly understood to be an Honor Code violation, you'd be out on the street. So there were certainly incongruities.[34]

Kevin McHugh encountered a situation that exposed those same incongruities of "playing the game," and how that experience demonstrated to him that honor and ethics are, in fact, both critical aspects of acting with integrity.

I made a mistake with the Honor Code at the end of the first semester, third-class year. One Friday night—I think it was in late-November or December—a snowstorm hit, and we were all restricted to the Academy. My former roommate from the previous semester told me that his girlfriend from Colorado State University, who he had been dating all doolie year, was breaking up with him. He

Kevin McHugh
CS-09

told me that he just had to go up to Fort Collins to talk to her. I warned him not to go, but he insisted that he had to go try and talk her out of leaving him. So he actually left in the middle of the snowstorm, when everybody was restricted to the base. This was on a Friday night.

He hitchhiked and somehow managed to get a ride to Denver. Once he got there, he called me and told me he was continuing on to Fort Collins. He said 'I know I'm probably going to get thrown in jail, or at least kicked out, when this is all over. But I've got to go see this girl.' Again I tried to talk him out of it but he was adamant. This was a really good guy and I wanted to do what I could to help him out and keep him from getting in trouble.

I was the only one who knew he left, as his roommate was on a trip that weekend. I heard that upperclassmen on restrictions would sometimes stuff their beds so they could leave their room and go watch TV somewhere. That way, when the CQ looked in the room, he'd see what he would think was a body asleep in bed. I didn't think that was really ethical but, in this situation, I thought my loyalty was to my friend more than to the system.

The next morning, we had Saturday training. A lot of times they'd take roll, and I decided, if they did that, I wasn't going to sign his name or cover for him because that would be an Honor Code violation. Fortunately, they didn't take roll that Saturday.

When my friend came back Sunday night, he was prepared to be arrested. But, when he found out no one knew he had gone, he started bragging about it to a couple of *guys. One guy he talked to asked whether he left the card outside his door marked 'authorized'[35] and, if so, wouldn't that be an honor violation? He said he hadn't thought of that—it was a completely unintentional oversight on his part. But, after thinking about it, he turned himself in for possible honor violation. He was investigated and cleared. So, as it turned out, there were no disciplinary consequences for his unauthorized absence.*

As a disciplinary matter, they couldn't touch him because that would be using the Honor Code against him to enforce regulations. Still, I always felt guilty about my role in all that because it certainly wasn't ethical.[36]

As John Stefonik pointed out, we all recognized that the Honor Code was to be strictly interpreted and uniformly applied. While the Code's administration has evolved over the years, in 1973, the consequences of a violation tended to be binary: you were either in or out.[37] He explained the system we lived under at the time.

During our time at the Academy, we had an Honor Committee composed of honor representatives elected from each squadron. Each 'Honor Rep' was given supplemental training. If an honor violation was alleged, an investigation was commenced and, if there was deemed to be sufficient basis, an Honor Board was convened

John Stefonik
CS-20

35 | Each cadet had a nametag outside his dormitory room. There was a card next to his nametag with two selections, "authorized" and "unauthorized." When a cadet wasn't in his room, he was required to adjust the card to explain his absence as being either authorized or not.

36 | Interview with Kevin E. McHugh, April 16, 2021.

37 | See Appendix B, "The Honor Code and the Class of 1973."

to determine 'guilt or innocence' (the 'guilt or innocence' language was later changed to 'violation'). A cadet found 'guilty' of a Code infraction was asked to resign, and most did. 'Discretion' was possible but rarely used; under discretion, the cadet could be retained at the Academy. However, a fully developed graduated response to honor deviations was not available until many years after we graduated.

Although a universal commandment, the Code had a personal and profound meaning to each of us. Although the Code applied to all of us, each of us had a different experience with and reaction to the Code.[38]

THE TOLERATION CLAUSE

While the first tenets of the Honor Code—"we will not lie, steal, or cheat"—were very familiar to the majority of us, the admonition that we will not "tolerate among us anyone who does" added a new twist. Mike Arnett explained the challenges this concept presented and the important role moral courage played in its implementation.

Mike Arnett
CS-09

For me, the Honor Code was nothing new because that's how I lived my life. However, the toleration clause was certainly a big issue. We lost a couple of guys in the honor scandal [of 1972].[39] Fortunately, I didn't know anything about the guys who were implicated. I know it would have been tough to have turned them in but, in the end, I

38 | Stefonik, John R. "Living the Honor Code, 1969-1973." Undated.

39 | In January 1972, 39 members of the Class of 1973 were found to have violated the Honor Code and subsequently resigned from the Academy. What became known as the honor scandal of 1972 is described in Appendix B.

hope we all would have screwed up our courage and done the right thing.

Looking back, the Academy was a great leadership laboratory. But, in terms of honor, we tended to learn things through negative experiences—that is, we learned by seeing people being caught, as opposed to having been taught those important lessons in life through a more positive approach.

One of the key advances in today's Academy is the National Character and Leadership Symposium (NCLS). The NCLS offers cadets insights that go beyond the Academy experience. Stories from NCLS speakers help cadets form in their minds what will be expected of them in the future. That is one of the reasons I support it so strongly.

Looking back at our honor system, there were virtues I think could have been emphasized more. One was moral courage. For instance, with respect to the toleration clause, it takes moral courage to stand up and turn in a classmate. But the reality is that you're going to face situations in your life where it's going to take moral courage to do the right thing, so this is a critical lesson to learn.[40]

OTHER LESSONS LEARNED

There were other issues we saw with implementation of the Honor Code that led to painful lessons learned. Rich Comer gave an example of a situation which, while not technically a violation of the Code, in retrospect left him feeling like he had fallen short of its ideals.

---

40 | Interview with James M. Arnett, March 8, 2021.

Rich Comer
CS-30

Neither my roommate nor I were Astronautical Engineering majors, and we hated the Astro core course. We didn't have engineering or math backgrounds, so we really struggled.

The Astro Department had set up a study room which, among other things, contained past exams. Anything in the study materials they provided was considered to be fair game. One day we had a graded homework assignment. In reviewing the materials in the study room, I noticed there was a problem from a previous exam that was very similar to the homework problem we had been assigned. Well, I just copied what was there—I figured that, by doing that, I would at least get 80% of the problem right, which was what the previous student had gotten on his exam.

My roommate asked me whether I was able to do the homework assignment. I said, 'Yeah, in fact I found the exact problem in the materials in the study room.' So he copied it as well. Neither one of us looked at why the previous student had gotten 80 percent, rather than 100 percent.

As it turned out, the problem we had copied made a very basic math error. Because we had both copied it and were roommates, there was an honor investigation. As it turned out, we were exonerated. But I felt really dirty when it was all over. While the Honor Committee cleared me, I didn't feel clear.[41]

41 | Interview with Richard L. Comer, April 23, 2021.

On paper, the Honor Code was very straightforward; however, in execution it could become complicated and require difficult decisions with profound consequences. Bob Munson was an honor representative and related an Honor Board experience that left him feeling like there was a bigger picture that should have been considered.

Bob Munson
CS-34

We all learned from our first honor lessons as basic cadets that there was zero tolerance for honor violations. And, in subsequent years, we learned from 'Cadet X' reports of circumstances that led to cadets being found guilty of honor violations. But it wasn't until my first Honor Board as a member of the Honor Committee that I learned, firsthand, how strictly we cadets enforced our Honor Code—and how unforgiving the results were.

This particular case involved a first semester doolie who was approached by an upper classman in his squadron and told he was expected to support the football team. The upperclassman intimated that doolies in other squadrons had painted 'spirit signs' on bedsheets, and that he expected their squadron to be represented as well.

The question became how to get a bedsheet to paint the sign on. Each squadron had a linen rep who was charged with taking in dirty sheets, turning them into the cleaners, and putting out clean sheets. The clean sheets were left out unattended, with the understanding that each cadet would only exchange a dirty sheet for a clean one. The doolie in question went to the squadron linen exchange, grabbed a sheet and, with the help of his classmates, painted a sign and hung it from the staff tower in Mitchell Hall. Later he was asked where he got the sheet. He said he had taken it from the squadron linen cart. As a result, he was told to turn himself in for stealing.

The doolie was referred to the Honor Committee and met the Board I sat on. The eight-member Board asked detailed questions, but the facts of the case were straightforward. The doolie was scared and upset, and testified he thought he was being ordered to take a sheet, even though that was not explicitly stated. In the subsequent closed-door discussion, seven Board members thought it was clearly an honor violation. I was the only holdout, and the deliberations lasted two hours before I changed my vote. With the unanimous vote, the cadet was obliged to resign.

Looking back, my original 'not guilty' vote was technically wrong—the other seven cadets on the Board correctly understood the rules of the Honor Code as they were exercised in 1972. But what haunts me to this day is that this cadet was motivated to be at the Academy, would likely have done very well as a cadet, and I'm sure would have served honorably as an Air Force officer.[42]

BECOMING UPPERCLASSMEN

We had all heard stories about the dreaded Hell Week.

The stuff of legend and rumor, Hell Week marked the transition from doolie to upper classman. It was five days of unrelenting pressure, intense mental stress, and impossible physical demands. Although specific events varied somewhat by squadron, each day of Hell Week was

---

42 | Interview with Robert A. Munson, July 5, 2021.

designed to reinforce aspects of the hard-earned lessons we learned throughout doolie year, and to prepare us to assume our place in the Cadet Wing as upperclassmen.

Hell Week was far more than an initiation. While in form it was a return to BCT, in function it was a stark introduction to the responsibilities we'd be assuming to train the new class in the coming academic year. Conducted almost wholly by third classmen, Hell Week was also a natural mentoring activity—the first step toward integrating our class into leadership roles as upperclassmen. But that all lay ahead of us; for now, we had to make it through Hell Week.

As we lay in our beds Sunday night, nervously mulling over the rumors that had been circulating and contemplating the week that lay ahead, the rock group The Mamas and the Papas gave us a hint of things to come when Command Post played one of their popular songs over the loudspeaker system at Taps. The dire warning echoed through the empty hallways outside our doors:

> *Monday, Monday*
> *So good to me*
> *Monday mornin', it was all I hoped it would be*
> *But Monday mornin', Monday mornin' couldn't guarantee*
> *That Monday evenin' you would still be here with me*
> *Every other day,*
> *every other day*
> *Every other day, every other day of the week is fine, yeah*
> *But whenever Monday comes, but whenever Monday comes*
> *But whenever Monday comes, you can find me cryin' all of*
> *the time.*[43]

One classmate's diary of Hell Week described the week's events:

43 | "Monday, Monday" by The Mamas and the Papas. Lyrics.com. accessed 12 Jun 2021

Sunday, 26 April: Cleaned room, shined shoes, got uniforms ready for what's to come. No shower party[44] tonight, which was a relief. Probably going to have a run tomorrow morning, so need to be ready for that.

Monday, 27 April: Upperclassmen woke us up at 0400 by kicking on doors and blowing whistles. Ran us to parade field, up and down hills with rifles at high port [arms extended over our heads]. Two dropped out. Got back to dorm, uniform inspections and SAMI [Saturday Morning Inspection] before morning formation and IRI [In Ranks Inspection]. Uniform inspections after class in quadrangle—had to run up to room on sixth floor, change uniform, run back down six floors for inspection. Did that four times. Had a SI [Special Inspection] before evening meal formation for 25 minutes. Completely soaked my Alphas [dress uniform]—heavy sweat. Tables weren't as bad as I thought they'd be, but tough shower party after evening meal. Gonna be a long week…

Tuesday, 28 April: Thankfully no run before breakfast. Waxed floors during free period. Had intramurals after class, so no SI. Lots of screaming at evening meal, lost my voice. Shower party at 1915. Drop, get up, drop, get up, etc. etc. Really tough. Can hardly raise my arms. Don't know how long this can continue.

Wednesday, 29 Apr: What a day. Run this morning was long, but good—no one dropped out, no one puked. Waxed floors, had a SI, numerous uniform changes in

---

44 | The dreaded "shower party," conducted by upperclassmen and designed to put stress on doolies through intense physical and mental pressure, consisted of running in place, pushups, screaming interrogations, and impossible demands.

afternoon. Had another SI this evening. Really tough. Tables at evening meal formation were loud and hard. Surely tomorrow will be easier. Shower party tonight should be a bitch...

Thursday, 30 Apr: *No run this morning! Actually saw a glimmer of humor today. Was allowed to have a smoke after intramurals but had to be in a front leaning rest [push-up position] the whole time. Shower party tonight was hard but fun—lots of screaming, but some humor as well. Almost seems like third classmen are showing signs of humanity. The whole week has been worth it—only 1½ days left!*

Friday, 1 May: *Shorter run this morning. IRI at morning formation, knowledge at tables, but not mean—actually enjoyed it. Left us alone after class. No SI. Shower party was fun—obstacle course set up in hallway, lots of humor from upperclassmen. Tomorrow's the big day—Recognition! Can't imagine what that's going to be like.*

Saturday, 2 May: *Marched to breakfast, Command Post played 'It's a Beautiful Morning' over loudspeakers as we marched into Mitchell Hall. What a feeling! Tables were very laid back. Recognition Parade after breakfast. It was good but, after we marched back to the Terrazzo, third classmen descended on us again, just like on Monday. About 10 minutes of screaming, rifle drill, and harassment, told to fall out and they pinned prop and wings [symbol of upper classman] on our chests! Unbelievable. Actually got to walk back to dorm, third classmen told us to call them by first names! Don't know that I'll ever get used to that.*[45]

45 | Mosier, Michael L. Diary annotations from *Checkpoints Calendar*, 1970.

As we looked back, our doolie year at the Academy was something none of us will forget. As was the intent, the intense mental, physical, and emotional demands played a significant role in our character development.

While the fourth-class system has evolved and changed over the years, the demands today are no less onerous than the demands in our time. Steve Lorenz, our classmate and former commandant of cadets, reflected on the differences between our doolie year and the doolie year that contemporary classes have experienced.

Steve Lorenz
CS-15

I have a saying: the toughest doolie year is your doolie year. For instance, the Class of '59 probably thought the Class of '65 had it easy. So you have to consider things in the context of the times. Has the Class of '23 done the same things we did? Heavens, no. Ours was a different time and a different place. As a result of the pandemic, the Class of 23's time here at the Academy is, in some respects, totally different—and, from that perspective, tougher than it was in our time. As an example, they had to do classes on Zoom rather than going to Fairchild Hall every day as we did, so there was a definite socialization, as well as academic, impact there. Now, at some point down the road, they will be at a bar or at the Club, telling stories about how tough it was during the pandemic. Of course, we had tough experiences, too—but different than theirs. I guess the bottom line is that comparing our experience with theirs isn't particularly useful. It's neither right nor wrong—it's just different.[46]

46 | Interview with Stephen R. Lorenz, September 28, 2021.

THIRD-CLASS YEAR: A DAY IN THE LIFE

Mercifully, the intensity that was doolie year quickly faded as we found ourselves taking on new summer challenges and opportunities: Survival, Evasion, Resistance, and Escape training in the mountains of Colorado; and the Zone of the Interior field trip to a variety of operational Air Force units in the continental U.S. Best of all, we were rewarded with three glorious weeks of summer leave.

When we returned to the Academy to begin the new academic year, we all thought life would be sweeter as upperclassmen; however, we didn't anticipate the crushing academic load and the daily grind that was our sophomore year. Consider this description of a cadet's typical day during fall semester, third-class year.

I hate that alarm.

The obnoxious, ear-splitting buzz from my white Timex alarm clock shakes me out of a deep sleep. I lay in my bed for a minute to let my head clear, then struggle to a sitting position, swing my feet over the side of the bed, put my head in my hands. I finally heave a sigh and struggle to my feet. Welcome to another Monday morning at the Blue Zoo.

My roommate and I wordlessly toss our sleeping blankets back into our laundry bins and smooth out our permanently made beds. Doolie year we had to sleep under the covers but, now that we're upperclassmen, we sleep on top because it saves having to make our beds in the morning. We shave, dress, clear our desks, and wipe down the sink with a towel. Outside our door a doolie is standing at rigid attention by the mirrors at the end of the hallway, shouting at the top of his lungs: "SIR, THERE ARE

*TEN MINUTES TO FIRST CALL! UNIFORM IS SER-
VICE BRAVO WITH PARKAS, HOODS UP! THERE
ARE TEN MINUTES TO FIRST CALL, SIR!" We quickly
finish getting our room in inspection order, put on our
black wool parkas, tug our dark blue stocking caps over
our short-cropped hair, and join our squadron mates
streaming out of rooms and heading toward the doors at
the end of the hallway. Everyone crowds into the stairwell,
noisily clambers down the two floors, and exits out onto
the Terrazzo and the morning meal formation. The doolies are already formed up and waiting in the frigid air.
Bright lights from the dorm push back the early morning
darkness, illuminating the rows of uniformed cadets. We
stand at attention in formation, waiting for our turn as
the squadrons ahead of us to march to Mitchell Hall.*

*We march to all three meals, seven days a week. While
the breakfast formation tends to be more perfunctory, the
noon meal march-on is more formal: uniforms and hair
are inspected, squadron and flight commanders carry
sabers, the Air Force Academy band sets the cadence, and
all 40 squadrons march in sequence to our dining facility in Mitchell Hall. It's a ritual we've followed since we
came to the Academy, and one we'll repeat each day until
graduation. Tourists line the Chapel wall to witness the
ceremony. Some gaze in respectful silence, some point and
laugh at the formalities below. I find that annoying. The
way I look at it, tourists are an unnecessary and unwanted
distraction.*

*As we march through the open doors, I'm greeted by a blast
of warm air, the faint smell of bacon, and the din of 4,000*

cadets moving to their assigned tables. Doolies continue to march at attention, eyes straight ahead; upperclassmen casually stroll, sometimes stopping to yell at a doolie who has lost his way among the maze of tables. Like everything else, it's a ritual we've all come to take for granted.

Mitch's is a huge, open structure, framed by huge aluminum-and-glass walls and a three-story high ceiling. The 1.7 acres of floor space holds an array of 400 precisely aligned tables, each set with white hard plastic plates, silverware, and glassware on white tablecloths. Each table seats 10 cadets, typically three doolies at one end, the senior cadet "table commandant" at the other, and additional upperclassmen filling in. We stand at our seats until all 4,000 cadets are at their places. The Wing Adjutant calls the Cadet Wing to attention, then gives the orders and announcements of the day from his perch on the Staff Tower—a small collection of tables for Wing Staff and dignitaries on a second-floor mezzanine overlooking the expanse of tables below. If there's an official visitor, he/she is introduced. We hate these introductions, as we only have 23 minutes to eat, regardless of how long the preliminaries last. We remain standing at attention until the Adjutant commands, "Gentlemen, take your seats." That's followed by the simultaneous scraping of thousands of chairs and the resumption of conversations as everyone is seated. An army of waiters emerges from kitchen doors, wheeling stainless steel carts around to each table and simultaneously distributing the gleaming serving containers to each doolie sitting at rigid attention at the end of the table. The doolie passes the steaming containers to the table commandant, then passes around the containers of orange juice, milk, and coffee to the rest of the table.

What Mitch's food lacks in sophistication, it makes up for in quantity. I heard once that a typical cadet burns more than 4,500 calories per day, so our waiters are quick to refill food containers as many times as we require. This morning's breakfast is typical of most: scrambled eggs, sausage links, bacon, toast, pancakes, and a variety of cereals. When not serving or responding to a question or comment, doolies are required to sit upright, shoulders back, eyes down on their plates. As they silently eat, they're occasionally corrected for appearance and conduct, and peppered with general knowledge questions, like 'How many days until graduation?', 'Name the cadets at the table and where they're from,' or 'Who's the commander of Tactical Air Command?' As a result, they don't have much time to eat. At some tables, the upperclassmen are harsh, but at our table, the firstie table commandant takes an interest in our doolies and asks how they're doing. One of the doolies at my table is heading for academic probation in Chemistry, so the firstie directs him to 'drive around' to his room after the evening meal for counseling. Our 23-minute meal ends with the doolie at the end of the table asking the pro-forma question: 'Sir, do you or any other gentleman at the table have any remarks or suggestions for the Form Oh Dash Nine Six?' Hearing none, he dutifully checks the required boxes on our waiter's O-96 critique form: 'fast,' 'neat,' 'average,' 'friendly,' 'good,' 'good,' and then writes 'None' in the 'Remarks' and 'Suggestions' sections—always with periods. We leave only when formally dismissed. Within 30 minutes of our entry, *the massive dining facility is empty except for the army of waiters policing up the tables.*

I have a first period class so, after eating, I leave the dining hall and proceed directly to Fairchild Hall with its six stories of classrooms, laboratories, and lecture halls. As I stroll across the Terrazzo, I can see the horizon starting to brighten across Black Forest, far to the east. It looks like it's going to be another clear Colorado day. Except for the occasional car on I-25, there's no sign of civilization in the distant hills, which heightens our sense of isolation.

As with every other aspect of cadet life, even walking to class involves a ritual: doolies run along the Terrazzo's light gray marble strips, stopping whenever they pass an upperclassman to yell a greeting such as, 'Good morning, Sir!' Most carry heavy, scuffed brown leather attaché cases issued to basics during in-processing. The ugly and cumbersome bag is filled with books, and it swings awkwardly as the doolies stop and start on their narrow marble pathway. Between the dorms and Fairchild Hall, doolies may stop and start 20 or 30 times to shout the required greeting. Their yelling echoes across the Terrazzo. The process is hardly efficient, but it's a recognized part of the training regimen. Some upperclassmen hold their arms out with two fingers extended. The two fingers mean 'as you were,' signaling the doolie to continue without stopping.

Finding my way through Fairchild Hall was confusing at first, but by now I don't even think about it or even look where I'm going. As I enter through one of the heavy aluminum doors, my gaze settles on the glassed-in bookstore across the foyer. I'm in luck: the 'Bookstore Lady' comes into view. A rare female in a sea of young men, the beautiful girl with the long hair and dazzling smile reminds us of girlfriends in hometowns across America. She smiled at me once; the sight of her always cheers me up.

Our typical academic day is a complex mixture of lectures, formal classroom instruction, and hands-on laboratory sessions. The schedule is organized into separate 'M' and 'T' days, which alternate throughout the academic year. While there's no formal posting or announcement of what day it is, I intuitively know 'M' vs. 'T' now, without any reference. Academics are very difficult. Back home, my high school buddies are taking 12 hours each semester and have time to goof off after class. Not us—this semester I'm taking 20.5 semester hours of classes, all from the core curriculum. I can't wait to get into my major courses next year so I can pull my GPA up; in the meantime, I've got to make it through the core courses. My lightest semester so far has been 16.5 hours, my heaviest was 24 hours and, at this rate, I'll graduate with more than 210 semester hours. Even if I decided to major in liberal arts, after four years I'd accumulate enough of the required science and engineering hours to graduate with a Bachelor of Science degree. My original plan was to major in Astronautics, but my toughest course this semester has been Engineering Mechanics 361, so I won't be going the Astro route. Let's face it—Mech isn't fun. It's not intuitive, and it takes up 80% of my study time.

My favorite course by far has been Human Physiology, so I've decided to drop Astro and sign up for Life Sciences

(Life Sci). Life Sci is currently the most popular major at the Academy, with more cadets enrolled in that major than any other program, including all engineering disciplines. But, regardless of how interesting a class may be, with our hectic schedule and lack of sleep it's always a struggle to stay awake. Cadets who nod off are directed by the instructor to stand at the back of the classroom. That doesn't always work for me—one time in Econ I fell asleep standing up. I managed to catch myself before I collapsed on the floor, but it caused a real commotion.

Our academic instructors are all captains and majors. They're PhDs and recognized experts in their subject areas, but many are pilots with recent combat experience in Southeast Asia. I guess they realize that in a few years we'll be working for and flying alongside them, so they take a genuine interest in us. We're not shy about trying to lure them into telling us stories about the 'Real Air Force.' They're happy to do that, but only if we've covered all the required material and still have a few minutes left in the 50-minute period. Their stories are important to us, because they remind us that there's a life after the Academy. That helps us stay motivated.

My last class this particular day is Mech. My instructor is at the board at the front of the room, chalk in one hand and eraser in the other. He's in continuous motion, side-stepping his way across the board, scribbling equations with his right hand and erasing with his left, dryly commenting as he goes. It's a mind-numbing progression of numbers and symbols. As hard as I try to concentrate on what he's saying, my thoughts wander to intramurals after class today. It's fall season—the first of three intra-mural seasons in the academic year—and I'm playing tackle football. Because most of us played football in high school, it's a pretty high level of play. Today we'll be playing the reigning Fourth Group champions, 32ⁿᵈ Squadron. I thoroughly enjoy intramurals; they're a great way to let off steam and clear the head. Penalties are rarely called, so play is always aggressive and everyone hits hard. It's also an equal opportunity program, as there's no distinc-tion made between year groups on the athletic field. That means we can hit anyone without repercussions.

As the final bell rings, we all quickly pack up our books and hustle out of the classroom and into the wide marble hallway. I follow the highly polished floors past a succes-sion of classroom doors to my right. On my left, a solid wall of glass windows gives me an expansive view of the fading green parade field below. I climb a stairwell and exit Fairchild next to the Cadet Library, glad to be out into the crisp Colorado afternoon. Up against the mountains, the shadows are already lengthening, and I can feel the temperature starting to fall. I'm headed to the dorm where I'll drop off my books and hustle down to the Cadet Gym, another quarter mile from the New Dorm ⁴⁷.

The football game is a good one. We lose by three points, but everyone plays well, and our squadron team is proud to have made a good showing against 32ⁿᵈ Squadron. I quickly shower and change, then leave the gym and climb

---

47 | Although construction on the New Dorm was completed in late 1968, it wasn't formally named until 1976 when it was dedicated to Captain Lance P. Sijan, Medal of Honor winner from the USAFA Class of 1965.

the stairs leading toward the cadet area. Now it's starting to get dark, as the sun has dropped behind the mountains. My black wool parka wards off the chill.

On the way I decide to make a quick detour to the mail room in Vandenberg Hall. The mailroom is a gloomy concrete enclosure on the ground floor, but it's a welcome refuge for cadets because it represents a vital lifeline to girlfriends, family, and friends. I quickly walk past the rows of tarnished bronze mailboxes, envelopes occasionally visible behind small windows. I generally average a letter only once every two weeks, but I'm hoping this will be my lucky day. I finally come to Box 2546 and eagerly peer through the window. No luck, empty. Well, maybe next time. I hustle up the stairwell to the Terrazzo, take a short-cut through the Air Gardens—forbidden territory when I was a doolie—and head back to the New Dorm to get ready for the evening meal formation.

After the evening meal, I leave Mitch's and head back across the Terrazzo to attend to my squadron additional duty; this semester I'm the Linen Rep. It's easy. We put our clothing in individual mesh bags to be sent out to the 'Denver Destroyers,' so-named because the Denver-based laundry company somehow manages to crush shirt buttons or wear small holes in our t-shirts on a regular basis. A tag on each laundry bag has our cadet serial number on it. Mine is 734827K, and every bit of my clothing has that number stamped somewhere on it. Even my wooden coat hangers are stamped with the number. Once the laundry is returned, our squadron doolies deliver the neatly pressed items to our rooms. As the designated Linen Rep,

I'm also responsible for collecting the dirty sheets and tow-els everyone has dumped into the large gray laundry cart. When I get the clean linen back from the Denver Destroy-ers, I set it out to be picked up on a one-for-one exchange, using the honor system.

After I complete my Linen Rep duties, I walk through the quiet hallway back to my room. On the way I pass by the CQ office. All third classmen serve as CQs on a rotational basis, and today it's my former roomie Mike. As the CQ, Mike's duties consist of manning the duty phone, acting as squadron security, and attending to a myriad of minor administrative matters. Outside the CQ office, there's a large light brown bulletin board with announcements, daily information, and a variety of rosters. Today there's a sign-up list for a Ski Club trip to Breckenridge, along with a list of cadets who have been reported for missing a class. My name is on the list, so I enter a code for 'excused CQ duty' to avoid any disciplinary repercussions. There's also a computer printout alpha roster listing all '73 squadron members, and I initial next to my name to show I've com-pleted my dental appointment for wisdom teeth screening. Had I missed the appointment, I'd have been written up on a Form-10, which is used to document infractions and assign disciplinary actions. That's something I'm familiar with, as I briefly held the record for the most infractions and weekend confinements in the squadron. Confine-ments are no fun—stuck in my room for one hour per confinement, with no TV, radio, or entertainment of any kind. The only upside is that when the CQ or my AOC isn't peering in through my open door, I can sneak in a nap while sitting at my desk.

The seven-story New Dorm only opened year before last [1968], so we were among the initial cadre to move into our newly formed squadron. Our squadron area has 115 cadets living in three hallways arranged in a 'U' shape. Although cadets come from almost every state, our squadron's senior leadership last year all came from Arkansas, which is why our newly designed squadron patch has an Arkansas Razorback on it. The cadet squadron commander and his operations officer are in a centrally located room, right across from the CQ office. To a large extent, our squadron life is defined by these two cadets. The squadron is divided into three flights, and my room is in the C Flight hallway.

Our AOC is an A-7 pilot and he's a good guy. He's not particularly enthusiastic about this assignment. He views it as not much more than a glorified babysitter and he's anxious to get back to the cockpit. He generally stays in the background, guiding where necessary but otherwise letting us run the squadron. He does pull people into his office occasionally to get to know us better, check for problems, and offer advice. Given my reputation as the 'confinement king,' he's gotten to know me pretty well.

Outside of our generic leadership/management classes in Fairchild Hall, I don't think there's a particularly well-defined cadet leadership program. No one has ever told me what my third-class cadet responsibilities are with respect to training the fourth class. Our first and second classmen haven't formalized a program, let alone assigned us any specific responsibilities. Because we really don't have any guidance, my classmates and I tend to manage our doolies the way we were treated when we were doolies. So I do what I think makes sense: correct appearance and actions, often raising my voice; occasionally check their rooms; and organize a bit of manpower when there's a need for a detail, such as passing out laundry. Today I've been giving them heat for not coming up with an original spirit prank to support the football team for the upcoming game this weekend.

So far, we haven't lost too many classmates in my squadron. We started with 34, and 31 are still hanging in there [though only 24 will eventually graduate]. Skip Sanders is my roommate by mutual choice. While I'm not a particularly motivated cadet, the Academy is where Skip always wanted to be. From that perspective, he's definitely good for my attitude. He's also a gregarious guy, which probably isn't so good for my study habits. By now Skip knows my life story and helps me out without being asked. Unlike me, he takes every advantage the Academy offers, such as trying out for the Academy Parachute Team. He also loves intramurals and, being a good athlete, he excels in both. Despite our lack of funds (our monthly pay jumped from $28 per month as doolies to a whopping $43 as third classmen), Skip pumps a lot of change into one of two pay phones in the squadron to make expensive long-distance calls to his girlfriend. He says they're going to get married at graduation.

We don't have a lot of opportunities for outside distractions. The sound system in our room is rudimentary; I have a cheap Sony reel-to-reel tape deck and Skip has a turntable to play records off my basic speakers. Cadet

Store albums seem expensive at $2.10 each, so we don't have much of a collection. Skip's Sansui tuner allows us to listen to KKFM, which plays alternative rock from obscure albums, rather than following the typical Top 40 format. We only get four Off Duty Privileges (ODPs) each semester, which means we're allowed to leave the Academy after training on a Saturday or Sunday morning and sign back into the squadron by Taps at 2230. Best of all, now that we're upperclassmen, we can wear civilian clothes, rather than the official gray wool slacks and dark blue Academy blazers that all doolies are required to wear on the rare occasion they're allowed off-base. As upperclassmen, we also get one weekend off this semester, although we'd get more if we were on the Dean's List with a 3.0 average, which neither of us are. Although we rarely get off-base, Skip is good for getting me out of the room at every chance. We go to the snack bar in Arnold Hall to hang out and occasionally attend a concert. Last weekend we saw the band Chicago. We have a home football game this weekend and, if we win, we'll hopefully get a free ODP. If we do, we'll probably go to our sponsor's house where we'll be welcomed with unlimited refrigerator privileges.

Skip and I do some studying after 1900 Call to Quarters but, after Taps plays at 2230 we go shower, as the six-head shower room is usually empty then. We won't go to bed for at least another hour or so because that's about the only free time we get. If any of our classmates are up, we'll join them to shoot the breeze on most any subject, but our sessions generally revolve around girls and our plans for the upcoming Christmas break.

My classmates and I are already bonded by doolie year, and the bonds grow even tighter as we struggle through our third-class year. As third classmen we're at the peak of our cynicism, and we often criticize what we see as pointless Academy rules and routines. That's always a lively topic of conversation. Rings, cars, and graduation are other frequent topics of conversation, but they all seem like a lifetime away. That adds to the feeling that our third-class year is a year in purgatory. It also fuels our cynicism.

We return to our room around 0100 and get ready for bed. As we do that, Skip again reminds me we'll both choose OV-10s at the end of pilot training, a distant four years away. We both were impressed with that airplane on a field trip we took this last summer. First things first, though—we have less than two months to go before Finals Week, and then Christmas break. With a sigh, I pull the stem out on my alarm clock, make sure the wake-up time is set for 0545, climb onto my permanently made bed, and pull my sleep blanket over my exhausted body. Sleep always comes fast and deep.

Only two-and-a-half years to go.[48]

ALTERNATE PATHS: WHY SOME LEFT

While we all started out with the intention of graduating, it didn't work out for all of us. Gen. Olds wasn't far off in his prediction: of the 1,406 who entered, 844 of us graduated—right at 60 percent.

Lack of motivation was the deciding factor for many. Some quickly

---

48 | Munson, Robert A. and Mosier, Michael L., "A Day in the Life of a Third-Classman." April 22, 2022.

discovered that the harsh reality of Academy life didn't match the pictures in the catalogues and brochures. For others, it was due to either a growing awareness that life in the Air Force wasn't what they wanted, or because their primary motivation for going to the Academy was to meet parental expectations. Either way, it became impossible to endure the demands, pressure, and stress of four years at the Academy.

Academic shortcomings accounted for many of our losses. "Grading on a curve," the practice of comparing academic performance to one's peers and awarding grades according to the "bell curve" distribution, vs. establishing set percentage thresholds to define grades, meant that some of us were bound to fail on any given exam. Given the high academic standards for admission, grading on a curve made for a highly competitive academic environment. At the same time, the byproduct of this grading practice was a drive for excellence.

Some of life's most valuable lessons are learned through failure, as much as through success. As traumatic as it is to be dismissed for academic shortcomings, it can also contribute to character development. One of our former classmates, Bob Pineiro, is a prime example. He explained how he was able to convert failure into long-term success.

Leaving the Academy was a traumatic experience for me because I flunked out. It happened at the end of the first semester of our third-class year. Going into the Christmas finals I didn't study at all, and I paid a high price for it.

Bob Pineiro
CS-34

In the end, the failure taught me a number of important lessons. One of the most obvious was to be more disciplined about studies and completing assignments. I also learned that I could do a lot more than I thought I could do, whether it was intramurals or all the other activities, in addition to academics. From that perspective, the biggest thing I learned was the ability to accomplish a great deal in a short amount of time—the Academy taught us all to prioritize our days and accomplish a great deal in those 18 waking hours.

In my career after the Academy, I strove to complete my assignments on time or early. But even more important, I learned how to fall down and get back up again. So, while leaving the Academy was a hard lesson, it prepared me to survive difficult situations in later years.[49]

TAKING THE LEAD

Leadership development was, in one form or another, an essential component of all aspects of cadet life, but it really came to the forefront when it came time for us to take our place in the Wing as upperclassmen. While we were taught the academic concepts in the classroom, we ended up learning the most enduring lessons in our squadron areas, on the Terrazzo, and on the athletic fields. Some lessons were learned from positive examples, some from negative. John Wigington considered how his perspective changed when he became an upperclassman.

John Wigington
CS-14

As I look back, there were three things that impacted my leadership style. The first was 'how not to' lead. We all saw cadet squadron commanders or AOCs using the hammer to make cadets conform or behave. Others took the approach to reason with cadets to help focus our actions. The positive interactions we had with academy officers helped set the tone that we would use as leaders.

49 | Interview with Roberto Pineiro, April 29, 2020.

During our four years at the Academy, we saw the beginning of the shift in how fourth classmen were treated. During our doolie year, I can remember being in the 'front

leaning rest' [push-up] position for what seemed like hours (although I never figured out the 'rest' part). By the time we became firsties, that approach had changed in that the emphasis shifted to positively motivating and encouraging the fourth classmen. The lesson we learned was that people respond better to leadership that imparts understanding and encouragement, rather than to fear or coercion.

The second cadet experience that impacted me was when some of us transferred squadrons, in most cases during second-class year or just prior to our first-class year. We transferees were the new guys in the squadron and had to adjust to the new environment and existing interpersonal dynamics. We had to assess how we would fit in and what we needed to do to become a part of the squadron, aside from just wearing the squadron patch. This was like being reassigned to another unit when on active duty, and taught us the importance of a new leader taking the time to assess and understand the state of the organization and the mindset of its members.

As cadets, 'time' was our most valuable—and limited— resource. We learned to manage our time, weighing the risk and reward of our allocation decisions. We all had

*to make priority judg-
ments, such as focusing
time on an upcoming
paper at the expense of
not reading the lesson in
another course, where
there might be a pop-
quiz. There were other
trade-off decisions to be made, such as taking an ODP vs.
spending extra time on academics. We all learned to make
decisions and accept the consequences of those decisions.*[50]

Of course, as we look back with the advantage of more than 50 years
of hindsight and maturity, some of the lessons imparted through a rigorous disciplinary system are obvious. But, at the time, many—if not
most—of us had to learn through the occasional misstep and painful
experience. Joe Kahoe, now a retired colonel, was typical of many of us
in our cadet years.

Joe Kahoe
CS-07

*Overall, my memory of the Academy was that I
was a pretty mediocre cadet. My goal was just to
graduate and go off to the 'Real Air Force,' which
I thought had to be better than this place. I was
an immature teenager: rebellious, pushing back
all the time, and resisting guidance at every turn.
I was always envious of our contemporaries at
civilian colleges like Boulder [University of Colo-
rado], partying their butts off while we were out marching
or doing some other military-type activity that I wasn't
exactly fond of. What also stands out in my mind were*

50 | Wigington, John T. "What a Leader of Character Looks Like from a Joint Agency Perspective." March 21, 2020.

the one hundred tours I marched for disciplinary infractions. When I reflect on those times, I wonder how I even graduated.

In some ways I remember my Academy years with great fondness. In other ways, I don't know how I managed to get through four years of that. When I graduated, I threw my hat in the air and was on cloud nine but had every intent to be the first one to the door when I finished my pilot training commitment. And then, 30 years later, in what seems like a blink of the eye, came retirement. They had to pry me out of the Air Force.[51]

Bob Munson considered his cadet career to have gotten off to a slow start. However, looking back, he realized that not only was the learning taking place, but that his budding leadership skills had an impact far beyond what he understood at the time.

When I went through the Academy, for the most part I was mentally challenged by going to a place that really wasn't my first second or third choice. And the Academy really wasn't what I wanted in a college—it wasn't what I was hoping for in the way of a college experience. That affected me throughout the time I was at the Academy. In fact, I was one of the guys who just wanted to get through and graduate. From that perspective, I didn't take advantage of everything the Academy offered, such as trying for leadership positions. Looking back, though, there were obviously important things I learned.

Bob Munson
CS-34

51 | Interview with Joseph J. Kahoe, March 27, 2020.

For instance, in my second-class summer, I was an element sergeant in First BCT—not a particularly sought-after job. But, about seven years ago, I got an email from a newly retired major general who told me a story about that Doolie Summer long ago that I had forgotten about.

As it turns out, I had been this retired major general's element sergeant. Another element sergeant and I had been talking about how our basics had terrible attitudes and many of them wanted to quit. They were crying, they were whining—they hated what they were going through and doing badly. We knew something had to change. So, the other element sergeant and I decided to round up all the basics in our room late at night, after Taps. We quietly woke them up and told them to come on down the hallway to our room. We had them all sit down, and I told them, 'Look, as far as we're concerned, this session didn't happen. Don't say, 'Yes, Sir.' Don't say, 'No, Sir.' Don't say anything—just listen.'

My speech to them was basically that they would look back on these weeks as being the funniest time in their lives. They'd talk about how their classmates screwed up, how they screwed up, and how the upperclassmen screwed up. Then I told them that if all they did was try to do the best they could, in the end they would not fail. We were putting pressure on them to make it look like they were failing, but we knew they wouldn't be able to answer every knowledge question perfectly. It didn't matter that they couldn't hold their rifle at port arms for 10 minutes while we were screaming at them. No one could do it, and we knew that. We were putting pressure on them to teach them a lesson

*about effort, perseverance, and the importance of sup-
porting their classmates. In the end, that's what it's all
about. And then we dismissed them by saying 'Tomorrow we're going to be on your tails again but, if you want
to get through this badly enough, you'll get through.' And
apparently that, at least for one future two-star general,
made all the difference.*[52]

Leaders must hold themselves—and their people—accountable
for their actions. That's a difficult lesson for a young cadet to learn, but
essential in later years when the stakes are higher. A.J. Ranft described
the lesson he learned in accountability over his four years at the Academy.

*Initially I was doing very well both militarily and
academically, but in our third-class year I guess I
got a little cocky. At the time, I was rooming with
two other guys, so we had a three-person room,
which was pretty unusual. And, as it turns out,
that really wasn't good for any of the three of us,
because it was more like a frat house. One night
all three of us decided to go Over the Fence [leav-*

A.J. Ranft
CS-11

*ing campus without authorization]. We got caught and, as
a result, had to meet a Commandant's Disciplinary Board.
The outcome was that we were restricted over Thanksgiv-
ing—no leave. I'll never forget calling my mother about
a week before I was supposed to go home for Thanksgiv-
ing and telling her that I wasn't going to be able to attend.
'Why?' she asked. I said, 'Because first, I'm on academic
probation. And second, I just got a formal punishment
and can't leave anyway.' She started sobbing.*

52 | Interview with Robert A. Munson, July 5, 2021.

Now there are some guys in your squadron who could do bad things and never get caught. But then there are guys like me: if you do something bad, you'll get caught, guaranteed. What I learned from that experience was that if you're going to do the crime, you need to be willing to do the time, and you need to know that upfront. So that was a strong—but painful—lesson in accountability for me.[53]

The higher up you go in the chain of command, the broader your perspective—and the greater your responsibility to the institution. We learned this first-hand when our new commandant, Gen. Vandenberg, decided to change the role of our squadron AOCs from actively leading cadets, to remaining in the background and simply advising the cadet chain of command. Having the direct responsibility of running the wing was a fundamental change, as Kees Rietsema, our cadet wing commander during our first-class, year recalled.

Kees Rietsema
CS-14

In the months of the 1972-1973 school year, I spent a great deal of time in the commandant's office. In fact, I only attended about 50 percent of my classes; most of the rest of the time was spent dealing with the Cadet Wing on one hand and the commandant's staff on the other. Gen. Vandenberg wanted the cadet chain of command to become the focal point of Wing leadership, and the officers (the commandant's military staff in particular) were there only to support. Consequently, on a majority of issues, I often found myself sandwiched between the Cadet Wing and the commandant's officers. I was held accountable. Since Gen. Vandenberg's objective was to hold the

53 | Interview with Andrew J. Ranft, April 27, 2021.

cadet chain of command responsible for the leadership of the Wing, a hot line from his desk directly to my room was installed and I was regularly summoned to appear in his office at all hours of the day. We often met early in the morning before the normal breakfast meal at Mitchell Hall where he would, in his words, 'pump me full of thousands of ccs of blue and silver.'

Gen. Vandenberg was a product of his times, and his style was that of a traditional military leader. He was very conscious of his family's lineage and role in USAF history.[54] It was important to him to be viewed as 'hard core' and he expected that of us as well. I recall, on more than one wintry morning when the rest of the faculty and commandant's staff were excused from arriving at the Academy for work, Gen. Vandenberg would rail about the fact that only the hard core (he) had the toughness to make the trip through the snow and be present for duty...a true example of what he expected of others.

He was not particularly thrilled with having to be the commandant of cadets. He saw little alignment between his military background and the needs of this posting, where he was in charge of the training of roughly 4,000 young men. However, for me and the cadets he interfaced with, he was a window into the 'Real Air Force.' We understood his vision of being hard core and even had calling cards printed up with the words, 'Lead Follow or get the Hell Out of the Way!'

---

54 | Brigadier General Hoyt S. Vandenberg, Jr. was the son of General Hoyt S. Vandenberg, the second Air Force chief of staff.

One fine day, the telephone in my room rang and Gen. Vandenberg was on the line. He wanted me in his office— now. I sprinted across the Terrazzo and breathlessly arrived in his office, where he was standing at the large glass window overlooking the Academy grounds. He had a pair of binoculars in his hand that he thrust at me and pointed out a sole cadet crossing between buildings. I trained the binoculars on this individual and listened to the general tell me in no uncertain terms that this cadet was dressed in pants that were of the high-water variety [too short], and not acceptable. I responded that I would make this a point of emphasis in future meetings with the cadet staff.

As the cadet wing commander, I was obliged to eat meals on the Staff Tower in Mitchell Hall. During the winter months, when cadets wore their parkas to meals, the parka hood was worn over the top of a watch [stocking] cap. Routinely, as cadets marched into the dining hall, they would reflexively toss back the parka hood, but retain the watch cap on their heads until reaching their assigned tables. On the occasions when he attended meals, Gen. Vandenberg would stand on the Staff Tower, hands gripping the railing, knuckles turning white, with a frown on his face. The cadets were remaining 'covered'—wearing hats—indoors, which ran counter to USAF rules requiring hats to be removed as one entered a building. This was a particular irritant to the general, and he would often make that clear to me. One day, knowing that I could not continue to absorb the pain of the general's daily exhortations, I decided I'd make an attempt to demonstrate to *the general that removing one's watch cap while carrying books enroute to the table was simply inconvenient and not that important. My roommate, Deputy Wing Commander Ken Womack, and I made the trip to the general's office, in full parka regalia and arms loaded with books. Less than five seconds into my presentation on how inconvenient this all was, the general exploded, 'Rietsema, I don't care if it's raining s**tballs from heaven, you get those cadets uncovered in the dining hall!' After a meeting with the rest of the cadet staff and informing them of the gravity of the situation, the issue disappeared the next day in a flurry of Form-10s. Here was the lesson learned for me: had I been the least bit sensitive to what was obviously an ongoing irritant to the general, who was determined to promote the traditions of the service, I could have avoided the confrontation in his office and spent the green stamps I squandered there on something a bit more consequential.*

As cadet wing commander, I also learned of the loneliness of leadership. I was a member of the 14th Cadet Squadron. The prevailing attitude in the squadron was one of rebelliousness within the limitations of the USAFA system, and the perception was that I had moved to the so-called dark side of cadet wing leadership and aligned myself to some degree with the commandant. There were times when I wished I was back in the squadron![55]

With responsibility comes obligation, and not all the leadership lessons were easy to learn. Oftentimes, the cadet chain of command found

---

55 | Rietsema, Kees W. "What a Leader of Character Looks Like from a Former Cadet Wing Commander's Perspective." Undated.

themselves being put on the spot and having to make difficult and often unpopular decisions. Rowe Stayton cited an example of a difficult choice he faced between friendship and loyalty to the institution.

Rowe Stayton
CS-36

I was the commander of Fourth Group during our senior year. We were the first class, I believe, where the cadets, rather than the AOCs, ran the wing. It became our job to mete out punishments and privileges. We were also responsible for hiring the cadets in our chain of command. Because we were the first to be given these responsibilities, it was important to prove to the officer corps that we were up to the challenge. As the group commander, I wanted to demonstrate that we had the capability and maturity to do it. But that also meant that I had to make calls that oftentimes weren't popular. I have to say that, looking back, I made a few calls I regret but, at the time, these were the calls I felt I had to make to demonstrate that cadets could truly run the wing.

To illustrate the point, a situation arose in one of the squadrons involving the perceived integrity of their AOC— evidently, he had lied to the cadet squadron commander and had been difficult to deal with overall. The squadron commander came to me and basically demanded I take action. In his view, the AOC was violating basic values and the sense of duty we all cherished. The situation was particularly difficult for me to deal with because of the bonding and the relationships that we first classmen had among each other. After all, these were all really good, decent guys who were trying to do what they thought was the right thing. After consulting with other people about this situation, I decided it was in the best interests of the institution to relieve the squadron commander. Making it even more difficult, he was a good friend of mine.

Now, looking back, in the big scheme of things I don't know how important that decision was in our development as cadets and then, later, as officers. But I do think that one of the important lessons learned was the need to subordinate friendships to duty. We all develop friendships with people in the service, but sometimes you've got to make hard choices. In this particular situation, I don't even know if I made the right choice—but it was a choice I felt I had to make at the time. That's the nature of leadership development—it's easy to question certain calls when we can look back with experience, but we have to have the courage to make the tough calls. We do the best we can with the understanding we have at the time, then use that understanding to inform future actions.[56]

NEW HORIZONS

As the end of our second-class year approached and our excitement grew, two eagerly anticipated events represented our transition to the first class and eventual commissioning: rings and cars. Our class ring represented far more than graduation from an elite institution: it was symbolic of our joining the ranks of the fourteen classes that had graduated before us. It was also a symbol of permanence—the everlasting symbol of our membership in not only the growing graduate community, but also the officer corps of the United States Air Force. A new car, on the other hand, represented unprecedented freedom, as well as the first time most of us had owned such a coveted symbol of independence.

56 | Interview with Rowe P. Stayton, September 8, 2021.

Furthermore, because only first-classmen were allowed to have cars, this was a symbolic rite of passage. Rings and cars were exciting and tangible carrots that helped many of us endure the constant grind of academics and military training.

For most—if not all—of us, graduation couldn't come too soon, as the desire to live in a less-structured and less-regimented environment grew with every passing day. But even during our first-class year, the Academy's strict rules didn't allow much room for deviation. Gary Anderson looked back on one instance when he ran afoul of the disciplinary system just prior to graduation, and the consequences that left a strong impression on him.

Gary Anderson
CS-34

I felt responsible for one of the guys in my squadron having to go through an honor investigation first-class year. He had an accident on my motorcycle—which I was not allowed to own at the time. In an attempt to protect me from disciplinary action, when he was asked how his injury occurred, he avoided telling the whole story. That resulted in an honor investigation.

I ended up testifying on his behalf at his Board. During my testimony I confessed that I was the one who owned the motorcycle. I subsequently had to meet a Commandant's Disciplinary Board for violating the 'no motorcycle' rule. As punishment, I ended up spending the last months of my first-class year marching tours and serving confinements; consequently, I missed some pretty significant events, like Hundredth Night.[57] While everyone else was out celebrat-

57 | Hundredth Night is a milestone that marks one hundred days until graduation for the senior class. In our day, it was typically celebrated with a formal dinner, copious amounts of alcohol, and firstie rooms being gleefully trashed by fourth-class cadets.

ing one hundred days to graduation, I was confined to my room. At that age, a lot of us had a tendency to rebel against authority anyway. So, when I left the Academy, there were a lot of things I was glad to leave behind. The strict discipline was one of those things.[58]

As our first-class year passed, our excitement about being commissioned and going out into the real world grew. But the prospect of assuming our role as second lieutenants also had a sobering effect as we thought about our responsibilities as commissioned officers. This is where all our military training classes became less theoretical and more real. To Rocky Avvento, it was a growing awareness of the need for maturity and sound judgment in a gray world.

I remembered talking about moral dilemmas in military training classes. It was good that we were exposed to potential situations in a training environment, but it was rather academic. In discussing gray-world situations in the classroom we'd talk about what we thought was the right way to respond or the right decisions to make. Looking back, that was a very sterile, clinical environment. On the other hand, it was certainly important to understand that situations will come up in which there isn't a clear right or wrong answer, and that you're going to face difficult choices.[59]

Rocky Avvento
CS-02

First-class year brought most of us the ultimate prize: a pilot training slot and the chance to select an Undergraduate Pilot Training (UPT) base through a class-wide lottery system. Each of us took turns drawing

58 | Interview with Gary L. Anderson, April 19, 2022.
59 | Interview with Gennero J. Avvento, April 20, 2021.

numbers from a box, and the number drawn determined the order we would each select our UPT base and class start date from available assignments.

To help us prepare for the selection process, we scrutinized video presentations on each base in the spring of our first-class year. While pilot training was highly standardized at all bases, these videos helped us compare base facilities, local attractions, and most importantly, access to a long-repressed social life. When the highly anticipated moment arrived, we assembled in a lecture hall to make our base selection.

Denny Merideth remembered his growing excitement as graduation drew near and the operational Air Force was tantalizingly within reach.

Denny Merideth
CS-08

I felt the Academy prepared us well, not only for pilot training but for our responsibilities as Air Force officers. Operation Third Lieutenant[60] was particularly beneficial. I was fortunate to be assigned to Ramstein Air Base in an intel shop where I had the opportunity to work alongside airmen, non-commissioned officers, and junior officers. Then, as we progressed in our years at the Academy, we continued to be exposed to the bigger picture by talking with faculty and staff members about their experiences. So it was critical to develop those relationships with the captains, majors, and lieutenant colonels who helped us mature from cadets to Academy graduates.

60 | Operation Third Lieutenant was an opportunity for second-class cadets to be temporarily assigned to an Air Force unit, shadow Air Force personnel, and observe their daily routine.

I remember the excitement and anticipation of pilot training, but it was also the lure of flying fighters, which is all I had wanted to do for an exceptionally long time. All in all, it was a euphoric feeling as I thought about graduation.

We all realized that the war in Vietnam was winding down at that point and that the principal threat was now the Soviet Union. We were excited to step up and do our part. And I think the Academy experience convinced us that we could make an impact but, as part of a much larger team, rather than as individuals. We all felt that we had a role to play, and that it was our responsibility to do the best we could in whatever role we were assigned.

Of course, our near-term objective was to get to UPT, and maximizing our chances of success was an important consideration as we sorted through base options. A lot of us in my squadron decided to try to go to the same place, so we all wound up at Laughlin AFB in Del Rio, Texas. That ended up being a smart move because it provided us with a great mix of common shared experiences from the Academy and comradeship with our squadron mates in a healthy, competitive environment.

We respected one another and, having spent four years together, we knew each other's idiosyncrasies. There were a couple of classmates who felt this was just a step in the career ladder, but most of us were just focused on doing our best at the task at hand and just seeing where that may lead.[61]

61 | Interview with Denny J. Merideth, August 25, 2021.

Not everyone took a UPT slot. Those who went into non-flying specialties had differing motivations and experiences. For instance, Mitch Mitchell was not pilot-qualified and therefore had to consider other options.

Mitch Mitchell
CS-31

I took a look at the list of non-flying jobs that were available. At that time, the missile field had an advanced degree program so, if you went into missiles, you could get a master's as part of your job. In fact, alert tours were scheduled around the class schedule, so it was a great program. I was a mechanical engineering major at the Academy, and one of the advanced degree options was in engineering. So that looked like an attractive option. By the time I got to my first duty station at Grand Forks AFB, the master's program had changed from engineering to a Master's in Business Administration, but that turned out to be quite useful.

As far as preparing for commissioning was concerned, that was minimal for me as I was going into the Intercontinental Ballistic Missile (ICBM) field. Frankly, we never spent time at the Academy talking about strategic systems, or non-aircraft-related systems, for that matter. In fact, I don't even remember the term 'ICBM' ever being discussed in class. We may have talked about the nuclear triad, but only in terms of the manned bombers.

In those days, the Academy was very flying-oriented, to say the least. Those going on to pilot training were

well-prepared through the T-41 program[62], but it was
totally different for guys going into areas like acquisition,
finance, personnel, or missiles—there was no training at
the Academy to prepare us for those jobs.[63]

In Bob Allen's case, the decision to go into meteorology was a defin-
itive choice, rather than an inability to qualify for a UPT slot. Bob
explained his reasoning for taking a non-flying assignment.

Bob Allen
CS-12

As we approached graduation, I was a bit con-
flicted on what I wanted to do. Like most of my
classmates, I had completed the T-41 program
and had the opportunity to take a pilot training
slot. I thought long and hard about what I really
wanted to do after graduation. Pilot training
seemed to be the common expectation and, even
leading up to graduation, I felt pressured to take
that career path. Although I'd taken the T-41 program, I
just felt that my passion was in meteorology. Why meteo-
rology? The conclusion I came to was that I was probably
not smart enough to be a math major, a physics major, or
a chemistry major. But meteorology touched on all those
subjects and, as a guy who had a passion for the sciences,
that really appealed to me. So I turned down the UPT slot
and went to North Carolina State University in an Air
Force Institute of Technology-sponsored program to get
an undergraduate degree in meteorology. After gradua-
tion, my first duty assignment ended up being Fort Rucker,
Alabama as a staff meteorologist, which was an Air Force

62 | The T-41 program was a prerequisite for UPT entry, and consisted of very basic
training in a Cessna-172 aircraft.

63 | Interview with Robert V. Mitchell, September 14, 2021.

billet. So, from that perspective, I felt well-prepared for commissioning.[64]

Orderia "O" Mitchell also ended up turning down a pilot training slot, but it was a difficult choice. He reflected on the rationale that led to his ultimate career choice.

"O" Mitchell
CS-22

I had to make a tough decision coming up on graduation. Having majored in pre-med, I had applied to medical school. I knew that, if I were accepted, I'd have to choose between med school and pilot training.

Our commandant at the time, Gen. Vandenberg, told me he'd rather see me go to pilot training, but said the choice was up to me. But the war in Vietnam was over, and everything was de-escalating. So I asked Col. Carter, the head of the pre-med program at the Academy, for advice. He told me, 'You can go fly. But I think med school is the direction you ought to go.' I had always sought advice from people I trusted, so I decided this was the direction I ought to go.

I had applied to six medical schools and decided that I'd accept the first one that offered me a slot. I was fortunate enough to be accepted by all six schools, but Tulane was the first one to notify me, so that's the one I selected.[65]

Regardless of the initial assignments, excitement began to build as we worked our way through first-class year. For some, it was a time to

64 | Interview with Robert H. Allen, January 19, 2022.
65 | Interview with Orderia F. Mitchell, February 8, 2022.

plan a June Week wedding at the Cadet Chapel immediately following graduation. For others, it was a chance to resume a long-denied social life. Regardless, the closer we got to June 6th, 1973, the more our anticipation grew.

Graduation was now real.

PART II

BECOMING LEADERS OF CHARACTER

Many of us had our share of ups and downs as we transitioned from the Academy to the operational Air Force. In fact, the "Real Air Force" we had all heard about required a greater adjustment than many of us expected. The following chapters describe the stark reality that confronted us: life is rarely black or white, but rather painted in shades of gray.

3

OUR EARLY CAREERS

Regardless of our selected career field, after graduation we all reveled in the freedom we had been denied during our four years at the Academy. For some, that meant settling into married life. For others, it was the opportunity to regain an active social life that our civilian counterparts had enjoyed since high school. But, for all of us, our new Air Force responsibilities became a primary focus as we transitioned from cadets to commissioned officers.

PILOT TRAINING

For most of our class, UPT was the first step in our Air Force careers. In many ways, the rigor and intense pressure of pilot training was simply a continuation of our experiences at the Academy. We were constantly evaluated and tested on procedural knowledge before every flight and simulator event. During formal morning briefings in the flight room, a random student was called upon to stand up in front of instructors and peers. The unlucky selectee was then given a hypothetical aircraft emergency and grilled by a senior instructor on how to properly deal with the situation. The objective was to not only test the student's procedural knowledge, but to replicate the stress experienced in an airborne emergency. Incomplete or inaccurate responses resulted in the student being grounded for the day, so the stakes were high.

From Charlie Felton's perspective, the intensity of the flying program easily matched those of his Academy experiences, and in some ways, were more demanding.

Charlie Felton
CS-10

I got off to a rocky start in pilot training. I always felt like I was chasing the airplane, never mentally ahead of it. I was always wondering, 'Why isn't this airplane doing what I want it to do?' So, as I came up for solo in the T-37, I was last in my section, and I was thinking that, if I didn't get my act together, I'd be gone. My instructor was as frustrated as I was—he couldn't figure out what I was doing wrong. So, he decided to put me with another instructor in our flight, Lieutenant Gary Wood.

Gary was known by all of us as the infamous 'Lieutenant Doom,' because when his magnetic name tag on the scheduling board was flipped upside down, it spelled 'DOOM.' He was intimidating—a huge, no-nonsense guy who had a habit of grabbing your oxygen hose at the base of your mask and jerking your head around so he could chew you out face to face. So, when I saw that I was scheduled to fly with Lt. Doom, I knew I was in real trouble.

So off we went. I was so nervous, I was sweating through my gloves. We flew out to the work area, and he said, 'Okay, show me a spin prevention.' As I climbed to altitude, I mentally rehearsed the maneuver: slow to the edge of the stall, add a little rudder to initiate a spin, and then recover. But, as the airplane started into the spin, I stomped on the wrong rudder and the airplane literally went over on its back and snapped into a terrifying inverted spin. Gary grabbed my oxygen mask, pulled my face to within an inch of his, and screamed, 'No one has EVER put me in an inverted spin!' At that point, I was desperately trying to suck air through a crushed oxygen hose. He glared at me angrily and barked, 'Now, recover this damn thing!' He threw my head back over to my side of the cockpit.

Somehow, I managed to recover from the spin—how, I don't know. We then flew back to the traffic pattern at the base, where my problems continued. My first approach and landing were horrible. I did a touch-and-go, then came back around for another approach. Despite my best efforts, the same thing happened: airspeed off, altitude erratic, poor heading control. Mentally, I kept thinking, 'Come on, airplane, come on! What the heck is the matter with this thing?' Finally, Gary had seen enough and said, 'I have the aircraft.' He landed and we taxied in. At that point I remembered thinking, 'That's it; I'm done. Wow, that was a short Air Force career.'

Gary taxied to an open area of the ramp, shut down the right engine, and started unstrapping. As I started to unstrap along with him, he put his hand on my shoulder and said, 'Sit still.' Next thing I know, he climbed out, came over to my side of the cockpit and said 'Stop making f***ing excuses. Just put the airplane where you want it. I know you can do it. You did it in the spin recovery. Now, go solo.'

That simple statement changed me. My solo consisted

*of three of the prettiest patterns and landings I've
ever made.*[66]

Many of our instructors, particularly in the primary (T-37) phase,
were experienced combat pilots with multiple tours in Southeast Asia.
While most were friendly and approachable, some were harsh and
demanding. Steve Lorenz remembered one T-37 instructor who was
typical of some combat pilots-turned instructors—one who had a profound impact on his future. As he told the story,

Steve Lorenz
CS-15

*I had busted my ride prior to initial solo in the
T-37, and my flight commander decided to
make a change and see if a new instructor could
bring me up to speed. To my absolute horror, he
assigned me to the one IP we all dreaded, the
most difficult and demanding in the flight. He
was legendary, having flown OV-10s in Vietnam
and receiving the Air Force Cross for heroism. He
was also a product of his times: he flew hard and played
hard. Every other word was a swear word, and about once
every six weeks he got thrown out of the Officers' Club for
imbibing too much.*

*He also demanded the best from his students. His debriefs
were brutal, and he wouldn't tolerate anything less than
maximum effort from anyone, regardless of the circumstances. He flew his own way—flight suit sleeves rolled
up, gloves off, and checklist stuffed in the leg pocket of his
flight suit.*

66 | Interview with Charles Felton, February 4, 2022. Charlie was the only one of our
classmates who didn't have his picture taken for our senior yearbook—he broke both
arms in a bicycle accident during Spring Break and was unable to wear the parade
uniform for the senior class picture. This is his picture from second-class year.

I'll never forget our pre-flight briefing. He started out by saying, 'Always be hot and high, never be low and slow.' He must have said that ten times. We finished the brief, got our parachutes and helmets from the 'chute shop, and walked out to the flight line. I was nervous as a cat. Since I had busted my last pre-solo flight, I knew this would be my last chance.

He told me to get in the airplane and he proceeded to do the walkaround. Then he climbed in, quickly started the engines, and we taxied out. We took off, and he set me up for a straight-in approach, a single engine, and then a no-flap pattern and landing. After the last approach, he turned to me and yelled, 'Lorenz, you're going to kill me. Put her on the deck!' My heart sank; I was sure I had busted the ride and was on my way out the door. We landed, taxied to the hold area, and he directed me to shut down #2 engine. Then he turned, made a rude hand gesture, and repeated his mantra: 'Always be hot and high, never be low and slow.' That was when I realized he was going to let me solo. I was elated. I took off and flew a very uneventful solo sortie.

This IP had realized that I lacked confidence and just needed the right kind of instruction and motivation to succeed. He was rough, his techniques were unconventional, and he was a screamer when his students didn't perform up to his expectations. But he was a product of his Vietnam experiences and wouldn't allow me to fail. For that, I'll always be indebted.[67]

67 | Interview with Stephen R. Lorenz, January 13, 2022.

THE "REAL AIR FORCE": TRANSITIONAL SHOCK AND INCONGRUITIES

Once we completed the initial training for our chosen career field, we left the classrooms behind and took our places in Air Force organizations around the world. But that transition wasn't always smooth or easy.

The Honor Code undoubtedly had the greatest influence on our early development as leaders of character. The Code had been integrated into all aspects of our daily rituals, from taking unmonitored exams, to leaving valuables in unlocked rooms, to assuming absolute honesty from fellow cadets. It also led to the expectation that decisions, actions, and assumptions would be based on the same framework of integrity once we transitioned into the "Real Air Force." Unfortunately, we quickly discovered that the Academy we had left behind was different than the post-Vietnam environment we encountered on active duty. Bob Munson described the incongruities he discovered in his first assignment.

Bob Munson
CS-34

Like most of my classmates, I went into pilot training right after graduation. The program was really intense, with little room for additional training of any kind. As my classmates and I became accustomed to the 'fire hose' routine, we would occasionally hear IPs advise each other to 'do what you can; log what you need.' In other words, even if a student hadn't accomplished a required training event on a particular ride due to IP oversight or lack of opportunity, make the paperwork reflect a complete sortie. There just wasn't room in the curriculum for an extra ride just to make up a single maneuver.

That led to an integrity trap. In theory, if every single requirement on the student's two-page grade sheet wasn't completed, it could be completed later—that is, if there was an opportunity to do so on another sortie. But sometimes there wasn't. In those cases, the IP's default position became, 'Well, I know you can do it, so we'll just check it off.' Coming from the Academy environment, we had a hard time understanding that philosophy. The term 'pencil whipping' was something we weren't familiar with, but we all eventually discovered that it was an all-too-common practice in the Air Force.

After we got our wings, there later came an analogous integrity challenge with a different form of pencil whipping. In my unit, we dreaded the end of each fiscal quarter and, worse yet, the end of the fiscal year. We were expected to 'zero out the flight time,' which meant we should make the paperwork reflect the number of flying hours our unit had been allotted, whether actually flown or not. If there were insufficient flying hours on the last day of the quarter to accomplish mandatory training events, pilots were often directed to take the time necessary to complete the training sortie, but to document a shorter flight time, to ensure the paperwork would match the allotted flying time. Conversely, if there was more flying time available than required by a given sortie, the pilot was expected to log the 'correct' flying time to make the paperwork come out right.[68]

A.J. Ranft explained how difficult it was for him to maintain the black-or-white worldview from the Academy once he transitioned to his operational unit, and the importance of learning how to recognize important distinctions.

68 | Interview with Robert A. Munson, January 7, 2022.

When we were commissioned in the 'Real Air Force,' we found the world was not often black or white—it tended to be shades of gray.

A.J. Ranft
CS-11

To illustrate that, in the aircraft I was flying, we were constantly tested on visual recognition of Warsaw Pact [Soviet Union and their allies] aircraft and weaponry. And the truth was that, unlike when we were at the Academy, we collaborated on those tests. The prevailing attitude was that we were collaborating as a squadron because we would be going to war as a squadron, never by ourselves. Given that rationale, this commonly accepted practice didn't seem wrong to me. But then, in different circumstances when confronted with a true integrity issue, you had to be able to turn a switch in your mind and say, 'Okay, now this is different.' For instance, when we got an Operational Readiness Inspection (ORI), we had to take individual tests. We knew you didn't cooperate on that test—we all knew that. So, looking back on those gray areas, we had to learn when it was appropriate to cooperate as a group, and when it wasn't. Where it was accepted behavior and when, as in our Academy days, it was an integrity issue.[69]

Many of us encountered situations in which our foundational beliefs in honor and integrity from the Academy were directly challenged. Mike Mosier described one particular incident that illustrated the difficulties he faced.

After pilot training, I was assigned to Beale Air Force Base

69 | Interview with Andrew J. Ranft, April 27, 2021.

as a B-52 copilot. While at Beale, our Wing was hit with a no-notice ORI. My crew had been on alert when the ORI team hit our base, so we were launching off alert to fly our assigned mission.

Mike Mosier
CS-34

Right before engine start, the windshield panel in front of my aircraft commander (AC) suddenly shattered, with large cracks running from the center of the windshield toward the outer edges. My AC called the command post, described the situation, and asked for maintenance to come take a look. When the technician arrived and inspected the damage, he advised us that, if the cracks didn't extend to within an inch of the windshield frame or the glass didn't become too distorted, it would be safe to fly. So, we went ahead and launched.

The windshield got progressively worse as we flew the mission. While we were on the navigation leg, for some reason, I decided to draw a picture of the windshield, to include all the cracks, bubbles and resulting surface distortion. We completed the mission and landed uneventfully.

That was on a Friday. Next thing I knew it was early Saturday morning and the phone rang in my apartment. I answered the phone and it was my squadron commander. He said, in a cold voice, 'Mosier, come into the squadron, right now. Meet me at my office.' I didn't have any idea what was going on, but I threw my flight suit on, hurried out to the base, and hustled to the squadron commander's office. He and the operations officer were sitting there, arms crossed, waiting for me.

My squadron commander said, 'Mosier, I understand you drew a picture of the windshield that cracked on your aircraft.' And I said, 'Yes, sir.' He demanded, 'Where is it?' I said, 'Sir, it's in my locker.' He said, 'Go get it and bring it to me.' I did.

I handed it to him, he studied it, and said, 'Is this the way it really looked?' I responded, 'Yes, sir, that's accurate.' He reached over, grabbed a blank piece paper, and slyly said, 'Let's redraw this.' He drew the outline of the windshield and then drew a couple of small cracks. Then he gave me a knowing look and said, 'It looked pretty much like this, right?' I glanced at his drawing and said, 'No, Sir. What I drew in my picture is exactly what it looked like.' That was followed by a long, uncomfortable silence.

I think it was the ops officer who finally said, 'You do realize they might take away your bomb scores because you guys flew with a safety violation? Our wing could bust the ORI because of you.' That was followed by another long silence.

Finally, the squadron commander said, 'Then are you absolutely positive this is what it really looked like?' And I said, 'Yes, Sir.' There was another long pause. Finally, he dismissed me with an abrupt, 'Get out of here.' I left the office thinking to myself, 'Wow, that wasn't a particularly career-enhancing move.'

Fortunately for me, our wing passed the ORI. A few days later, the wing director of operations called me into his office and assured me that my efficiency report would not be adversely affected because of what I did. I was stunned. I can remember thinking to myself, 'Well, of course it wouldn't be adversely affected, because I told the truth. Why would that reflect badly on an efficiency report?'

This was my first experience confronting the incongruity between the Academy's Honor Code and the real world. And that, quite frankly, was a bit of a shock to me. It all worked out in the end, but it was a disillusioning lesson for a young, idealistic lieutenant to learn.[70]

As a young lieutenant, John Mann was stationed at Holloman AFB. He also remembered the challenges of transitioning from the Academy environment to the "Real Air Force," and reflected on the importance of finding like-minded allies to help work through the difficult situations he faced.

John Mann
CS-25

Prior to graduation, we heard the Air Force was having some issues with integrity, and that we needed to go out and be part of the solution. I remember thinking to myself, 'I'm going to be a second lieutenant. I don't know exactly how I can be part of this solution if I'm going to be the lowest ranking guy in the squadron.' I didn't understand how to take the things we were trying to learn from the Honor Code into the 'Real Air Force,' make a difference—and survive.

What I discovered is that you've got to pick your battles, the ones you can win as a second lieutenant. You need to find allies, find out where your support group is, and don't take things on by yourself. Get your wingmen out. Get your support going.

There were certainly times when I didn't know what I should do. In those cases, I'd go find one of my support group members, a like-minded person, and just bounce ideas off them. For instance, Mike Francisco, Class of '65 at the Academy, was a really good influence and helped me understand those things. I thought a lot of him—he was a great guy, a F-4 pilot in Vietnam, and an Air Force Cross recipient. He really helped me out.

Here's a real-world example. I was a first lieutenant sched-uler at Holloman. The wing commander at the time would not go sit in a simulator and do his required simulator events. He told me to get someone else to sit in the simu-lator for him, put his name and Social Security number on the forms, and log the event for him. I didn't feel like that was the right thing to do. So I went to my ops offi-cer, who was a major, and explained that to him. He said, 'Lieutenant, it's very clear what you're going to do. You're gonna go get someone to sit in the simulator for the wing commander and log the event for him.' And I thought, 'Huh…how am I going to fight this battle?'

As I turned to walk out, the assistant ops officer, who also happened to be in the room, spoke up. He was a '64 Acad-emy grad. He said, 'Stop. You'll do no such thing.' Then the ops officer said, 'Yes, he will.' And the assistant ops officer said, 'No, he won't.' It was an interesting moment. Then the assistant ops officer looked at me and said, 'Leave the room. Shut the door behind you.'

I did. I really wanted to hang around and listen to this one, but I wasn't afforded that opportunity. About a half-hour later, the assistant ops officer came out and said, 'You'll do nothing like that. Don't worry about it. It's not your problem.' So I didn't.

At the end of the month, the wing commander still needed eight hours in the simulator. But, on the following Monday, all his requirements had been met. I don't know what happened or who did what. But I do know that I had no part in it. That was an example of finding allies to help you figure out what to do and what battles are worth fighting.[71]

Mike Edwards gave an example of integrity issues he ran into as a young captain, also at Holloman AFB, and his attempt to navigate around the integrity challenges he encountered.

Mike Edwards
CS-13

While at Holloman, I was crewed with my original back seater from F-4 training at MacDill AFB. He was a talented guy, I knew him well, and we had a great relationship. We worked hard to be the best crew in the wing. But we ran into problems with the limitations in our automated bomb delivery system, and it turned out to be an integrity trap for us.

Whenever you were delivering a bomb in the F-4, there were two options: a dive-toss delivery, which relied on an automated system controlled by the back seater, or manual delivery, which relied on the pilot for both maneuvering and release. The difference between the two deliveries had a lot to do with aircraft survivability: in a dive-toss delivery, we'd be able to drop a bomb with G-loading on the aircraft, which enabled us to do evasive maneuvering. But, in manual delivery mode, our G-loading parameters were much lower. For instance, in a 45-degree dive bomb with an automated delivery, we'd be able to drop a bomb at up to 4 Gs and still be able to hit a target. With a manual delivery, we'd have to be at about 0.7 Gs, which would only allow for minimal maneuvering.

During that time at Holloman, we worked hard on dive-toss type bomb deliveries because that was the more survivable approach for the aircraft. Unfortunately, because of maintenance problems we'd been having with the dive-toss system, it was also the least accurate delivery, so our bomb scores suffered.

Whenever we practiced the automated dive-toss deliveries and got a bad bomb score, we'd write up the airplane. At that time, the coordination between operations and maintenance was problematic. From the operations perspective, good bomb scores were the ultimate objective and were key to a good rating. Maintenance, on the other hand, wasn't rated on the bomb scores—they were only concerned about write-ups on the aircraft systems. As a result, if we had a bad bomb score due to a faulty dive-toss system and wrote up a discrepancy on the aircraft, maintenance would always come back with a CND [Could Not Duplicate] as corrective action, indicating that they couldn't identify a problem with the system. The CND entry would preserve their statistics. That maintenance practice became widespread knowledge at Holloman. The wing supported the approach because they wanted to preserve the maintenance ratings. But the result was that they weren't doing anything to improve the quality of the bomb delivery system for the Air Force.

One day, our ops officer pulled us into a pilot meeting to address the dive-toss maintenance problems we had been having. He basically stood up there in front of all of us and said, 'When it comes time to do dive-toss events, if I catch you actually using the dive-toss system, there's going to be a problem. If you do that, you're going to cost the wing a good maintenance rating.' Instead, he told us to do manual deliveries—which were more reliable from a bomb score perspective—but to log the event as a dive-toss delivery. In other words, we were being pressured to falsify the records. In his view, doing that would result in a win-win for both ops and maintenance. But it was an integrity trap for the aircrews.

Faced with that dilemma, and what was basically a direct order from a lieutenant colonel operations officer, my back seater and I decided to look for a practical workaround solution. We decided to do exactly what the book said to do—that is, to use the dive-toss system and log dive-toss events. But we also discovered that, if my back seater delivered the bombs using the automated system while I kept us within the maneuvering parameters for a manual delivery—that is, if I maintained minimal G loading—we could still end up dropping pretty good bombs.

Well, lo and behold, one of our back seaters in the squadron finally lodged an inspector general complaint. As it turned out, that complaint resulted in a much wider-ranging investigation into overall wing procedures. It wasn't just the dive toss situation, because the resulting investigation also looked into how back seaters were being rated on Officer Effectiveness Reports and being treated as second-class citizens, as well as a number of other questionable wing leadership practices.

I ended up having to testify during the formal investigation. I told the truth about what we had been directed to do, as well as our workaround solution. We ended up losing the wing commander, as well as the vice wing commander. We also lost our squadron commander and the ops officer. This ended up being a leadership decapitation of the biggest F-4 wing in the United States.

Fortunately, I never felt like I suffered any career consequences. I felt like my back seater and I came through under pressure, in that we didn't falsify our delivery events and, at the same time, we didn't disobey any orders from our squadron leadership. Most important, I always felt like I could look myself in the mirror and feel good about what we did.[72]

Integrity problems weren't limited to the flying world. Ron Scott spent his early years as a personnel officer. As a second lieutenant, he found himself in the position of having to investigate an alleged criminal act by his unit commander. As difficult as the situation was, his unwavering sense of integrity told him what he had to do.

My first duty assignment was the 861st Radar Squadron

72 | Interview with Mike Edwards, May 24, 2021.

in Aiken, South Carolina. This was an Air Defense Command remote site, even though it was in the continental U.S. Our parent command was the 20th Air Division in Fort Lee Air Force Station, Virginia, about 500 miles away. Our site had four officers and was commanded by a captain who was in the zone for major. My primary duty was as a personnel officer but, because our unit was so small, I had a host of additional duties, from social actions to finance. I was also the unit inspector general, which ended up putting me in an awkward position.

Ron Scott
CS-34

It was brought to my attention that our installation commander had been seen taking wood paneling from the civil engineering yard—he'd been seen backing his station wagon up to the storage facility, loading up the paneling, and driving away with it. About the same time, our civil engineer came to me with some paperwork the commander had signed authorizing the purchase of some lawn mower parts on the local economy for the civil engineering folks. But, according to the civil engineer, no one in his shop had requested the parts—they were unnecessary. In looking more closely, he discovered that, instead of purchasing lawn mower parts, the commander had personally used government funds to buy chain-link fencing and had installed it at his home. These were two potential criminal acts I had to deal with as the unit IG.

I ended up reporting the situation to the division vice commander. He came down to our site, talked to the

commander, and directed him to retire. He told the com-
mander that, if he didn't retire, he'd be court-martialed.
And that's how I ended up becoming the installation com-
mander as a second lieutenant.[73]

Our experiences transitioning from the Academy to the "Real Air Force" varied, according to time, place, and circumstances. But in fulfilling our obligations as Air Force officers, we were left to individually draw from our Academy experiences and values to deal with the gray world situations we encountered. However, that process became much easier with Chief of Staff Ron Fogleman's introduction of the Air Force Core Values.

73 | Interview with Ronald J. Scott, Feb 1, 2021.

4

THE CORE
VALUES: A
WATERSHED
MOMENT

A s the military struggled to rebuild and adapt to the post-Cold War world, newly selected Air Force Chief of Staff General Ron Fogleman (USAFA '63) was viewed as a stabilizing force. As he recalled in an interview with Dr. Richard Kohn in a Spring 2001 *Aerospace Power Journal* article:

> *When I became the Chief, I received a number of letters from people…who essentially said that they thought the Chief needed to restore the soul of the Air Force. That caught me somewhat by surprise because I was not sure exactly what the soul of the Air Force was, or what was required to fix it. But my conclusion was that somehow we had found ourselves, or allowed ourselves, through a series of decisions and actions, to lose sight of our values.*

The trouble came, not from some overriding set of prin-
ciples, but more from employing situational ethics (i.e.,
cronyism) and other things that made it seem as though
the institution lacked integrity. So, in the back of my mind,
there seemed a necessity, or charge, if you will, to work
this issue on my watch.[74]

DEFINING THE CORE VALUES

On November 13th, 1996, Gen. Fogleman formally introduced three bedrock values: Integrity First, Service Before Self, and Excellence in All We
Do. What became known as the Air Force Core Values reaffirmed and
cemented the institutional commitment to increased accountability at all
levels. At the same time, Gen. Fogleman announced an effort to "infuse
those values across the Air Force and weave them into the fabric of the
Air Force institution[75] The accompanying "Little Blue Book" explained
the four reasons for articulating and emphasizing the Core Values, as
well as the strategy for implementation.

The first reason is that the Core Values tell us the price
of admission to the Air Force itself. Air Force personnel,
whether officer, enlisted, civil servant, or contractor, must
display honesty, courage, responsibility, openness, self-re-
spect, and humility in the face of the mission. All of us
must accept accountability and practice justice, which
means that all Air Force personnel must possess Integrity
First. At the same time, a person's self must take a back
seat to Air Force service: rules must be acknowledged and

---

74 | Kohn, Richard H, "The Early Retirement of Ronald R. Fogleman, Chief of Staff,
United States Air Force." *AeroSpace Power Journal*, Spring 2001, p. 10.

75 | "Air Force Core Values," Memorandum for All MAJCOM/FOA/DRU
Commanders, HQ USAF/CC, 13 Nov 1996.

followed faithfully; other personnel must be respected as persons of fundamental worth; discipline and self-control must be in effect always; and there must be faith in the system. In other words, the price of admission to the Air Force demands that each of us places Service Before Self. And, it is imperative that we all seek Excellence in All We Do, whether it be product/service excellence, resources excellence, community excellence, or operations excellence.

The second reason for recognizing the Core Values is that they point to what is universal and unchanging in the profession of arms. Some persons are bothered by the fact that different branches of the service recognize different values; other persons are bothered by the fact that the Air Force once recognized six values and has now reduced them to three. But these persons need not worry. It is impossible for three or six or nine Core Values to capture the richness that is at the heart of the profession of arms. The values are road signs inviting us to consider key features of the requirements of professional service, but they cannot hope to point to or pick out everything. By examining Integrity, Service, and Excellence, we also eventually discover the importance of duty, honor, country, dedication, fidelity, competence, and a host of other professional requirements and attributes. The important thing is not the three road signs our leaders chose. The important thing is that they have selected road signs, and it is our obligation to understand the ethical demands these road signs pick out.

The third reason for recognizing the Core Values is that they help us get a fix on the ethical climate of the organization. How successful are we in trying to live by the Core

Values? Our answer to this question may not be the one we'd like to give. All of us have heard about the sensational scandals—senior officers and NCOs [Non-Commissioned Officers] engaged in adulterous fraternization; the tragic and senseless crashes of the Ramstein CT-43 and the Fairchild B-52; contractor fraud and cost overruns; and the shootdown of the two Blackhawk helicopters over Iraq. We all have read about these incidents and experienced the shame associated with them. But these big-ticket scandals didn't just happen in a vacuum, and they weren't always caused by evil people acting on impulse. The people involved knew the difference between right and wrong, and they knew what professionalism demands in these situations.

These big-ticket scandals grew out of a climate of ethical corrosion. Because we believe our operating procedures or the requirements levied upon us from above are absurd, we tend to 'cut corners,' 'skate by,' and 'get over.' As time goes by, these actions become easier and they become habitual until one morning we wake up and can no longer distinguish between the 'important' taskings or rules and the 'stupid' ones. Lying on official forms becomes second nature. Placing personal interests ahead of the mission seems sensible. And we develop a 'good enough for government work' mentality.

In such a climate of corrosion, the Core Values are like a slap in the face. How far have you strayed from integrity, service, and excellence? What about the folks with whom you work?

Fortunately, there is a fourth reason for recognizing the Core Values: just as they help us to evaluate the climate of our organization, they also serve as beacons vectoring us back to the path of professional conduct; the Core Values allow us to transform a climate of corrosion into a climate of ethical commitment. That is why we have developed the Core Values Strategy.[76]

While identifying and articulating these three specific Core Values may have been new to the Air Force as an institution, the same values were familiar to us as Academy graduates. Denny Merideth considered the parallels between the values we were raised with, the values at the Academy, and the subsequent Air Force Core Values.

When I look back on it, the Core Values Gen. Fogleman announced in 1996 were very familiar. While they may have been a turning point for the Air Force as a whole, from my perspective, these Core Values had been a way of life from the time we entered the Academy.

Denny Merideth
CS-08

Part of that may have been generational. For instance, the idea of cheating in high school never crossed our minds. Obviously, there were a few notable exceptions, but, for the vast majority of us the importance of integrity had been instilled by our parents from the very beginning. So that was nothing new. Once we got to the Academy, it was very easy to see that we were in a group where the vast majority felt the same way, and had been raised with the same values. Whether we came from rural America or from the cities, it didn't make any difference—we all had

76 | "United States Air Force Core Values." 1 January 1997.

the idea that we wanted to be able to trust one another. And so those same foundational values were something that most of us came to the Academy with and that the Academy helped mold.

Obviously, times change. In the light of some high-profile failures and lack of accountability, I think Gen. Fogleman saw the need to get back to basics, to identify the values that are so critical to our institution, and to start working on them. But, from my perspective, the Core Values simply reflected what had always been expected of us at the Academy.[77]

Mike Edwards described the impact Gen. Fogleman and the introduction of the Air Force Core Values had on his organization at the time.

Mike Edwards
CS-13

Gen. Fogleman was very well thought of, not just across the active-duty Air Force, but across the Air National Guard as well. This was particularly true, given that he was an Academy graduate.

That 'Little Blue Book' sat on all of our desks because it was that important to us. In my view, it was a total reinforcement of our experience at the Academy. It gave those of us who are not as articulate as Gen. Fogleman a clear reference we could use to mentor our people, and for all of us to refer to whenever we were dealing with difficult issues. It was a great reference because those are our values and what we stand for. The Core Values are still out there, which tells you the impact that Gen. Fogleman had on our United States Air Force.

77 | Interview with Denny J. Merideth, August 25, 2021.

The Core Values have been particularly helpful for me as a commander when I had to deal with difficult situations, such as sexual harassment. The Core Values are a great basis to talk about moral courage, which is what it takes to deal with something that's not right.

Thinking back on our Academy experience, the role moral courage plays in upholding our Core Values reminds me of the toleration clause in our Honor Code. In fact, I also use toleration as the example to my people in talking about sexual harassment because, in most cases, investigations find that, although there is an awareness of what's going on, people are not willing to step forward and say, 'That's not right.'[78]

Now that the Core Values had been clearly articulated and disseminated by Gen. Fogleman, the next challenge lay in weaving them throughout the cultural fabric of the Air Force. It was now time for us to do our part.

78 | Interview with Howard M. Edwards, November 30, 2021.

PART III

APPLYING THE CORE VALUES

Gen. Fogleman's announcement of the Core Values in 1996 confirmed what we already knew from our Air Force Academy experience: the foundation of effective leadership is Integrity, Service, and Excellence. Living those Core Values, on the other hand, requires strong commitment and difficult decisions.

As outlined in the "Little Blue Book," each of the three Core Values is supported by several underlying virtues. The following chapters help illustrate the role the Core Values and supporting virtues have played in our development as leaders of character.

5

INTEGRITY FIRST

Integrity is simply doing the right thing, all the time, whether everyone is watching, or no one is watching. It is the compass that keeps us on the right path when we are confronted with ethical challenges and personal temptations and it is the foundation upon which trust and respect are built. An individual realizes integrity when thoughts and actions align with what he or she knows to be right. The virtues that demonstrate one truly values integrity include:

HONESTY

Honesty is the hallmark of integrity. As public servants, we are trusted agents. Honesty requires us to evaluate our performance against standards, and to conscientiously and accurately report findings. It drives us to advance our skills and credentials through our own effort. Our word must be unquestionable. This is the only way to preserve the trust and respect that we hold so dear for one another, and the population we serve.[79]

Kevin McHugh gave an example of honesty—and the lack thereof—he encountered as the commander of a T-37 squadron at Laughlin AFB. As he explained, quickly and directly confronting dishonesty within the

---

79 | "A Profession of Arms: Our Core Values." 16 May 2022, p. 9.

ranks is essential in maintaining an organizational culture of integrity and ethical behavior.

Kevin McHugh
CS-09

I got a call one day from an Air Education and Training Command detachment commander at Carswell AFB who said he had gotten a report from Minnesota that a T-37, possibly from Carswell, had made a very low, unauthorized pass over a lake—just above the water, as fast as it could go—and then pulled up and did an aileron roll at the far end. After checking, he said he was able to confirm that it wasn't one of his guys but wondered if it might have been a T-37 from my squadron at Laughlin.

I checked with my scheduler. As it turned out, two of my young captain IPs from check section[80] had been on a cross-country up in that area at the time of the alleged incident. So, I called the detachment commander back and let him know that it appeared to be two of my guys and told him I'd deal with it.

I called the two IPs in individually and asked each of them about the situation. Both denied having been in that area, which I knew wasn't true. Because the detachment commander had identified a specific lake where the unauthorized flyby had taken place, I pulled out a map and challenged each of them directly. I said, 'Are you sure you didn't fly out of this airport and make a low pass over this

---

80 | Check section is the office within a flying training squadron tasked with giving "check rides"—flying examinations—to UPT students. Check section pilots are typically among the most highly qualified and experienced instructors in the squadron.

lake?' They both swore that they absolutely didn't do it. So, I had them each give me written statements to that effect.

Later one of the guys came to me and said, 'Sir, I lied. The other IP had a grandmother who lived on a different lake in that area. We did make a low pass and pulled up at the far side, but it was on a different lake than the one you showed me on the map. I guess technically I didn't lie, but I know I misled you. I know I shouldn't have done it and wanted to tell you the truth.'

Armed with this information I called the other IP in and said, 'Why don't you tell me one more time? Did you fly low over <u>any</u> lake in Minnesota, and make an unauthorized low pass?' He told me, 'Absolutely not. I wouldn't do that. I didn't do that.'

I went to my wing commander to let him know about the situation I was dealing with. I really appreciated the fact that he didn't tell me what to do or how to handle the situation. He just asked me, 'Well, what are you going to do about it?' And I told him, 'Sir, I gotta think about it.' I thought about it for about a day. Then I went back to my wing commander and said, 'I'm going to fire both IPs from check section, with no chance of moving back up for at least a year. And I'm going to make them talk to all the IPs in the squadron about their error in judgment, and more important, about not telling the truth.' The wing commander agreed with my approach, but what I really appreciated is that he never attempted to micromanage the situation at all. He let me handle it and be accountable. And I, in turn, made these guys accountable.

The first IP who confessed to me that he had lied turned out to have a great Air Force career. In fact, he later became a Thunderbird pilot. The lesson he learned was to always tell the truth, regardless of the ramifications. But the second IP who had continued to lie to me just didn't seem to get it.

Once I had all the details, I had both IPs talk to the rest of the squadron. I didn't preach to everyone about honesty and air discipline—I had the two IPs do it. But the best testimonial came from the first IP who had come clean about the whole situation. He said 'We screwed up in making that low pass. But the worst thing we did was to lie about it.' So, for that IP, this was certainly a good learning experience.[81]

Bob Allen described a situation he ran into as a colonel in which dishonest behavior threatened to complicate a critical decision-making process, with significant operational repercussions. He described the circumstances:

Bob Allen
CS-12

I was commander of the Air Force Weather Agency, a field operating agency under the Air Staff. We had a newly developed program that was being considered for deployment, one that I and many others in my organization strongly supported for operational reasons. It was a hard sell for budgetary reasons, but in our view was very worthwhile.

The primary opponent of this program sat on the Air Staff.

[81] | Interview with Kevin E. McHugh, April 16, 2021.

I had no problems with his opposition, but I did have a problem with the way he made his case: rather than arguing from a tactical or technical perspective, he told our deputy director that some arguments I was using to defend the program were not only misleading, but patently untrue—which wasn't the case. In effect, he was attacking my integrity to bring the program down. As it turned out, this wasn't unusual, as he had a reputation for shading the truth to suit his own purposes. In thinking about it, I realized if I went head to head with him, I'd probably create a whole lot more friction and divert attention from the real issue at hand. The other approach was to have the confidence in my staff and others to defend what I knew to be a very strong and worthwhile program.

I decided to let my staff and the merits of the program make the case, rather than becoming embroiled in personal attacks. I called up my counterpart at the Air Staff to tell him I was stepping aside from my program advocacy and letting my staff make the case, and that I didn't want my personal disagreement with my Air Staff opponent to affect the decision-making process. Although my counterpart urged me to stay engaged, I held firm. As it turned out, it was a good decision, as the program was deployed and succeeded on its own. Just as important, my Air Staff opponent paid the price: the program not only survived, but he suffered a loss of reputation and credibility.[82]

COURAGE

Courage is not the absence of fear but doing the right thing despite fear.

82 | Interview with Robert H. Allen, January 19, 2022.

Courage empowers us to take necessary personal or professional risks, make decisions that may be unpopular, and admit our mistakes; having the courage to take these actions is crucial for the mission, the Air Force, and the Nation. A person of integrity does what is right even if the personal cost is high.[83]

John Mann recalled an incident that put his moral courage to the test as a young fighter pilot stationed at Holloman AFB, New Mexico.

John Mann
CS-25

Holloman AFB in the mid- to late-seventies was notorious for having issues with integrity, primarily leadership-driven things. For instance, there were issues with the way fitness reports were being written, in that raters were given top-down guidance: 'This is how you rate this guy.' So Holloman in the summer of 1977 was a challenging place to be.

In September 1977 I was leaving the squadron on a Friday afternoon. As I walked by the duty desk the enlisted guy said, 'Hey, Captain Mann, the Judge Advocate General (JAG) office is ready for you.' I said, 'What are you talking about?' He replied, 'The JAG. They're ready for you. They want to see you.' I said, 'I've got nothing going on with the JAG. Tell him he's got the wrong guy.' He said, 'Well, all right. But, you know, they were there looking for you.'

The JAG's office was right across the street from where my car was parked, so I thought I'd go in there and find out what was going on. I walked in the door and, before I could even inhale, the secretary behind the desk pointed to a door and said, 'Captain Mann, please go right through there.' So I did.

83 | *A Profession of Arms: Our Core Values.* 16 May 2022, p. 9.

118

I stepped into a soundproof-type room with acoustical tiles all around it. There was a reel-to-reel tape recorder and a one-star general sitting in the room, who I immediately recognized as the Tactical Air Command inspector general. He said, 'Come on in.' He pushed the record button, said, 'Please state your name.' I thought to myself, 'Wow, I've just gone from being totally in charge of my own destiny to being totally at someone else's mercy.'

He asked about my squadron scheduling job, and I told him. Then he went through a litany of questions, such as, 'Have you ever logged a dive toss event when you actually made a dive bomb delivery?' I answered, 'yes.' He asked a second similar question about air-to-air training events, and I again replied, 'yes.' I thought to myself, 'That's what everyone does. That's what you have to do to survive in this wing.'

The third question was about the nuclear weapons training (our wing had a nuclear delivery mission in the event of World War III). He asked whether I had ever pencil-whipped a nuclear training event. These events were more important than the typical training event, such as a touch-and-go or an instrument approach. So I was a little bit nervous. I said, 'Sir, can you turn that machine off for a second?' He said, 'Sure,' and punched it off. I asked, 'Do I need a lawyer?' And he said, 'Oh, I'm sorry; I've been here all week, and I didn't give the preamble. We know you guys are doing all this. We know exactly what's going on. We're just trying to find out who's making you do it. Is it your squadron commander? Wing commander? Where's *the pressure coming from?' I said, 'That's easy—it's the wing commander.'*

What followed was a genuine, honest conversation about training events and integrity within the fighter community. I gave him specific examples. And I added, 'This isn't just happening at Holloman; it's happening across the Air Force.' He kind of surprised me by saying, 'I understand. We're very aware of that. We're going to make an example of Holloman to fix this.' And so, right there, on that Friday afternoon, I discovered that I might have an ally in the inspector general. Then he hit the record button again and we went through that same conversation, and I was on record.

As I walked out, the enormity of the situation really hit me. I thought, 'Boy, I don't know how this is going to end up. I could be driving a car in Thule, Greenland.' But I knew I did the right thing. As it turned out, they came back and fired the wing commander, the vice wing commander, and other lower-level commanders. They made an example of Holloman, just as the IG said they would.[84]

Telling truth to power takes tremendous moral courage because candor can demand a high price, depending on who's in charge. But it's our duty to speak truth to power because the consequences of dishonesty or failing to speak the truth can have catastrophic repercussions for an organization and its culture. Larry Faber told about an experience he had involving loyalty and service parochialism that demonstrated both the need for speaking truth to power, as well as the moral courage it required to deal with a sensitive situation.

---

84 | Interview with John C. Mann, April 2, 2020.

I graduated from the Armed Forces Staff College in 1987 and, as a follow-on assignment, I became the deputy commander of the Joint Reconnaissance Center (JRC) at Atlantic Command.

Our direct boss was the J3 [director of operations], a Navy one-star. One of the most difficult issues we were dealing with at the time involved the SR-71. The Air Force wanted to get rid of this high-altitude, high-speed reconnaissance aircraft because, in their view, it wasn't cost-effective. But, from our perspective in the JRC, that capability was critical—the SR-71 was the only asset that could get decent coverage in some areas.

Larry Faber
CS-05

One day, we got a call from the office of the commander-in-chief of Atlantic Command. The commander wanted someone to come over and talk to him about whether we needed the SR-71 or not. Being a U-2 pilot and the JRC's reconnaissance expert, the job fell to me. I thought, 'I know he's going to expect me to give the Air Force position.' I put everything together for the meeting and, as was standard practice, went to the J3 for a pre-brief. I walked into the admiral's office and, to my surprise, he just grabbed his hat and said, 'Let's go.' As we walked over to the commander's office, I said 'Sir, don't you want to know what my recommendation is?' He said, 'No, let's just go do this.'

When we got to the commander's office, my J3 boss absolutely floored me—he just said, 'Sir, on this SR-71 issue, I'd just go with Larry's recommendation.' And I thought,

'Holy cow, that's a lot of pressure on me, but it's also a lot of support.' I later found out that the Air Force had been pressuring the commander to relinquish his control of the SR-71. But, from my perspective in the JRC, it really was a serious problem—Atlantic Command was getting intelligence from the SR-71 that no other platform could provide. That was the bottom line in my brief to the commander.

After my briefing, the Air Force decided to send a team to try to convince the commander to reverse our position. My J3 boss called me and said, 'I want you to attend that session, along with the Air Force. Essentially, you'll be debating with an Air Force two-star.' I was a major at the time so, needless to say, I was at a distinct disadvantage.

As we were walking into the briefing, the Air Force two-star looked at me and said, 'Major, don't forget what color uniform you're wearing.' That threw a big red flag up, and I thought, 'Wow, I could pay dearly for this in terms of my career.' But I also thought, 'I'm going to paint a complete picture here by presenting the other side of the argument. If the two-star says something that's true, I'll agree with him, but I'm not gonna lie about anything just to support an Air Force position that runs counter to Atlantic Command interests.' And I didn't. As we left the briefing, the two-star said, 'You seem to have forgotten which service you're in.' I just walked away.

About two days later, things fell apart. I was called into an Air Force colonel's office at Atlantic Command Headquarters. I didn't even know who he was—I was in J3 (Operations) and he was in J5 (Strategic Plans and Policy). It was *not a pleasant conversation—he accused me of making false official statements, all relating to the SR-71 issues before us. Shortly thereafter, I received notice that I had been 'red-lined' (removed) from the lieutenant colonel promotion list, which had already been approved/confirmed by the Senate. I was then removed from my job at the Atlantic Command JRC, my clearances were revoked, and I was transferred to Langley AFB with no job. Finally, I was directed to meet an administrative discharge board.*

There were three people on the board, but none of them had the background I did or really understood the issue we were debating. Several of my fellow U-2 pilots and other colleagues wrote letters on my behalf, and some testified before the board; however, in the end, the board voted to separate me from the Air Force with a general discharge.

It took me seven years to get that straightened out. I was never so humbled as to see all the people who supported me, particularly my former J3 boss. At the time of the administrative hearing, he was the carrier group commander in Mayport, Florida. Unbeknownst to me, he heard about the hearing. He flew up and barged in, right in the middle of the proceedings. And he said, 'If you don't want Larry in the Air Force, I'll take him on the Navy—right now. He can fly on my wing anytime.'

I eventually ended up submitting a request for review with the Board for Corrections of Military Records. One year after my request for review, my discharge was overturned—of the 3,800 cases reviewed that year, only three

*were overturned, of which mine was one. My promo-
tion to lieutenant colonel was reinstated, and I got all my
back pay. So it all worked out in the end. The important
point, though, is that, if I had to do it all over again, I'd
do exactly the same thing because I know I did the right
and honorable thing.*[85]

ACCOUNTABILITY

Accountability is the responsibility to an audience. That audience may be the American people, our units, our supervisors, our fellow Airmen, our families, our loved ones, and even ourselves. Accountable individuals maintain transparency, seek honest and constructive feedback, lead and live with respect for themselves and others, and take ownership of the outcomes of their actions and decisions. They are responsible to themselves and others and refrain from actions that discredit themselves or our service.[86]

Maintaining an environment of strict accountability often requires difficult decisions. Kees Rietsema described a situation in which his sense of accountability directly conflicted with that of his boss.

Kees Rietsema
CS-14

*I was serving at the Pentagon on the Joint Staff.
Not long after I arrived, I was asked to lead a
branch that dealt in issues of nuclear weapons and the Single Integrated Operations Plan
(nuclear war plan). As a fighter pilot in this
office, I was a fish out of water among Strategic Air Command professionals and I wondered
how I had landed here, but I thought of it as a
career-broadening assignment.*

85 | Interview with Larry E. Faber, June 3, 2021.

86 | "A Profession of Arms: Our Core Values." 16 May 2022, p. 9.

Not surprisingly, quite a bit of Top Secret (TS) paper-work was involved. I became concerned when I realized that it was not all being properly logged in and was scattered across the office; frankly, I was worried that some of the documents were not being properly controlled. Even though we worked in a very secure location, I initiated an audit. Shortly thereafter, I was called into my boss's office (a general officer) and informed that an Article 15[87] was prepared with my name on it and sitting in his top drawer, waiting for me should I continue the audit and find something 'untoward.' When confronted with his 'offer,' I acknowledged his concerns and returned to our office, chastened but determined not to call off the audit. Given the circumstances, I knew it was the right thing to do. Fortunately, after several days of audit, all the TS documents were back to where they should have been, and nothing was missing.[88]

While the term "toleration" isn't specifically mentioned in our Core Values, the principle of not ignoring bad ethical behavior is clearly spelled out, as it is the bedrock of accountability. Frank Klotz, who served as the chairman of the Cadet Wing Honor Committee during his time at the Academy, explained why the toleration clause is still an essential element in the Academy's Honor Code, and how the Code directly translates to accountability in Air Force organizations.

The most difficult decisions we're forced to make don't always involve choosing between right and wrong. Most

87 | An Article 15 is a tool used at a commander's discretion to resolve issues of minor misconduct, rather than resorting to judicial proceedings.

88 | Rietsema, Kees, "What a Leader of Character Looks Like from a Former Cadet Wing Commander Perspective." Undated.

rational and reasonably educated people can discern the difference between the two. Rather, the tougher challenge is having to decide between two relative 'rights.' That is where integrity can really be put to the test.

Frank Klotz
CS-04

The toleration clause brings this dilemma into sharp relief. I think we'd all agree that loyalty to friends, to classmates, to fellow squadron members, to athletic teammates—in and of themselves—are good and noble things. After all, no organization can survive without a large measure of internal cohesion, characterized by protecting one another, defending one another, taking care of one another. We in fact ask you…encourage you to be a 'good wingman.' And, any combat veteran will tell you, courage on the battlefield usually involves more than military discipline, more than a devotion to duty. In the end, it generally boils down to fighting for the person beside you, willing to risk your life for your comrades—in the foxhole, or in an aircraft formation. The problem comes when the 'right' of loyalty to friends and colleagues comes into conflict with the 'right' of loyalty to the Academy, the Air Force, or some other higher purpose.

So, the thinking behind the toleration clause—its rationale, its purpose, its efficacy—is not simply an artifice of the character development program at the Academy. Rather, it's fundamental to how organizations maintain good order and discipline; how they regulate themselves; how they keep events from spinning out of control. When I was a cadet, there was a 'we versus they' dichotomy here.

The 'we' were the cadets...you know...the good guys. The 'they' were the officers, the AOCs, the faculty; in a word, 'the system.'

When you graduate, you actually become part of 'the system.' Even as a second lieutenant, you automatically outrank almost 80% of the Air Force.[89] You'll operate highly precise and lethal weapons systems; you'll exercise control over space and cyber capabilities that are integral elements of our critical national infrastructure; you'll lead young men and women in combat; you'll oversee the spending of millions of dollars. You are going to be part of the system; you'll directly affect how well it works, how well it runs. If and when you observe conduct that does not meet Air Force standards or violates established procedures or tech data, the crucial test of integrity will be whether you take positive actions to correct the situation— even if people you know, or work with on crew, or are part of your social circle—may ultimately be held accountable.

In some cases, this will be a 'no-brainer.' For example, blatantly criminal behavior. But sometimes it may not always be so easy, especially when you're a newly arrived lieutenant and are still trying to assess how things are done in the new outfit. But it doesn't matter if you are the 'new guy' or the 'rookie.' You'll be an officer and, by your own actions and behavior, you need to set a tone of moral,

89 | As of January 1, 2020, there were 63,626 active-duty officers, and a total active-duty force of 328,255. National Academies of Sciences, Engineering, and Medicine. 2021. *Strengthening U.S. Air Force Human Capital Management: A Flight Plan for 2020-2030.* Washington, DC: The National Academies Press. https://doi.org/10.17226/25828.

principled leadership, seeking always to do what is right and what is good. That's the only way our Air Force can carry out its mission and, at the same time, maintain the trust and confidence of the American people, as well as our international partners. I simply cannot overemphasize how critically important this aspect of integrity is to our Air Force and to our national security—the willingness to set and enforce high standards, and to hold ourselves accountable for our actions.[90]

In practice, accountability also requires everyone in the organization to embrace the mission and take ownership of his or her actions. A.J. Ranft considered how his experience on the Air Education and Training Command's Inspector General team highlighted the important role accountability plays in unit performance.

A.J. Ranft
CS-11

In my experience, accountability is directly linked to performance. I always told people I worked with that what we want is organizational performance. On the individual level, everyone needs to understand his or her role and what's expected. But organizational performance also assumes maximum effort. I quickly learned that, when you had people working for you who weren't putting out the maximum effort, the organization always suffers.

My last active-duty job was as an inspector on the Air Education and Training Command IG team. As the support branch chief, I was responsible for everything that

90 | Klotz, Frank G. "A Former Wing Honor Committee Chairman Reflects on the Honor Code." Undated.

was not operational. All the people on my team who worked for me had skills in specific areas, such as transportation, communications, or firefighting. As IG inspectors, our attitude was, 'We're not here to judge you on your effort—we're here to evaluate you on the results of that effort.'

One of the things I did was sit in the command post and observe the unit response to exercises, such as a robbery or major aircraft accident. It was instructive to watch how the leadership at each base handled their group and how they responded to problems. Using that same approach, when our graduates go into the Air Force, they need to observe what their bosses do, both good and bad. Make mental notes for yourself about those traits as you advance in rank. You'll find yourself reflecting back on the lessons they taught you, both good and bad. Those lessons will make you a better leader.[91]

HUMILITY

A person of integrity grasps and is sobered by the extraordinary task of defending the Constitution of the United States. We practice humility by putting others before ourselves. We seek to add value through community and humanitarian support. We serve with gratitude and without arrogance.[92]

Leaders of character instinctively recognize the mutual dependency between integrity and humility, and build a foundation of integrity by putting others before themselves, which is the essence of humility. That

91 | Interview with Andrew J. Ranft, April 27, 2021.

92 | "A Profession of Arms: Our Core Values." 16 May 2022, p. 9.

humility, in turn, builds trust and respect within the organization and inspires "close teamwork, rapid learning, and high performance."[93]

Nort Schwartz is an exemplar of the humble leader. In terms of position and responsibility, he reached the pinnacle of Air Force leadership, having served as our 19th Air Force chief of staff. However, regardless of his high visibility and extraordinary career accomplishments, he's always quick to credit others for his success. He recently reflected on the value, the nature, and the role of humble leadership in public service.

Nort Schwartz
CS-34

In my experience, there's a visible link between integrity and humility. I've known a number of humble men and women over my years in public service, and they've all demonstrated tremendous integrity. Arrogance, on the other hand, has a corrosive effect. An arrogant leader is off-putting to most everyone. But, even worse, the self-interest that characterizes arrogance undermines the very foundation of integrity in an organization, which is trust and respect. In fact, I'd go so far as to say that don't think I've ever met an effective, honest, arrogant leader.

When I was at the Academy, I recall watching an AOC who was self-interested in the extreme. It seemed like he thought he was well connected and, as a result, was pretty arrogant about his station in life. As a result, he was a negative role model for those who knew him—exactly the opposite of what an AOC should be. And now, more than 50 years later, I still remember that. On the other hand, I was fortunate enough to have been around many

93 | Shellenbarger, Sue. "The Best Bosses are Humble Bosses." *Wall Street Journal,* October 9, 2018. https://www.wsj.com/articles/the-best-bosses-are-humble-bosses-1539092123, accessed August 1, 2022.

remarkable people during my four years at the Academy. They all had their own unique strengths and, as a group, they made me profoundly grateful to be a part of the institution. That led to my strong belief that we all need to recognize how fortunate we are.

While humility is certainly an essential aspect of integrity, you could also make a good argument that humility is an all-encompassing virtue, one that has application in all kinds of human interaction. I think it's also important to remember that just because a leader is humble doesn't mean he or she is weak, soft, or indecisive. And it also doesn't mean that the leader lacks self-confidence. Quite the contrary, because the humble leader is secure enough in his or her abilities to listen intently to subordinates, look for better ideas, and be quick to credit others for organizational success. That's what builds trust and respect. From my experience, it's no different in the business world, because successful organizations let their products and services speak for themselves. That kind of an attitude tends to permeate the best corporate cultures.

Unfortunately, at this moment in time, there's a great skepticism about government. That's why genuine humility, the kind that puts others first and builds trust and respect within organizations, is so important in public service. From that standpoint, our country is in great need for the humble leader, men and women of integrity who feel a keen sense of obligation to serve others and the Nation well.[94]

94 | Interview with Norton A. Schwartz, August 1, 2022.

6

SERVICE
BEFORE SELF

Service Before Self tells us that professional duties take precedence over personal desires. The call to serve is a call to live according to a higher standard. It is not just a job; it is a commitment that takes energy, dedication, and sacrifice. We do not "work" in the Air Force; we serve in the Air Force. A heart and mindset for service allows us to embrace expectations and requirements not levied on the American public or other professions. The virtues that demonstrate one truly values service include:

DUTY

Duty is the obligation to perform what is required for the mission. While our responsibilities are determined by the law, the Department of Defense, and Air Force instructions, directives, and guidance, our sense of duty is a personal one and bound by the oath of service we take as individuals. Duty sometimes calls for sacrifice in ways no other profession has or will have. Airmen who truly embody *service before self* consistently choose to make necessary sacrifices to accomplish the mission, and in doing so, we honor those who made such sacrifices before us.[95]

95 | "A Profession of Arms: Our Core Values." 16 May 2022, p. 10.

In the profession of arms, duty may ultimately call for sacrifice in ways only a few professions will. Airmen who truly embody Service Before Self consistently choose to make necessary sacrifices to accomplish the mission. In recognition of their unselfish devotion to duty, we honor those who made the ultimate sacrifice.

Charlie McMillan
CS-03

Among the members of the Illustrious Class of 1973, one of us who made that ultimate sacrifice was Captain Charlie McMillan II, who perished in the Joint-Services mission code-named DESERT ONE, also known as OPERATION EAGLE CLAW. Charlie was one of eight Americans killed April 25, 1980, in the attempt to rescue 53 U.S. hostages who were being held by Iranian radicals at the U.S. Embassy in Tehran. He was killed when a Marine RH-53 helicopter, operating in the dark with blowing desert sand, struck his EC-130's vertical stabilizer with its main rotor and crashed into the EC-130's wing root. The eight Americans who died that day are memorialized in a small monument in Arlington National Cemetery. Presiding over the memorialization ceremony, General Henry Shelton compared the Iranian mission to the 1804 raid on Tripoli. 'Just as the Tripoli raid was the most daring act of its age, Eagle Claw was one of the most daring acts of our age,' Shelton said. 'That it did not achieve its objective does not detract in any way, in any measure, from the heroism of those who tried.'[96]

Through our four years at the Academy, we were instilled with a deep instinct to "go the extra mile" in pursuit of mission objectives, regardless

96 | East Tennessee Veterans Memorial Association—McMillan II, Charles T. (etvma. org)

of the circumstances. During his 34 years of flying Air Force helicopters and fixed-wing aircraft in Special Operations and Combat Rescue roles, Dave Ellis saved the lives of several dozen people, often under extreme conditions. However, one single mission—and the regret he carries about a failed search for a lost aircraft—is a graphic illustration of his devotion to our Core Values.

Dave Ellis
CS-32

On a winter's day in the northern U.S., I was tasked to search for a lost Cessna that had disappeared on a cross-country flight with a single young pilot aboard. I had a crew of six in my HC-130 Combat King. We had been given the coordinates of the pilot's flight plan, and our mission was to search his planned route of flight.

Once airborne, one of my crewmembers starting whining about the potential mission duration, saying that he had commitments he had to meet that night. Later, another crewmember joined in, complaining that he needed to get back to the base in time to catch a ride home with his wife. I noted their complaints but directed them to remain focused on the task at hand.

Hours later, after fruitlessly searching for a lost white aircraft on the snow-covered white ground, we came to the end of our planned search track in the waning daylight. As I banked to return to base, I could just barely see a lone hill in the distance off to the side of our search track, sticking up from the white plain like half of a giant football. I had a nagging instinct that made me wonder whether a disoriented or lost pilot might turn toward a landmark like that in what was otherwise a featureless area. I estimated the hill to be 50 miles away, 10 minutes flying time at 300 knots. A search around that hill would add 30 minutes to our mission, at most. As aircraft commander and the leader, I could have told my crew we were going to search a while longer. Despite my gut telling me I should do this, I decided not to extend the mission beyond our tasked search area. We returned to base. Three days later, the lost aircraft was found. It had landed next to that half-football hill and the young pilot had frozen to death.

In my flying career, 'going the extra mile' to achieve mission success was an essential feature of our culture. As a leader, I've made unpopular calls more times than I can count but, in this one case, I didn't follow my gut instinct. Years later, I still question my decision to end our search that day. What if I had demanded another search mission the next morning? If the Air Force Rescue Coordination Center declined to task it, what if I had added a training line to the schedule and sent out a search crew anyway? Would they have found the downed aircraft? Would the pilot have survived?

I'll never know, but those questions haunt me to this very day.[97]

LOYALTY

Loyalty is an internal commitment to the success and preservation of something bigger than ourselves. Our loyalty is to the Nation first, the values and commitments of our Air Force second, and finally, to those with whom we serve. Loyalty to our leaders requires us to trust, follow,

97 | Interview with David T. Ellis, July 26, 2022.

and execute their decisions, even when we disagree. We offer alternative solutions and innovative ideas most effectively through the chain of command. Leaders demonstrate loyalty by respecting those who serve and treating them with dignity, compassion, and true concern for their wellbeing. Ultimately, loyalty is demonstrated by helping each other act with respect and honor.[98]

Loyalty is most graphically demonstrated in peoples' willingness to make day-to-day sacrifices for the mission and for their team, working under exceptionally challenging conditions. That's a demonstration of Service Before Self in action. Craig MacPherson described the loyalty his unit demonstrated to the mission and each other during DESERT SHIELD/DESERT STORM.

Craig MacPherson
CS-39

When you talk about loyalty, I think the most defining moment for me was DESERT SHIELD/ DESERT STORM, while I was the commander of the 5th Military Aerial Port Squadron. Our job at the time was to execute deployments to forward operating bases and operate cargo and passenger operations.

In the first week of August, Saddam Hussein invaded Kuwait and things got pretty dicey. We got the call to deploy the entire squadron to Dhahran. That deployment really taught me to appreciate the tremendous work ethic, integrity, and dedication of our airmen and NCOs.

We had deployed with 12 hours-notice, ending up living in Saudi elementary school rooms for three weeks and then tents for an additional seven months. These Airmen and senior NCOs landed at 0700, then took over an operation

98 | "A Profession of Arms: Our Core Values." 16 May 2022, p. 10.

which, a week prior, had only been handling three to five aircraft per week. In a matter of about 24 hours, they were handling 60 aircraft per day. Our operation grew from 80 people initially, to nearly 400 people from 13 different aerial port squadrons from around the world. That included six or seven reserve units as well. Our people worked 12-hour shifts. While the goal was six days on and one day off, frequently it was seven days on and no days off. The whole time, they were living in tents in Saudi Arabia. It was so hot they had to do shift changes at noon and midnight.

Our people worked more than 10,000 missions over a five-month period. Many were young men and women, 18 to 20-year-olds, supervised by staff sergeants to make sure everything happened. It was not hard to feel dedicated to them. It was impressive to watch that young cadre of NCOs and young airmen accomplish so much. I didn't teach them that. They learned the basics of dedication, professionalism, and integrity growing up, but it was reinforced by their Air Force training and experiences leading up to that defining moment.[99]

RESPECT

Respect encompasses self-respect, mutual respect, and organizational respect. This three-dimensional view requires us to embrace the unique value of all individuals and treat everyone with dignity. We must always act in the certain knowledge that all Airmen must be treated with respect and boldly speak up, even when it is uncomfortable, to assert this truth. Further, respecting others requires a commitment to recognize and root

99 | Interview with Craig K. MacPherson, March 27, 2020.

out prejudices, biases, and stereotypes. We must engage genuinely, honestly, and with an empathetic and open mind. We must honor the Air Force and others by following our words with actions.

Respect must be embraced mutually by military and civilian personnel in all grades or positions and demonstrated in the everyday actions of all Airmen. Without it, we simply cannot stand strong in the defense of our Nation. Mutual respect strengthens teamwork, supports increased communication, reduces stress, and diminishes conflict. Put simply, it means treating others the way you would want to be treated and creating an environment, through your words and actions, where all Airmen can serve to their full potential.[100]

It's difficult, if not impossible, for leaders to earn trust without respecting their people. While it's important for leaders to talk with their people about the importance of respecting one another, the way leaders treat their people sends the most powerful message of all. Larry Faber explained how his AOC, Captain (later Lt. Gen.) Michael C. Short, demonstrated respect for him when Larry was a struggling doolie at the Academy, and the impact that respect had on his life.

Larry Faber
CS-05

As several of our classmates have attested to, academics were a tough hurdle for some of us. I spent most of the first half of our Academy time on academic probation. Graduating from the Academy was a long-time dream of mine, but that dream almost crashed and burned my doolie year. My GPA in several semesters was well below 2.0. Instructors offered tutoring and extra instruction, but it seemed I never got out of my dorm room, particularly on weekends. Our AOC at the time was a '65 grad, Capt. Michael C. Short. Capt. Short would step into my

---

100 | "A Profession of Arms: Our Core Values." 16 May 2022, p. 10.

dorm room while I was studying on the weekends and offer encouragement. He never said anything discouraging to me. But, as time passed and we advanced through our upper-class years, I forgot how Capt. Short had supported me.

Many years later, following the deaths of my parents, I was going through my parents' file cabinet, and I discovered two letters Capt. Short had written to my parents. I had never seen these letters before. The first letter stated that he had never seen a fourth classman work as hard as I did to get through academics. But, despite my efforts, he didn't think I was capable of bringing my GPA up enough to survive our fourth-class year. But there was a second letter, written at the conclusion of our fourth-class year, telling my parents they had a son to be very proud of, and that hard work and determination had enabled me to survive that first year of academics. Capt. Short added that he was 'amazed by my determination' and that he felt certain I would become a fine officer one day. After reading those letters, it dawned upon me that I had not even noticed Capt. Short's extraordinary leadership.

Sometimes we have great leaders in our midst and, because they lead quietly and effectively, we don't realize the impact they've made until much later. In fact, I never was able to thank Gen. Short for his support and leadership because I hadn't seen his letters before he passed away in 2017. Hopefully he knew just how much I would one day appreciate what he had done for me.[101]

---

101 | Interview with Lawrence E. Faber, January 26, 2021.

Leaders can't build trusting relationships without treating their people with respect and engaging with them on a personal level. Denny Merideth learned about the influence he and his classmates had on underclassmen in his squadron—influence he didn't discover until many years later.

Denny Merideth
CS-08

About four years ago, I ran into a '76 graduate who had been in our squadron as a doolie. I had been a flight commander during that year. He told me that our class—the Class of '73—had a big influence on him. He didn't specifically mention one event but said the overall leadership example my classmates and I provided had made a huge impact on him. That is something I'll always cherish.

In thinking about being a leader, most people assume that the position requires them to stand apart from their people. In reality, though, you can't neglect building the one-on-one relationships and getting down on a personal level with your people. It's important to develop expertise in that area, just as it's important to develop technical expertise in your career field. In my opinion, that's really what carried our class forward in the Air Force.[102]

---

102 | Interview with Denny J. Merideth, August 25, 2021.

7

EXCELLENCE IN ALL WE DO

Excellence in All We Do does not mean that we demand perfection in everything from everyone. Instead, this value directs us to continuously advance our craft and increase our knowledge as Airmen and Guardians. We must have a passion for continuous improvement and innovation that propels America's Air Force and Space Force in quantum leaps toward accomplishment and performance.

MISSION

Mission encompasses operations and excellence in stewardship. The complex undertaking of the Air Force mission requires us to harness the ingenuity, expertise, and elbow grease of all Airmen. We approach it with the mindset of respect, pride, innovation, and a continued commitment to anticipate and embrace change. Our work areas, our processes, and our interpersonal interactions must be undeniably professional and positive. Our people are the platform for delivering innovative ideas, strategies, and technologies to the fight.[103]

Regardless of the organization, one of the leader's primary

---

103 | "A Profession of Arms: Our Core Values." 16 May 2022, p. 11.

responsibilities is to establish and maintain a culture of outstanding mission performance. Toward that end, he or she must embody the standard of excellence. Jay Beard gave an example from his flying career.

Jay Beard
CS-18

When I was a young lieutenant growing up in the Strategic Air Command, I had commanders and leaders who may have been effective administrators, but they were lousy aviators. And I said to myself, 'If I'm ever fortunate enough to be in a position to command a unit, I want to be the best pilot in that unit, period.' That was my philosophy.

I eventually got the opportunity to command a B-52 squadron. I replaced a guy who was very smart but, as a pilot, he was maybe a strong four on a scale of one to ten. His predecessor, by the way, was maybe a two on a ten-point scale. Both of them ended up as general officers but, from my point of view, they were lousy pilots and the squadron reflected that.

My goal as a squadron commander was to be the best pilot possible, not only because that's what I expected of myself, but because I knew I'd be setting an example to my crews. I constantly told my people that I expected them to be the absolute best they could be, regardless of their crew position. When it came to unit evaluations, that really paid off—we always came out near the top.[104]

"Excellence in All We Do" goes beyond meeting high standards—it also means challenging traditional assumptions and beliefs when there's a better way. As a pilot-physician, Bob Munson worked in the Human

104 | Interview with John H. Beard, March 2, 2021.

Systems Program Office (HSPO), an Air Force Materiel Command organization whose job was to ensure human factors were considered in the acquisition process. He recalled one particular struggle to overcome bureaucratic resistance in pursuit of excellence.

Bob Munson
CS-34

Airmen have been wearing leather boots since the dawn of military aviation. Leather is fire-resistant, with little obvious damage after exposure to flames; consequently, for more than five decades the Air Force has required that all flying boots be 100% leather.

In 1998, the HSPO received a $10,000 grant to test flying boots against commercial industry standards. Despite the minimal funding, two dedicated civilians, Linda Hamilton and Art Gonzalez, were determined to find a safer standard. After exhaustive tests, they determined that commercial boots made with treated nylon fabric would provide superior fire protection to our aircrews. In addition, the commercial boots proved to be lighter, more comfortable, and the material breathed.

Challenging a long-established rule is hard, and this was no exception. As it turned out, the resistance to the change came from our own chief engineer. His objection: the Air Force regulation called for all boots to be leather and, from his perspective, it was 'case closed.' Plus, any new boot would need additional life support testing, and he wasn't willing to go to that additional expense.

I worked for almost two years to find ways to overcome his resistance. Finally, with two weeks left in the HSPO,

I concluded that the chief engineer's strategy was to just wait me out. So I decided to go over the chief engineer's head and ask the HSPO director for a decision brief. He agreed to hear both arguments.

I made my presentation of Art and Linda's test results: that the current USAF boot had failed the fire test, whereas the commercial boots had passed. The chief engineer in turn gave his presentation on the importance of following extensive life support testing protocols to ensure absolute safety. My response was that the additional testing the chief engineer was proposing was largely unnecessary. The example I gave was that testing every commercial boot in a high-speed rocket ejection simulation test was unnecessary and a waste of money, as the commercial boots' configuration was the same as the leather ones. So, we already had the data we needed to make a decision.

When I sat down, there was a brief pause while the HSPO director gathered his thoughts. He then turned to his chief engineer and announced his decision with a simple statement: 'Get over it.'

Reason had triumphed over bureaucracy. The new boots were approved.[105]

The drive for excellence, even when inconvenient or near impossible, is what distinguishes leaders of character. While serving as a member of an accident investigation board, Dave Ellis found that the relentless pursuit of excellence among board members was key to unraveling a years-old mystery of tragic aircraft accidents, undoubtedly saving many lives.

105 | Interview with Robert A. Munson, December 17, 2021.

The Sikorsky H-53 'Super Jolly Green Giant' helicopter had been flown by the USAF since 1967 in combat rescue, special operations, and tactical air support roles. When a handful of my classmates and I finished helicopter training in late 1974 and headed for initial operational assignments in H-53 squadrons, the H-53 fleet had suffered through several years of loss of control mishaps that invariably led to a smoking hole and the deaths of all aboard. Investigations into these mishaps were hampered by a lack of physical evidence and no surviving crewmembers to interview. Therefore, accident investigation board (AIB) conclusions and remedies were only best guesses. Still, these H-53 loss of control mishaps continued.

Dave Ellis
CS-32

On St. Patrick's Day in 1976, one of my unit's H-53s was in a 15-foot hover at the base helipad when it went out of control and crashed on its side. The 650-gallon sheet metal auxiliary fuel tank on the side of the giant helicopter burst, causing an explosion and fireball that consumed the aircraft and its four occupants. An AIB was convened, of which I was a pilot member. The wreckage had barely cooled when a board member from Warner-Robins H-53 Depot located two halves of a flight control bolt among the now-hardened pools of melted aluminum. We didn't touch the fractured parts of the bolt—we packed it up and sent it to the Air Force Safety Center to have the bolt analyzed by metallurgists. They sent word back to our AIB that expert analysis determined the bolt had broken in the post-crash fire, and therefore could not have caused the accident.

Deflated with this news, we nevertheless redoubled our efforts to determine a cause of the mishap. With every new piece of information we compiled, causation kept pointing back to this broken bolt that had connected a flight control rod to the pilot valve on one of the three massive hydraulic pistons. These pistons tilt the helicopter's main rotor swashplate, which in turn changes the pitch and angle of attack of the H-53's six main rotor blades at different points in their rotation. As the end of our 30-day investigation approached, our AIB concluded that the flight control bolt had indeed broken in half during flight and backed out of its intended position, rendering the helicopter uncontrollable. Our final report stated this conclusion, even though it was in direct opposition to the metallurgists' findings. Our report also recommended that all the current flight control bolts, which were manufactured by a sub-contractor and quite high tech with a self-retaining feature utilizing an internal spring and ball bearings, be replaced by 'old school' bolts that featured a castellated nut safety wired to the bolt shaft.

When our AIB briefed the commander of the U.S. Air Forces in Europe on our report, he asked how many of these high-tech bolts connected the flight controls on an H-53. I told him there were 77. He didn't hesitate. He ordered they all be removed and replaced with the tried-and-true low-tech bolts we had recommended, and that his H-53 fleet was to get back into the air as soon as possible, as grounded H-53s would have a wide-ranging and detrimental effect on the command's mission. Other USAF commands operating H-53s followed his lead.

In the months that followed, H-53 crews all over the Air Force held their collective breath, wondering if the real cause of so many loss of control mishaps had finally been identified and corrected. To everyone's great relief, no more unexplained mishaps occurred. Then six months after our AIB report was released, a box of 500 of the suspect high-tech bolts arrived at the McDonnell-Douglas manufacturing plant in St. Louis for installation on new F-15 fighters they were building. Two of the high-tech bolts were found to have broken in half during shipment. That was bittersweet vindication for our AIB.

As you can imagine, the aviation industry was gravely concerned with this discovery. It was determined that improved processes were needed in case-hardening bolts to prevent a phenomenon called 'hydrogen embrittlement,' which could make a steel or alloy bolt as brittle as glass. Also, better inspection and quality control processes were required. These changes were implemented, aviation safety was greatly improved, and today's high-tech flight control bolts are widely used throughout the aviation industry without problems.[106]

DISCIPLINE

Discipline is an individual commitment to uphold the highest of personal and professional standards. Airmen commit to a life of discipline

106 | Interview with David T. Ellis, July 28, 2022. Other Improvements to the H-53 fleet were made in subsequent years, such as replacing the 650-gallon sheet metal auxiliary fuel tanks with those made of wound Kevlar that would deform but not burst if the aircraft rolled over on them. Main rotor blades were upgraded to those made with a titanium spar. Most of the Air Force H-53 fleet was upgraded to the MH-53 Pave Low configuration with its incredible capabilities. The MH-53 fleet was retired in 2008 and replaced with the CV-22B Osprey.

and self-control. We demonstrate it in attitude, work ethic, and effort directed at continuous improvement, whether it be pursuing professional military education or nurturing ourselves physically, intellectually, emotionally, or spiritually. Each Airman represents the entire Air Force. Our appearance, actions, and words shape the culture of the Air Force and the reputation of the entire military profession.[107]

Tim Cooper reflected on an important aspect of discipline, which is perseverance. His medical career in the Air Force illustrates the point. Despite numerous setbacks, he continued pursuing his goal of becoming an infectious disease specialist. He described the long and arduous process that led to that distinction.

Tim Cooper
CS-40

The Academy gave me the attitude of perseverance. There are certain things I know I'm worthy of and, with enough effort, I know can do them. The opportunity may not present itself the first or the second, or maybe even the third time, but I'm going to do everything I can to pursue the goal.

I didn't end up going to medical school until I was 29 years old, having already been in the Air Force for seven years. I started medical school in 1980 and graduated in 1984. I then became a 30-year-old intern—not an easy job itself. I did get into a residency immediately but, by then, I had decided that I wanted to specialize in Infectious Diseases, a sub-specialty of Internal Medicine.

It took me three application cycles before I was accepted—a total of three more years to get into an infectious disease program in the Air Force. I decided that's what I wanted to do, what I enjoyed, and that the Air Force could benefit from my training and knowledge.

107 | "A Profession of Arms: Our Core Values." 16 May 2022, p. 11.

It was just perseverance that enabled me to accomplish my goal. I just kept pushing until it came through.[108]

Steve Lorenz also credited his career success—as well as graduating from the Academy—to determination and perseverance. As a former USAFA commandant, he observed that:

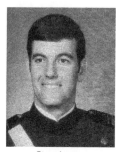

Steve Lorenz
CS-15

The most important thing to remember is that tenacity and perseverance will win out in the end. Even my struggles with academics taught me a lot and helped make me what I am. As the old saying goes, '90% of life is just showing up.' So don't ever stop showing up. You take the two by fours in the face, then pick yourself up, dust yourself off, and keep moving forward. And that's what the fourth-class system teaches us all.

Of course, the Academy teaches us many other things. But one of the most valuable lessons is that you have more ass than anybody can chew. That's a bit graphic but, during my time as the commandant, I put it that way to cadets so they'd remember it, particularly when they were put in a tough situation.[109]

TEAMWORK

Teamwork is essential to triumph at every level. Airmen recognize the interdependency of every member's contributions toward the mission and strive for organizational excellence. We not only give our personal best but also challenge and motivate each other to perform their best.

---

108 | Interview with Timothy W. Cooper, May 3, 2021.

109 | Interview with Stephen R. Lorenz, September 28, 2021.

We gain respect through our actions and strong work ethic to build team trust, and we give respect to others for their contributions. We carry our own weight and, whenever necessary, help our wingmen carry theirs. We serve in the greatest Air Force in the world, and we embrace the idea that our part of the Air Force meets the world-class standard.[110]

Learning to be an effective team member is critical, but leaders quickly discover that the key to building an effective organization is to leverage the knowledge and expertise of others. Bob Allen described how he learned the importance of identifying and utilizing experts, both inside and outside of the organization, to achieve mission success.

Bob Allen
CS-12

I think a lot of my approach to building well-functioning teams came from my time at the Academy. We had numerous opportunities, both in and outside of the classroom, to try different approaches and see what worked and what didn't.

Once on active duty, I found that my team extended to people I knew, some who were in my chain of command, some who were not. Over time I learned to call people I knew I could depend on, describe a problem I was having, see if they had experienced something similar, and what their experience had been.

Even as a senior officer, I continued to learn important lessons in teamwork. The leader can't be an expert in every area, nor is she/he expected to be. There's always a wealth of talented people in any organization, and the leader's job is to find them and put them to work. In my experience, there were many people in the organization who knew more than I did, or who were better than I was at solving a

110 | "A Profession of Arms: Our Core Values." 16 May 2022, p. 11.

given problem. Many times, it was the most senior enlisted person, whether a chief, the first sergeant, or just an informal leader in smaller units. But I didn't find that threatening—in fact, it built my confidence and helped build a culture of organizational ownership, accountability, and problem-solving.[111]

Every member has a role to play in an effective team. Charlie Felton quickly learned that, in the flying environment, the teamwork principles he learned at the Academy still applied. He also discovered that the costs of a dysfunctional team can be life-threatening.

Charlie Felton
CS-10

While the Academy taught me a great deal about teamwork, I don't think I understood its full ramifications until after I became a crew member on a B-52. To have a properly functioning crew, it's not enough that everyone be qualified and competent in their crew position. The best crews share a mutual respect for each other, no matter their education or rank. Everyone has a voice, everyone shares information, and everyone respects those inputs. For example, if the electronic warfare officer, a lieutenant colonel, calls, 'Break, right,' you'd better break right. There's no time to say, 'I don't see an imminent threat. I don't see a surface-to-air missile anywhere.' At that point, your whole crew is dead. The same is true if your gunner, a young airman, tells you, 'Break hard left,' you don't question it. You break hard left.

As an aircraft commander—or any team leader for that matter—you're leading a group that needs to act as an

111 | Interview with Robert H. Allen, January 19, 2022.

integral unit. If everyone does their job, and shares respon-sibility for the team's success, you have the highest odds of succeeding and completing your mission. Soliciting inputs from every member of your crew, or your team, is not a 'nice to have'—it's an absolute necessity. If you disregard or disenfranchise any member of the team, you increase your risk of failure.[112]

112 | Interview with Charles Felton, February 4, 2022.

PART IV

LEADERS OF CHARACTER FROM AN INSTITUTIONAL PERSPECTIVE

What does a leader of character look like from the perspective at the highest level of the institution? Why is having leaders of character so important to maintaining the health and well-being of the force? What role does character play in the military ethos? The following chapters present the perspectives of a variety of our classmates who held key leadership positions in our Air Force.

8

AN AIR FORCE CHIEF OF STAFF'S PERSPECTIVE

by General (Ret.) Norton A. Schwartz

Gen. Norton A. Schwartz served as the 19th Air Force chief of staff. From the time we entered the Academy, we knew Nort was destined for great things. His strength of character and quiet determination to do the right thing in all situations marked him as a standout performer from day one. As he rose within the ranks, he was an inspiration to all who worked for and with him. In recognition of his

Nort Schwartz
CS-34

extraordinarily significant contributions to our Nation and Air Force, he was honored by the Academy and the Association of Graduates with the Distinguished Graduate Award in 2019.

On March 14, 2020, I was in the parking lot at the Fort Myer commissary in Arlington, VA, loading my car. A younger man approached and asked, "What is your name?" I said, "Schwartz." He asked, "General Schwartz?" I said, "Yes."

He said he had been a much younger security forces Airman at Elmendorf AFB in the early 2000s, and that his wife had just retired two days earlier as a senior master sergeant. He also told me that one reason he had remained in our Air Force was because I had apparently stopped at the main gate at Elmendorf and had taken the time to interact and connect with him. He asked for a selfie and indicated that he was soon to retire as well, but wanted to express appreciation for that experience almost 20 years before—an experience that for me derived from a pair of NCOs at the Air Force Academy and a career flying a crew airplane.

Allow me to tell a story about two NCOs whom I met at the Air Force Academy and the impact they had on my life. TSgt. Mort Freedman was the NCOIC of the Parachute Team at USAFA in the early '70s. A combat controller, Mort was a veteran of the evacuation of Cam Duc, Vietnam in March 1968. He was one of three Airmen who were mistakenly left on the ground there after execution of the airlift evacuation. Lt. Col. Joe Jackson earned the Medal of Honor for returning to Cam Duc in his C-123 to bring those three great Americans home. Mort earned the Silver Star for that same mission. He was a demanding soul. All who knew him respected this original "Battlefield Airman." For whatever reason, Mort took an interest in me. His high standards inspired me, and it affected the way I served for more than 40 years. MSgt. Gene Rineartz was a "sergeant major" for Fourth Group when I was at the Academy, and was one of the first to serve as an NCO role model for the Cadet Wing. And a role model he was. I remember vividly one day Gene came up to me and asked about my sideburns. All of us pushed the limits back then…it was an important "act of resistance" for many in those days. He asked me how important my sideburns were to me: "Are you a leader or a follower?" he asked. You can tell I've never forgotten that intervention.

I mention these two vignettes because they reflect one of the great lessons I learned at the Air Force Academy…that everybody counts… that standards are vital in any organization, but especially one that possesses the legal sanction to apply lethal force. As a lieutenant, I was stationed at Clark Air Base in the Philippines. I happened at one point to be president of the Clark AB Sport Parachute Club. MSgt. Mort Freedman was then the NCOIC of the Clark Combat Control Team. He was also the U.S. Parachute Association (USPA) area safety officer (ASO). The ASO was an individual who could certify the sport parachuting credentials of other jumpers…in my case, as a jumpmaster.

On the day of my USPA jumpmaster check ride, Mort "busted" me for a significant procedural deviation. To this veteran of Cam Duc, it didn't matter who Schwartz was or who he might become. There were standards on which lives might depend. He reminded me that day of the necessity for standards and the necessity for making hard calls, even when it involved a promising mentoree and someone he cared about. Yes, I was thoroughly embarrassed and sad that I had disappointed my mentor and that I had compelled him to enforce his high standards. But I never forgot that fateful day in the Cessna 172 aircraft in the many years that followed. It was a seminal moment that crystalized, for me, the importance of standards and expectations in the profession of arms.

CMSgt. (Ret.) Gene Rineartz has stayed in touch over the years. He and his wife followed Suzie's and my progress, encouraging us to stay the course. He is elderly now and I will be profoundly sad when this tall, rock of an Air Force Academy staff member returns to the hands of his Creator, because he and Mort Freedman left me with one indelible impression: that everyone in our Air Force counts…everyone contributes without regard to their individual discipline or rank or previous station in life. And that the United States Air Force is a family of wonderful individuals and families who dedicate themselves to public service in ways large and small.

I hope that, in some small way, the experience with the Airman in the Ft. Myer Commissary parking lot reflects that I internalized the lessons that SMSgt. (Ret.) Freedman and CMSgt. (Ret.) Rineartz hoped I would learn.

Did I benefit from the Air Force Academy experience? While some Academy memories are not as vivid as they once were, my collective recollection is one of friendship, promise, and lifelong lessons. It has been and remains an exciting, consistently memorable and a profoundly meaningful journey. I don't think I'd change a thing and am genuinely grateful for our blessings.

The wife of one of our classmates submitted to the book committee a clipping she had kept since 2008. It was a speech by the "new" chief of staff of the Air Force, published in the Air Force Times on June 30, 2008. Nort had not yet been sworn in, but the Times recognized his vision and introduced the speech with this statement: "Gen. Norton Schwartz, nominated to become the new chief of staff, will be expected to fix many of the problems that plague the service, [and] the leadership that he, and those under his command, provide will be essential to that task." The following are excerpts from that speech.

Leadership has certainly been essential to the success of our armed forces throughout our history and especially since Sept. 11, 2001. Key to those successes are the individuals who, by rank, position, or personal charisma, provide the way ahead, encourage, comfort, inspire, discipline and command the finest military in the world.

I don't have any illusions about being a great leader but, after 34 years in uniform, I've certainly seen my share of both good and bad ones.

All of you probably have a short list of qualities, skills and values that you've seen in leaders you admire and didn't see in those you don't. My list, my chemistry of leadership, contains five basic elements—character, situational awareness, credibility, interpersonal skills, and values and ethics.

CHARACTER

Leaders with character have vision. They refuse to let the daily battles interfere with the longer view that transcends today's issues and articulates a meaningful and productive path for the future. People follow leaders who see beyond today or the crisis of the moment.

Leaders with character are tenacious. Anyone can perform under ideal circumstances. If you give up in tough times, so will the people you lead. Leaders must have the discipline and perseverance to "stay the course," and inspire others to do the same.

Leaders with character are resourceful—they are problem-solvers. They help those they lead find effective solutions to the inevitable challenges faced in achieving goals. Their playbooks are full of options—if taking the ball straight up the middle isn't working, an end-around, a pass or even the unexpected trick play may provide the yardage needed to succeed.

Leaders with character possess good judgment and moral courage. People bring the tough decisions to their leader—a leader must be ready, willing and able to make the call and stand by his or her decision.

Finally, leaders with character are competent. A leader must know his or her job, especially the fundamentals. Judgment, personal credibility (the third chemical on my list), and the trust of one's subordinates, peers and superiors all rely upon professional competence.

SITUATIONAL AWARENESS

We have a concept in the flying business known as situational awareness. There are obvious, and some not-so-obvious, parallels in leadership. A good leader knows his people and the environment in which they interact, both within and outside the organization. Good leaders understand and remain aware of the "pulse" of their organizations; they know when things are going well and when they are faltering.

Rather than micromanage, good leaders choose where and when to apply their detailed attention to contribute most effectively. Good situational awareness enables a leader to give others freedom, the basis for empowerment. A keen understanding of what's happening around them affords the confidence necessary to let the co-pilot take control.

CREDIBILITY

The moment you step into a new organization or a new position, your credibility is "on the line." Though it certainly takes time to earn the genuine respect, trust and confidence of your organization, as a leader you are in the spotlight from the day you arrive to the day you depart. Your character forms the foundation of your credibility; your day-to-day professionalism and ability to do your job make up the rest. Without credibility, a leader is that in name only.

INTERPERSONAL SKILLS

Of course, leadership is about people and moving them toward an objective. So the fourth element of leadership chemistry is interpersonal skills. Great leaders know and care about the strengths, ambitions, capabilities, talents, and shortcomings of their people. They know when to motivate, when to cajole, when to discipline and when to comfort. To be an effective leader, you must be able to connect with people. This does not mean that you have to change your personality or your basic leadership style—General Patton, a man you would probably not refer to as genteel, was an effective leader, but so was Mahatma Gandhi.

VALUES AND ETHICS

The last, but certainly not least, element of my leadership chemistry list is values and ethics. The connection between these two and great leadership should be obvious. That said, it is surprising to me how often this connection is broken. I won't argue that one can't have successes without values and ethics, but in the large majority of cases those successes are short-lived, and the resulting downside is nearly always deeper and steeper than the potential upside.

Great leaders demonstrate a commitment to the honorable and ethical standards associated with their organizations; they set the example of professionalism and integrity and they avoid even the appearance of impropriety.

This is especially critical to those of us who are called to be public servants—we have a moral obligation to wisely use the resources with which we are entrusted.

If you want to improve as a leader, I encourage you to concentrate on enhancing your character, situational awareness, credibility, interpersonal skills, and values and ethics. I don't think you can go wrong with these.

ACCOUNTABILITY

As my final point, let me hit a topic that affects all of us in positions of leadership—accountability and the answer to the question "Are good intentions good enough?"

While plenty of leaders are willing to take credit for the successes of their organizations, I'm concerned that some are all too willing to avoid the blame that comes with under-performance or failure.

In my mind, there is no such thing as "no-fault" leadership. Leaders should be rewarded for success and held accountable for failing to accomplish appointed outcomes. It comes with the territory. But how many of you have seen no-fault leadership in practice in either your seniors or contemporaries? Is it enough just to have good intentions for success, or is a change in leadership sometimes the appropriate path for an organization failing to achieve objectives?

In the U.S. military, accountability is critical to maintaining a moral force and the shared values of the profession of arms. While we are certainly accountable to our country's elected leaders and laws, we also, as a profession, have an obligation to police our own in order to maintain the values of the profession. It seems to me that's true for any profession.

My views on successful leadership aren't rocket science. While there are many great "how to" books on successful leadership, the real stuff of effective, even inspirational leadership comes down to the more basic chemistry of leaders—who and what they are.

If you're going to lead your organization through tough challenges, develop and refine those key personal qualities that make up your character. Strive for maximum professional competence to maintain that credibility within your profession. Finally, have a vision for where you want to go and define a path to the future. Then…go for it.

9

A SUPERINTENDENT'S PERSPECTIVE

by Lieutenant General (Ret.) John F. Regni

Lt. Gen. John Regni served as the 17th superinten-dent of the USAF Academy. Whether in the class-room, on the athletic fields, or on the parade field, "Regs" led with infectious enthusiasm and unshak-able integrity. His tenure as Academy superinten-dent has had a profound impact, not only on the Academy itself, but on the future leadership of our Air and Space Forces.

John Regni
CS-28

The Academy's mission is relatively unchanged over the last decades—to educate, train, and inspire men and women to become leaders of character, motivated to lead the United States Air Force in service to our Nation. The mission is pretty straightforward with respect to education and training, but it also includes lofty words like "inspire to become lead-ers of character." Our mission also suggests that the Academy's work is not only focused on delivering a return on investment to the Air Force, but also on serving our Nation as a whole. From that perspective, our mission is broad and all-encompassing. After five years, or forty, when the graduate transitions, those same traits of character and leadership are carried with them into the private or non-military public sectors where (unfortunately, I have found) our traits of honor, integrity, and character can be lacking…and thus are in very high demand. So, our mission charts us with lifelong work and endeavors, serving the greater good.

The answer to the question "what a leader of character looks like" lies within the Cadet Honor Code, the Academy's Core Values, and across the Academy's three main and nineteen supporting institutional outcomes. These institutional outcomes go well beyond the foundation of honor and our values and form the benchmarks and quality standards we want each and every graduate to attain before he or she walks across the stage in Falcon Stadium. From that standpoint, a leader of character is a graduate who has internalized, embraced and, by his or her actions and decisions, demonstrated honor, our values and *all* of our institutional outcomes. The institutional outcomes I refer to are as follows:

COMMITTED TO SOCIETAL, PROFESSIONAL, AND INDIVIDUAL RESPONSIBILITIES

- Ethical Reasoning and Actions
- Respect for Human Dignity
- Service to the Nation
- Lifelong Development and Contributions
- Intercultural Competence and Involvement

EMPOWERED BY INTEGRATED INTELLECTUAL AND WARRIOR SKILLS

- Quantitative and Information Literacy
- Oral and Written Communication
- Critical Thinking

- Decision Making
- Stamina
- Courage
- Discipline
- Teamwork

GROUNDED IN ESSENTIAL KNOWLEDGE OF THE PROFESSION OF ARMS AND THE HUMAN AND PHYSICAL WORLDS

- Heritage and Application of Air, Space, and Cyberspace Power
- National Security and the Full Spectrum of Joint and Coalition Warfare
- Civic, Cultural and International Environments
- Ethics and the Foundation of Character
- Principles of Science and the Scientific Method
- Principles of Engineering and the Application of Technology

While that's a long list, and maybe a somewhat ethereal and lofty one, we have four full years to get there, and the Academy's officer development plan does just that...not all at once, but progressively. For example, in the cadet squadron, building skills of being a member of a team (as a doolie, calling minutes so "your" firstie doesn't sleep in), to gaining more responsibility (third-class CQ) and, as you progress through the ranks to being the cadet-in-charge of an element, or a flight, or a squadron, or even group or Wing staff! But, in all cases, that path begins with honor.

It is easier in the admission process to identify a prospective cadet who will excel in Math 400 or Astro; measuring heart is a much more difficult thing. It is safer to assume at the starting point of Basic Cadet Training that we have significant work to do with honor, and to begin at ground zero. That was annually reinforced on day #2 of BCT when I met with each new class in Clune Arena. After the usual comments of welcome and motivation to succeed in Basic, and all the fun that lies ahead in Second Beast with Hell's Half Acre (Assault Course) and more, I took an unofficial but very insightful poll. "How many of you told your parents you were going out to one place but actually knowingly went elsewhere?" (About 70% of the hands flew up.) "How many of you may have taken a piece of candy from a Quick Stop or may have shoplifted?" (Another 30% hands.) "How many of you copied a friend's work on a high school paper or had inside information on what was on a quiz?" (About half of the hands.) "And how many of your friends did one of those things and you saw it and did nothing to correct it?" (99% of the hands shot up.) "Well, in a nutshell, that is our Honor Code...*we will not lie, steal or cheat, nor tolerate among us anyone who does*...and, in six weeks, you will take the Honor Oath as you are inducted into the Cadet Wing as cadet fourth-class men and women...we have much to teach you, inform you, get you to not only grasp but internalize our Honor Code and way of life."

Our Honor Code was directly imported from West Point and adopted by the Class of 1959 (the Honor Oath was added in 1984). The Academy Core Values (Integrity First, Service Before Self, and Excellence in All We Do) were developed and accepted by the Academy in the early 1990s and later embraced by the Air Force as the service's Core Values. In the early and mid-2000s, it took several years for the Academy to finalize the three main and nineteen supporting institutional outcomes. During that process, each lesson plan, every cadet activity, every program was turned on its head to answer the question: does it directly support and relate to one or more of the outcomes? The acid test became, if a lesson did not, it was simply deleted as not relevant, or rewritten to be so (and in the process much of the "mickey mouse" we used to grouse about was removed). And, if you are ever bored, the Dean and the 21 permanent professors (as the institutional "keepers of the flame") can show you a

5-tiered "spaghetti chart" that traces every one of the thousands of lessons and activities across the Academy to one or more graduation outcomes—informing, explaining, reinforcing, building upon them—so, by graduation, we have nurtured and built that substantial base of character and leadership for the Air Force and beyond, in a second or third career.

Thus, the first significant lessons were on honor, and the core value of integrity. And, over the days and weeks and months ahead, the lessons blossomed to more honor and core values and, over time and in-depth, into all 19 institutional outcomes. If you think back over our four years, you will recognize some of the outcomes and even recall a cadet activity that reinforced them. As an officer, even 10 years removed from my firstie days, I sometimes had moments of déjà vu when faced with an issue…"so that's why they talked about this at the Academy…now I see why we had that…how did they know I'd need that one?"

Rather than be too lengthy, I'll close here by again answering the posed question. The superintendent's (and Academy's) primary objective—collectively across the faculty, the commandant, the athletic department, the airfield, the Air Base Wing, and the superintendent's staff—was and is to produce individual graduates who are leaders of character, grounded in honor, integrity, service and excellence. Graduates who also have in character, grounded in honor, integrity, service and excellence. Graduates who also have in their arsenal a dedication to the mission, to the welfare and well-being of the enlisted men and women, civilians and, in time, the officers under them; who appreciate the value diversity brings to an organization; who have a genuine respect for human dignity; who appreciate internationals and their culture and language; who can critically think in the face of complex technical situations; and have the stamina and courage to make solid decisions; who, while cadets, did everything to beat Navy and Army on the fields of friendly strife yet now professionally understand and integrate their contributions to joint and coalition warfare; and who are articulate and effective communicators; and more. A graduate who renders his or her first salute as a second lieutenant who embodies all those tenets is surely the leader of character. We expect them to be that throughout their military service and beyond as they continue to serve the United States of America.

10

A MAJCOM COMMANDER'S PERSPECTIVE

by General (Ret.) Stephen R. Lorenz

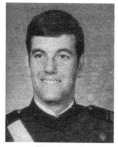

Steve Lorenz
CS-15

Look up "perseverance" in the dictionary, and you'll see a picture of Gen. Stephen R. Lorenz. His academic performance was less than stellar: six out of eight semesters on academic probation, two academic review boards, first-class summer on "R" flight (remedial academic classes), and innumerable hours of extra instruction over four years. But his perseverance and hard work paid off, as he commanded at the squadron, operations group, wing, and Major Air Command (MAJCOM) levels. In all positions, his tenure was distinguished by organizational innovation, outstanding performance, and an unmatched devotion to his people and the mission. In recognition of his outstanding service, in 2017 Steve was honored by the Academy and Association of Graduates with the Distinguished Graduate Award for "extraordinarily significant contributions" to our Nation and Air Force.

As I look back on our time at the Academy, my time as commandant of cadets, and my continuing involvement with the Academy as president of the Falcon Foundation,[113] it amazes me at how far we've come. While some things are very different for the Class of 2023 than what we experienced as the Class of 1973, others are very similar.

For the most part, the Class of 1973 was a homogeneous group. But today's diversity—which is the right thing to do, by the way—produces much less homogeneous entering classes. People enter from all walks of life—male, female, black, white, Asian, Hispanic. That diversity strengthens our Air Force, but it also means that the shared common experience of being at the Academy—the "bluing process"—is ten times more important than it was in our day. The "bluing process" also creates bonds between graduates that will last a lifetime.

THE NATURE OF CHANGE

As it turns out, everything is generational. Life experiences are based on the year you were born, and you have no say in it. If you would happen to have been born five or ten years earlier, or five years or ten years later, things would be very different. The people who are leading our Air Force—this generation of leaders—must deal with conditions as they are today. That said, while they have currency, we have perspective. We lived through the Cold War and saw the demise of the Soviet Union. We also saw how strong the military needed to be to succeed in those challenging times. Many of the bases we were stationed at or lived on early in our careers have long since closed. In our day, there were 600,000 to 700,000 people in our force structure. But today's Air Force has some 333,000 people, and the technology is vastly different. While the Class of 2023 does not have the former Soviet Union to contend with, they

---

113 | The Falcon Foundation is an organization that was established to further the opportunity for exceptionally motivated young men and women to attend the Academy through the award of Falcon Foundation Scholarships to select junior colleges and preparatory schools.

will have other global challenges, like Russia and China. Their job will be to survive during this very difficult period, to be the best they can be, and to meet their challenges.

That said, the Class of 2023 has to deal with some of the same challenges we did and, most fundamentally, they need to be good at leading. To do that, they need to have strong people skills and have high emotional intelligence, in addition to being leaders in technology and modern warfighting capabilities.

FUNDAMENTAL LEADERSHIP LESSONS LEARNED

Countless books have been written about leadership, but ultimately every aspiring leader must find what works for her or him in the working environment. I've learned a great deal over the years by observing good and bad leaders in action, or by evaluating my own effectiveness as a leader. I've also found that the process of journaling was a powerful way of developing my thinking and understanding about leadership. The following leadership lessons learned come from an article I wrote for the *Air & Space Power Journal* published in Summer 2005, and I offer them for your consideration. [114]

In 1987, I was commander of the 93rd Air Refueling Squadron at Castle AFB in Merced, California. Late one night, I sat down and wrote out a list of leadership principles. There was nothing magical about them—they were simply useful precepts I had learned over the years. Today, especially after the terrorist attacks of 11 September 2001, our leaders need to reflect on the principles that guide them. I do not seek to instill mine on the readers of this journal. Rather, I only ask that Air Force leaders reflect on what their principles are, regardless of whether or not they have written them down. That said, I offer the following for consideration.

114 | "Fundamental Leadership Lessons Learned" by Maj. Gen. Stephen R. Lorenz, USAF, was published in *Air & Space Power Journal*, Summer 2005, Volume 19, Number 2, pp. 5-9.

BALANCING SHORTFALLS

Shortfalls occur in our professional and personal lives. We never seem to have enough time, money, or manpower. The essence of this "scarcity principle" lies in accepting the reality of limited resources and becoming adept at obtaining superior results in less-than-ideal situations. Equally important, once people acknowledge the scarcity of resources, then they need not bemoan the situation any longer. In other words, they should "deal with it." Leaders must carry out the mission with the resources they have. They have to make it happen! This is part of being a military commander and leader. Commanders never go to war with all the resources they think they need—they balance their shortfalls to accomplish the mission.

KEEPING OUR EYES ON THE BALL

In order to prevail, leaders must always keep in mind what they want to accomplish, regardless of the task, and not become distracted. They must articulate the mission to their people. During my tenure as director of the Air Force budget, I didn't consider the budget the mission so much as I considered it a means for our service to defend the United States through the exploitation of air and space. In the Air Force, this means that leaders must connect actions and troops to the mission and never lose sight of this important relationship.

Leaders can assure their people's well-being (a major ingredient of mission accomplishment) by knowing how they feel and how they are doing. They should look them in the eye and ask how they are. Eyes don't lie. They reflect happiness, sadness, or stress. To get an honest answer, one should ask at least *three times*, and do so more emphatically each time: "How are you doing?"

The first response is always, "Fine." The second, "I'm okay." Finally, when they realize that their leader is truly interested, they respond honestly. By the way, the only difference between a younger person and someone my age is the amount of scar tissue. Because I have lived longer than most of my military colleagues on active duty and therefore have more scar tissue, I can probably disguise my feelings more effectively. But the eyes are the true indicator. Again, leaders must never lose sight of the primary objective: *to focus on the mission and take care of their people.*

THOSE WHO DO THEIR HOMEWORK WIN

The equation for this principle is simple: knowledge = power. Take, for example, the battle for scarce resources. The person who has the most compelling story, backed by the strongest data, gets the most resources. We have seen this principle, which applies universally to all other undertakings, demonstrated repeatedly throughout history—especially military history!

THE TOUGHEST WORD TO SAY IN THE ENGLISH LANGUAGE

According to an old adage, the most difficult word to say in English is *no*. But I have a contrarian's view. Saying *no* finishes the situation; saying *yes*, however, carries with it additional tasks, commitments, and responsibilities. For instance, when I agree to speak to a group, I have taken a more difficult path than I would have by declining. If I say *no* to a request for funding an initiative, my job is finished. If I say *yes*, then I must take on the task of finding resources.

Leaders should also consider the effects of a response on working relationships. If a leader responds affirmatively 95 percent of the time, his or her people will readily accept the fact that the leader has carefully considered their request before responding negatively. I never say *no* until I research the issue and look into all the alternatives. To this day, it still amazes me that most of the time I can say *yes* if I do a little work and make a personal commitment.

NEW IDEAS NEED TIME AND NURTURING TO GROW AND BEAR FRUIT

In order to overcome some of the challenges we face today, we need people to think and act out of the box. Furthermore, we must have the patience and faith to stay the course. Things do not happen overnight. People have to work very hard to make things happen. They must sell their ideas and do their homework without concern for who gets the credit. This principle is very important to remember as new generations of Airmen enter the Air Force to help fight the global war on terrorism.

LEADERS SHOULD NOT LOSE THEIR TEMPER— UNLESS THEY PLAN TO

To navigate the necessary course of action and ensure mission accomplishment, a leader must be willing to use more than one approach. Earlier in my career, I saw my boss—a mild-mannered, consummately professional four-star general—storm into a meeting and angrily bark out criticisms to his senior staff. When we left the room, he looked at me, winked, and calmly said that a person has to put across a different face in order for people to take him or her seriously. My boss had planned the whole incident. He had not lost his temper at all—he did it for effect. If leaders cannot control themselves, how can they control others? They must have self-discipline. They should never, ever lose their temper— unless they plan to.

ALL DECISIONS SHOULD PASS THE SUNSHINE TEST

Because leaders must make difficult decisions every day, it's important for people in the trenches to know that the process is fair and above reproach. Toward that end, we must be as open and accessible as possible and always act as if our decisions were public knowledge—as if they appeared in the newspaper, for example. If leaders are forthright about why they made a decision, their people might disagree, but they will understand the underlying logic and continue to trust them. As Air Force leaders, we need only look to our service's Core Values—Integrity First, Service Before Self, and Excellence in All We Do—to arrive at solid decisions that gain the public trust and instill faith in our processes.

EGO: BOTH FACILITATOR AND DETRIMENT

A unit's success depends upon its members keeping their egos in check. We cannot afford to let them run amuck. We need confident, capable people who work together to enhance the organization rather than individuals who pursue their own selfish agendas. As my father taught me, leaders need people with ambition—not ambitious people. Early in my career, I applied for a development program—the predecessor of the current Air Force Intern Program. I had confidence that I would be accepted, so not seeing my name on the list came as a shock. To make matters worse, another officer in my squadron did make the cut.

Inwardly, I withdrew from the organization and walked around several days feeling hurt and angry. Eventually, though, I realized that the Air Force only owed me the opportunity to compete. On the day the board met, my records did not meet its standards. Whose fault was that? Mine—no one else's. I put the issue behind me and embraced my squadron mate. This experience taught me the negative effect of allowing my ego to dominate my actions—specifically, my failure to realize that the Air Force had not promised to select me for the program. It did, however, guarantee me equitable consideration and fair competition. I should have expected nothing else. An Air Force person should compete only with himself or herself, striving for improvement every day!

WORK THE BOSS'S BOSS'S PROBLEMS

This principle goes one step beyond the adage "work your boss's problems." Most people make a decision through a soda straw but, if they would rise up two levels above themselves, they could open the aperture of that straw and get a strategic view of the decision. Taking a "god's eye" view—looking through the eyes of their boss's boss—allows them to make a much better decision. That is, leaders must become deeply committed to the organization and make their boss's challenges their own. If they can achieve this type of commitment—regardless of who the boss is or which political party controls the government—the only thing that matters is enhancing mission accomplishment by making the best decisions possible and doing the right thing under the circumstances.

SELF-CONFIDENCE AND MOTIVATION: KEYS TO ANY GREAT ENDEAVOR

We can attribute most successful endeavors to persevering and putting forth maximum effort. Whenever I speak about leadership, I always begin with a quotation from Sir Winston Churchill: "To every man, there comes in his lifetime that special moment when he is figuratively tapped on the shoulder and offered that chance to do a very special thing, unique to him and fitted to his talents. What a tragedy if that moment finds him unprepared or unqualified for that which would be his finest hour."

I am particularly attracted to this statement because of the great things Churchill accomplished, even though he faced failure and defeat many times. Regardless of the difficulty or hardship, he remained committed and motivated. He never gave up. Churchill's words represent a call to action that has helped me overcome such challenges as surviving engineering courses as a cadet as well as serving as a wing commander, commandant of cadets at the Air Force Academy, and budget director for the Air Force, despite having no prior experience in budgetary matters. Although I lacked in-depth knowledge of budgets and finance, perseverance got me through, as always. I never gave up. My best advice? Never give up. Never, ever give up!

APPLY OVERWHELMING COMBAT POWER TO THE POINT THAT WILL HAVE THE MOST EFFECT

I have a simple organizational method that has served me well for many years. I like to approach issues, goals, and tasks "big to small, top to bottom, or left to right." That is, I believe that one must be able to see the entire forest before working on individual trees. We must understand the big-picture issues before delving into smaller details. From a broad point of view, I find it helpful to pursue goals by progressing from the short term, through the midterm, to the long term. Leaders should make sure their subordinates have not only the "overall road map" they need for direction but also the resources to plan and complete tasks.

One of my favorite and most beneficial experiences involved an aircraft-sanitation worker at McGuire AFB, New Jersey. During a customer-focus class that I taught in an effort to counter what I perceived as lackadaisical attitudes prevalent in the organization, I noticed a lady in the audience whose body language was so agitated that she was figuratively *screaming* at me. I stopped the class and asked her what was wrong. Jeanie said she was frustrated because no one would help her with a work problem. I told her that, if she explained the situation to me, I would try to help.

According to Jeanie, the sanitation truck she operated was designed for servicing a KC-10, which sits high off the ground. Normally, she hooked the truck's waste-removal hose to the aircraft, flipped a switch, and gravity pulled the contents into her vehicle. At that time, however, McGuire also had the C-141, which sits only three feet off the ground. Consequently, when she attempted the same procedure on the C-141, the hose bent because it was not fully extended, as with the KC-10, and became clogged with waste. She then had to disconnect the hose, lift it over her head, and shake it to clear the obstruction—clearly an unpleasant task that she had to repeat multiple times if the aircraft's lavatory was completely full.

Although such a problem might seem trivial, on a large aircraft that makes extended flights, the lavatory is a mission-essential piece of equipment. Armed with the knowledge of Jeanie's problem, I organized a team to solve it—and the members did so by engineering and installing a 3.2-horsepower engine that proved more than capable of overcoming the clearance problem. But the greatest accomplishment in this case was neither the technical solution nor the vastly improved sanitation procedure, but the effect the process had on Jeanie. It revived and energized her. Thereafter, each time I saw Jeanie, she proudly displayed her truck, which she had polished and shined so highly that it would likely meet a hospital's sanitation standards. This story drives home the point that leaders must look for both verbal and nonverbal messages from the people in their organization. If they can reach the person who operates the sanitation truck, they can reach anyone.

STUDY THE PROFESSION AND READ— ESPECIALLY BIOGRAPHIES

During our Air Force careers, we have many opportunities to add to our education and knowledge. America's future depends upon our maximizing and complementing these occasions with our own regimen of reading and development. As a life-time student of leadership, I have an insatiable appetite for learning and regularly read two or three books at a time. I have dedicated myself to learning from other people's experiences so that I do not waste time trying to reinvent the wheel. Studying and learning how other leaders overcame adversity builds confidence in one's own ability to make tough decisions. I have found my study of Gen. Colin Powell and Gen. Henry "Hap" Arnold especially rewarding.

TAKE YOUR JOB (NOT YOURSELF) SERIOUSLY

To drive home the important concepts when I discuss leadership, I include comical—sometimes outrageous—videos and pictures to accompany each principle. Audiences seem both surprised and refreshed to see a general officer use David Letterman-style "top-10 lists" and irreverent videos ranging from Homer Simpson to bizarre advertisements as part of a serious presentation. However, I see these methods as the ideal way of delivering my message. Leaders must realize that, because they communicate with a diverse, cross-generational population, they need to speak in terms their audience will understand.

A leader must create a common, shared vision that everyone can comprehend and accept. I like to try to communicate my vision by talking about an experience or using an analogy that everyone can relate to, understand, and remember. It is critical that leaders deliver their message in easily grasped terminology. They should employ a type of universal device akin to the "Romulan translator" depicted in the *Star Trek* television series. The medium used by the communicator can take the form of an analogy, a video, or a story. However, the critical point is that the communicator package and deliver the message in a format that the varied groups we lead today will understand.

Today's leaders were born primarily during the last half of the 20th century. They could have been born 100 years earlier or 100 years from now. By accident of birth, most, but not all, American leaders were born in the United States. They could have been born in another country like Iraq or Cambodia, but most of today's leaders were born in America. The United States, whether it wants to be or not, is the world's greatest power, and air and space power is now the permanent instrument of that power.

CHART YOUR OWN COURSE

The above principles have worked for me, but ultimately each of you will have to chart your own course and over the years will discover what works best for you. But know this: I'd trade places with you in a heartbeat—even with your challenges. I have no idea what you're going to face down the road, but we didn't know what we were going to face either. But I do know this: the Air Force lets ordinary people do extraordinary things, and the Class of 2023 will make its legacy just as we did.

11

AN AIR AND SPACE FORCES ASSOCIATION PRESIDENT'S PERSPECTIVE

by Lieutenant General (Ret.) Bruce A. Wright

Bruce Wright
CS-39

Lt. Gen. Bruce "Orville" Wright had a long career as a combat-experienced fighter pilot and commander. He was the vice commander of Air Combat Command, and later served as commander of Fifth Air Force and United States Forces Japan. Following his retirement, he was selected as president of the Air Force Association, where he continues to serve our Nation by supporting dominant U.S. Air and Space Forces as the foundation of a strong national defense; honoring and supporting our Airmen, Space Force professionals, and their families; and promoting our enduring heritage.

More than 50 years have passed since the USAFA Class of 1973 raised our right hands and took an oath to defend the Constitution of the United States. Our shared four years of cadet training and experience, plus sustained friendships with classmates, have continued to inform, validate and encourage me ever since. The enduring resultant trust and confidence inspire continued commitment to the highest standards of integrity, selfless service, professional excellence, and courage. In fact, as I look back with a 50-year perspective, I realize that leadership development is something that never stops—it is truly a continuing journey and a lifetime gift that keeps on giving.

FORMATIVE TRAINING EXPERIENCES

In a long and varied career, UPT was one of my most unforgettable and formative experiences. While challenges and leadership experiences from the Academy certainly helped, pilot training introduced an entirely new challenge: how to make split-second, sound decisions at more than 200, or even 400 knots. As we all learned, the answer is to be prepared. Get out in front of the T-6 or T-38, or whatever it is you're flying. Be aggressive. Always be thinking about the next decision. Those enduring lessons on the importance of being prepared applied throughout my career: quickly develop answers to questions not asked yet. Identify solutions to problems before they become problems. Get ahead of the normal pace of decision making and take decisive action. Just as important, pilot training taught us the value of blunt self-assessment. There's absolutely no room for shallow or incomplete analysis, or self-promoting "spin." Appearance doesn't matter—results are what count.

The foundational lessons continued after graduation from advanced training. As a young lieutenant flying F-4 fighter aircraft, I found the more experienced pilots and weapons systems officers (WSOs) quickly became mentors in my professional and social life. My goal was to be as good as, or better, than my more senior and capable squadron members. Their Vietnam war stories left a strong impression that continues to define how I live my life today. They set an example of trust and personal accountability. They taught me to always strive to perform at a higher level and to demonstrate quiet but reliable courage in tough situations. They taught me that to build a reputation in peace and war, actions speak louder than words, and words must be true in every sense.

PREPARING FOR COMBAT

Realistic combat training began early in my career. The RED FLAG exercise series at Nellis Air Force Base in Nevada began in 1975 and it was exciting and an honor to participate as a young squadron pilot in 1976. Designed to realistically replicate the first ten days of combat operations, RED FLAG gave new pilots the opportunity to see, feel and survive the daunting challenges of enemy air and missile attacks with more aircraft in the nearby battlespace than in any previous training scenario. In the crucible of daunting combat training, documented performance was the discriminator for each pilot's credibility and trust across the squadron and wing.

Looking back on it, this was a natural extension of what the Academy taught us about personal accountability. Do the right thing, for the right reasons, under all circumstances. Not dissimilar from our Jack's Valley experience, there was no room, nor quarter offered nor given—for faking it as we prepared for combat. We were being trained to be accountable as warriors responsible for employing the most lethal weapons in the world. And, by the way, bragging about your in-flight performance was a sure way to be identified as a jerk. Giving credit to others was right and a respected leadership example.

It's essential that the American people have faith that we can perform at the highest levels of mental and physical toughness. We quickly learned that the only way to meet that high standard is to constantly hold each other accountable, and to recognize that you can't talk your way out of a less-than-perfect performance. So, as we sat through those post-mission debriefs, we all knew that candid feedback should never be taken personally. We're all in this together, and candid feedback is gold. It makes you a better person.

Following participation in RED FLAG exercises, I was able to also fly in equally realistic and challenging combat training in the Philippines-based COPE THUNDER exercise series. Combat aircraft from across the Pacific Air Forces, including F-4s from both Clark Air Base in the Philippines and Osan and Kunsan Air Bases in South Korea, took part. My classmate and good friend from Academy days, Captain Nick Pallas, was deployed to COPE THUNDER from Kunsan, and our F-4s were lined up together on the Clark ramp. As I returned from a morning COPE THUNDER exercise period, I met and talked with Nick as he walked to his F-4 for the scheduled afternoon go. I never saw him again. He was killed about an hour later as his F-4 malfunctioned at high speed and low altitude. Back in those days, everything we knew about avoiding advanced radar missile systems led us to believe that the lower and faster you could go, the better off you'd be in a high threat environment. Of course, the downside is that there's no room for error of any kind. In Nick's case, a leading-edge flap malfunction at 500 knots at very low altitude was what killed him.

While the pain of losing such a close friend was indescribable, there was some consolation in knowing that Nick was dedicated to serving what he considered to be the best part of his life. He wouldn't have called himself courageous; he would just say that he was doing his job. But he was willing to make the ultimate sacrifice—even though it was "just" a training mission—in defense of his Nation. That's the calling of our profession, one that motivates young men and women to put their lives on the line every day. So Nick's sacrifice made me further resolve that, regardless of the difficulty, I would always strive to give more.

My most humbling developmental experience over 50 years in uniform was the six months I spent as a student at the USAF Fighter Weapons School (now renamed the USAF Weapons School). Among fighter pilots of my generation, being accepted to attend the F-4 weapons school was itself considered a great achievement. This was the most demanding course for combat aviators, well-known for its daunting attrition rate. Flunking the course at the USAF Fighter Weapons School was the worst failure any F-4 pilot or WSO could imagine, but success was hardly guaranteed. One of our best and most demanding instructors was Captain Eddie Zwirko, my Academy classmate. Eddie graduated well in the bottom of our Academy class, but he was one of the best fighter pilots I ever flew with. Eddie demanded the absolute highest standards for combat flying performance. Classmate and friend though he was, he held me to the highest standards and made me a better leader in the toughest and most rewarding leadership course I ever attended. And he led all his students to be much more effective in the demands and higher calling of defending our Nation in future combat operations.

OUR SACRED OBLIGATION

Back at USAFA, we were blessed by the guidance of Colonel and Doctor of Philosophy Mal Wakin. He taught several outstanding courses and imparted the foundational principles for character, leadership, and professionalism in uniform. Almost 20 years later, when I commanded the 52nd Wing Support Group at Spangdahlem, Germany, Col. Wakin helped me once again. Our wing had experienced a significant increase in "blotter" incident reports—excessive drinking and other unprofessional conduct, and we needed to shake things up. Col. Wakin was good enough to travel to "Spang" and deliver a series of talks on military professionalism to a packed base theater. His message was clear and strong: When you wear the uniform of America's military, our citizens expect nothing but the best, and will hold you accountable for being a person of outstanding character with near-perfect professional accomplishment. The Constitution of the United States of America gives our military men and women the singular authority to kill the enemies of our Nation, a sobering responsibility that demands a higher level of conduct in how we lead our lives. For that reason, Americans expect us to live up to a reputation for always doing what is right. After Col. Wakin's visit, "blotter" entries at Spangdahlem Air Base decreased dramatically. His message was received and internalized.

From Jan. 1991 to early 1994, I was actively involved in leading combat air forces operations, including DESERT STORM, PROVIDE COMFORT, and DENY FLIGHT. The first-in-my-lifetime combat mission included leading sixteen F-16s attacking Iraqi-held airfields in Kuwait. Thanks to countless opportunities to compete under stressful conditions at the Academy and in Air Force combat training programs, I felt calm, confident, and prepared: when an SA-2 surface-to-air missile began tracking my wingman on that first combat mission, well-practiced radio calls kicked in. My former T-38 IP, Eddie Ballanco, now flying an F-4G Wild Weasel, fired an enemy radar-seeking "HARM" missile at the SA-2. As a result, my F-16 wingman, Phil Ruhlman, a USAFA grad, lived to fight another day. We continued to deliver lethal combat capability against the Iraqi army with tons of accurately targeted weapons and, along with our combat air forces teammates, decimated the Iraqi ground forces, weeks before the "100-hour" ground war.

Leadership in combat operations is all about operating at the highest levels of character, accountability, selfless resolve, and near-perfect performance. During DESERT STORM, PROVIDE COMFORT, and DENY FLIGHT in Iraq and Bosnia-Herzegovina, we were constantly required to make complex tactical decisions, with only seconds to decide whether to employ destructive weapons against enemy forces. America's most senior leadership, up to the level of the president of the United States, must be absolutely confident they can rely on the character and leadership of combat-engaged Airmen, who often employ the most destructive weapons in the battle space. In the American way of war, non-combatant civilian casualties, along with fratricide of U.S. and allied forces, are never tolerated. The singular objective to destroy the enemy while protecting our forces, allies, and partners always shaped and drove my actions and those of the F-16 squadron and group I led. The Rules of Engagement (ROE) we operate by are derived from multiple sources, but always founded on our oath to defend the United States Constitution. They constantly define who and what a combat pilot chooses to destroy in the heat of combat while facing lethal enemy opposition. As my classmate and good friend Nick Pallas understood, in Korea years ago, when we go into combat, we fully accept personal risks involved with destroying the enemy in strict adherence to established ROE.

Command at the more senior officer level in our Air Force always includes lessons and observations from associations with more senior officers over the decades of officer leadership development. Whether commissioned from USAFA, ROTC, or OTS, the senior officer leaders I served or partnered with could be relied upon for the highest levels of character in their professional and personal lives. Without exception, the shared fabric of character in all these leaders was selfless courage. You could absolutely count on them to engage the enemies of our Nation and know they would die trying. Each was promoted because their peers and superior officers knew they could count on them in a tough fight. There is no more demanding set of appraisers than those officers and NCOs one serves with in our military. While I have come to know many great Americans and leaders in the corporate and public world, the selfless courage of our military sets our USAF senior leaders apart. The public will always hold us accountable to that special nature and we will always be defined by our reputations and the promise to give our lives—or take lives—so that others may live to enjoy America's freedoms.

As the vice commander of Air Combat Command (ACC), one of my jobs was to teach the squadron commander courses we hosted. My boss at the time, General Hal Hornburg, taught the wing commanders. We both made the point that effective leadership requires three pillars requiring a lifetime of commitment and study: intellectual, physical, and spiritual strength. In the early 2000 timeframe, there was a good deal of public opposition to senior military officers sharing their personal faith in public. To talk about the importance of spiritual strength in one's leadership development, I was ably assisted by both our ACC lawyer and chaplain in the classes with me. I made the documented point to our squadron commanders that I was not "proselytizing." But then I went on to humbly offer, in my personal and professional experience, including combat time, that the Bible is an excellent reference for a leader's library. There were no documented course complaints. I will always believe in the Bible as a singular source of leadership guidance and encouragement, and a proven foundation for character development.

Whether training in Jack's Valley, learning to fly and lead as a U.S. Air Force combat pilot, a general officer, and a corporate and non-profit executive, the basics of leadership remain the same. When we set high standards and hold ourselves accountable, we inspire the same of those around us. Our credibility will always be founded on our shared commitment to our warrior ethos and our higher calling to defend the Nation.

A limited review of military history suggests that true warriors are a relatively smaller percentage of those who have worn the uniform of our Nation. But there's more to the story. In my view, the very personal commitment to those we train and serve with, plus the oath we all take to die for our country and each other, when necessary, define us all as America's warriors, regardless of rank or technical specialty. In my experience, a true warrior isn't strictly defined by facing enemy fire, but by making the deliberate decision to adhere to the highest standards of character and accountability—a willingness to give one's life for our military teammates and to preserve the future of freedom and opportunity for every American. Such decisions, strengthened throughout a lifetime, are what define us all as true warriors.

Thanks to the leadership examples of my USAFA classmates and USAF senior leaders and counterparts, the shared demands of accountability for employing the world's most lethal weapons, and the honor of serving in our United States Air Force, the answer to questions of character and leadership are simple. We will be exemplary and trusted in our commitment to give our lives for each other and to risk our "all in" defense of the Constitution of the United States of America. "So help me God," we took America's most sacred oath. We know that oath is always with us, always needed, and is a life-long responsibility.

12

A JOINT AGENCY PERSPECTIVE

by Colonel (Ret.) John T. Wigington, III

Character is a major emphasis in the Air Force, but what role does it play as we work alongside our joint service counterparts? With his extensive experience in joint organizations, Col. John Wigington brings a unique perspective on how and why leading with character is so essential in leading diverse organizations. His lessons learned have broad applicability within a variety of organizational cultures.

John Wigington
CS-14

I had the honor of leading two joint organizations: the Joint Intelligence Center Pacific (JICPAC), and the Missile and Space Intelligence Center (MSIC). Both organizations were tasked with producing intelligence products for a wide variety of customers, ranging from soldiers, sailors, and Airmen in combat units; to service acquisition agencies; to unified commands; and to the National Command Authorities. Needless to say, we had to have a customer focus. I never considered these units to be "staff" organizations because we were producers of intelligence, as opposed to those setting policy, planning, or working resource issues.

Both units included a large number of NCOs, junior officers, and junior/mid-grade civilians that gave the organizations a "unit-level" feel and called for a little different leadership focus as compared to an organization staffed by more senior personnel.

ANTICIPATING NEEDED CHANGES

In my experience, one of the key traits a leader must have is the ability to assess where an organization is in its development, understand where it needs to be, and know how to orient the unit members toward those objectives. That was largely my focus. As a result of winning the Cold War and downsizing in the intelligence community, JICPAC and MSIC were both the result of consolidation. JICPAC was the amalgamation of the Pacific Air Forces, Pacific Fleet, and U.S. Pacific Command intelligence centers. MSIC was an Army intelligence center that had been moved under the Defense Intelligence Agency. The personnel brought their respective organizational cultures, attitudes, processes, and customer focus with them. Not surprisingly, many members of both units had a "the way it always was" attitude that needed to be addressed. Both organizations needed changes.

Before making changes, the leader of a joint unit needs to understand the different service cultures, their traditions, and personnel and promotion philosophies. Service ways and traditions should be recognized, often celebrated, but never allowed to become competitive within the organization. To bring about cultural change in a unit, the leader must be out front and visible, setting the example, and leading the cheers. As we worked to establish unit identity, even the little things helped, like having unit ball caps, fielding athletic teams, and hosting social activities. A JICPAC dining-in with all ranks and services and civilian personnel did wonders to build unit cohesion and comradery.

UNDERSTANDING AND UTILIZING DIVERSE CULTURES

A joint unit can take advantage of the diversity of service cultures and experiences to improve mission performance and, as with JICPAC and MSIC, improve intelligence product for customers. In some situations, analysts were needed to work in areas they were not familiar with to support other services' units. That was a win-win, with the customer getting a better product and the intelligence professional becoming a more valuable member of the team, both then and in future assignments. But, occasionally, the leader must instill a sense of urgency in the workforce, particularly when a service member did not fully understand another service's intelligence requirements. In the case of civilians with no military experience, they had to be educated on the importance of providing time-sensitive, accurate information.

The leader must be customer-focused. Change was needed in our production processes to take advantage of rapidly changing technology and to improve the interface with customers. At JICPAC and MSIC, we increased direct contact with our intelligence customers. An educational process, frequent and meaningful customer interaction and cross-organization visits helped the intelligence producers understand the customer perspective. Often, you must accept customers as they are, constrained by technology or tactics, techniques, and procedures. Rather than trying to change the customers to accommodate our processes, we worked to integrate our products with their processes. Having a customer focus may mean that the leader must also play the role of a distant customer, becoming the customer's advocate with his or her own people.

Effective resource allocation often requires the leader to make tough decisions by trading off risk for opportunity. This typically happens with budgets, but also applies to the allocation of personnel. Trade-offs in unit members' time, energy, and effort can be disruptive to their lives, to unit production processes, and to some customers. For instance, when tensions on the Korean Peninsula rose and armed conflict with North Korea became a real possibility, we were required to shift a large number of JICPAC personnel to work the North Korea problem to bring the intelligence data (order of battle) up to date and to successfully integrate targeting products into the war-planning processes at the combat unit level. To do that, we had to accept a risk by stopping or reducing the intelligence production on other potential theater hot spots. We explained the refocus of resources to our customers, and they understood and were willing to accept the risk along with us.

While a leader personally may not be an innovator, he or she needs to recognize the importance of innovation and process improvement. The leader must champion innovation and good ideas. For instance, in each unit, we used internal resources to move innovation forward, and we freed innovators from other tasks so they could focus on developing and implementing new ways of doing business.

As with any other leadership role, the leader in a joint organization must be honest, fair, and impartial in dealing with people and issues. Subordinates and customers are very perceptive and, I think, are more critical in the joint world because they are always on the look-out for a service bias. Leaders must not only uphold high principles and guard against their own biases, but must also be aware of subordinate leaders' biases and weaknesses. He or she must be able to spot issues and help subordinates overcome them; otherwise, they will harm good order and discipline and the effectiveness of the organization. I had a couple of senior leaders in my organization from another service who believed in the old school of leadership by intimidation. As a result, I had to counsel a crusty, senior Navy captain—something I never thought I would need to do.

I found that sound character was essential in dealing with a variety of issues, challenges, and opportunities during my two joint assignments; however, the greatest issues and challenges typically involved personnel.

What is the best way to discipline someone? Do I use an Article 15 or an administrative tool? Should I motivate someone through mentoring? What about fairness and consistency? I found that each situation was different and required a separate assessment and decision. Long-tenured personnel can have long-held views, perceptions, and biases, which can lead to discrimination complaints. If the leader addresses those issues head-on and in an open and fair manner, the bureaucratic process can often be preempted with better results for the organization and all personnel involved. However, the longer the perception of being wronged persists, the harder an amenable resolution becomes.

A leader needs to be mindful of making opportunities available to others. We should work to grow the leadership and technical skills of our subordinates. It is a balancing act between taking an intelligence expert in a particular area and moving him/her into a position where he/she can grow as a leader. Job enrichment is important to all, even to senior personnel. When I was a junior captain, a brigadier general who at the time was a numbered Air Force vice-commander told me that, in his experience, the worse job in the Air Force was the "vice of anything." That was coming from an officer who had been a wing commander and air division commander. I remembered his comment, and always tried to enrich the job of those serving as my vice commander or deputy and of any other senior personnel in my units.

THE IMPORTANCE OF THE HONOR CODE

The Air Force Core Values and supporting virtues were just coming out as I exited the Air Force. However, the Honor Code has always been something I have tried to live by. In addition to the Honor Code, I called upon other guides to character, such as religious tenets I was taught, or the Scout Laws. It is easier for someone to follow and meet expectations when expected behavior is specifically articulated, rather than when a general statement, like "be an officer of good character" is made. I laid out my expectations and beliefs to the members of JICPAC and MSIC on my first day on the job. Those guidelines became the standards by which we measured ourselves and others. A leader in the joint world should look at the character guidance from all the services so that, when the leader addresses his or her expectations for character, performance, and behavior, the expectations ring true in the minds of the joint service members. The leader's expectations should provide a guide for subordinate decision-making so that, even when no one else is looking, they will make the right decisions.

LESSONS LEARNED

Some of the leadership concepts and practices I tried to employ during my JICPAC and MSIC assignments included making organizational assessments, maintaining customer focus, championing innovation, ensuring efficient resource allocation, growing the next generation, and articulating expectations. Additionally, I learned that it's important to avoid falling into a "staff" mentality and becoming trapped by paperwork in the office. Even staffers need to be led and they need to see their leaders. If you are getting a briefing, go to their place of work, and have the men and women doing the actual work give the briefing (not the division/department/flight/squadron supervisor). In all situations, the leader needs to be approachable, positive, and a good listener and learner. You should be receptive to input and feedback from all directions—your boss, your peers, and your subordinates. That input can come in more formal settings such as commander's calls or town hall meetings. The less formal venues, such as brown bag lunches with small groups, may be even better places to get straight input. Try visiting work sections unannounced, not as an inspection, but to talk with your people. I have found that the leader's personal interest in subordinates' work is one of the greatest motivators. I strongly advocate that you lead by "walking around."

13

THE ADJUTANT GENERAL'S PERSPECTIVE

by Major General (Ret.) Howard M. Edwards

Maj. Gen. Howard "Mike" Edwards is unique, in that he spent the vast majority of his career in the cockpit while commanding at the squadron, group, and wing levels. He was later selected as The Adjutant General (TAG) for the State of Colorado, where he was responsible for the command administration of over 5,000 Colorado Army and Air National Guard members. He also served as the Executive Director for Colorado's Department of Military and Veteran Affairs and was a member of the governor's cabinet.

Mike Edwards
CS-13

When I came to the Academy, my goal was to be a fighter pilot. As a kid, I was enamored with aviation in general, and fighters in particular. My desire to be a fighter pilot became even stronger at the Academy. Having Robin Olds as our commandant deepened my conviction that the fighter world was for me. Gen. Olds w.as larger than life, and the confidence he projected was really inspiring.

Vietnam was still in full swing until our first-class year. I can still remember my roommate and I sitting on the edges of our beds, talking about going off to war and doing our duty. He wanted to be a fighter pilot just as badly as I did. Looking back, I think we were both strongly influenced by the faculty and staff, many of whom had recently returned from combat tours in Vietnam or Thailand. But, typical of young guys, we also thought we were bullet-proof. Our attitude was, "Let's go do our patriotic duty and serve in the place where we're needed the most."

After graduation, I attended UPT at Reese AFB, Texas. Reese seemed like a great fit for me for a variety of reasons—some logical, some less so. I had heard the flying environment at Reese was demanding—a mix of cloudy weather (instrument conditions), clear skies, and strong winds. That was very different than places like Williams AFB Arizona, which always had ideal flying conditions, so Reese seemed like a great place for an aspiring fighter pilot. On the social side of things, Lubbock was also home to Texas Tech University, and Reese was the only UPT base that allowed a student pilot to live off-base. After four years of social isolation, that seemed like a great combination for me.

Once I got to Reese, I found that our Academy background had prepared us well for the fast pace and intense pressure of the UPT program. Unfortunately, I got off to a rough start due to airsickness. Lucky for me, my T-37 IP was willing to help me work through the issue. Between a bottle of Dramamine pills the flight surgeon gave me and my IP's patience, I managed to work through the nausea. Once I got to the T-38 phase, though, things really began to click. I was fortunate enough to get my dream assignment: fighter lead-in training at Holloman AFB and then MacDill AFB for upgrade training in the F-4. My childhood dream had finally come true.

JOINING THE FIGHT

Our involvement in Vietnam had ended at that point so, once I graduated from F-4 upgrade training, I decided to volunteer for a remote assignment in Korea, thinking that would be the closest I'd be able to come to a combat tour. I was assigned to Osan Air Base in South Korea, about 40 miles south of Seoul. From a flying perspective, my tour there was a good one. As a first lieutenant, I was assigned as a squadron scheduler and, not surprisingly, ended up flying quite a bit. I found there were always more senior guys who didn't want to fly as much as I did, so I ended up plugging myself into the schedule in every hole I could find.

Unlike what I had experienced stateside, the flying environment in Korea was as real-world as it could get. Kim Il-Sung was the North Korean premier at that time and, according to our intel briefs, was an unpredictable guy who posed a real threat. Due to the tense environment, our squadron had a 10-minute air defense alert requirement. I happened to be on alert one day in August 1976, when an incident along the DMZ almost sparked a shooting war. North Korean soldiers attacked and killed two U.S. officers who were trimming a tree blocking their view from one of our observation posts along the border. I was the senior alert pilot that day and my classmate Pete Gimborys was my wingman. Luckily, we both had experienced back seaters. I can remember sitting at my scheduling desk when the squadron commander hurried in, saying, "Get your G-suits on, grab your gear, and get to Intel." As they briefed us on the situation, I seriously thought we were going to get scrambled.

As it turned out, we didn't launch because of dense fog; the visibility was horrible, maybe 150 feet or so, and the dense fog hung around for a week or so. Looking back, had the weather been above minimums, I'm sure we would have launched. Meanwhile, there was a rapid force build-up on the Korean Peninsula. In fact, once the weather cleared, we ended up flying escort for B-52 sorties along the North Korean border.

Being tracked by surface-to-air missiles really gave us a feeling of imminent combat, but we never fired a shot in anger.

About the same time, I was scheduled to take leave back in the States to get married, but the political situation in Korea put that on hold. Although tension along the DMZ had calmed down a bit, all leaves were cancelled, and the entire squadron stayed on an alert footing. In fact, we slept in sleeping bags in the squadron area.

Then came the moment I had to tell my fiancée that our wedding was probably going to be postponed. I called her on our Military Auxiliary Radio System—which was awkward under the best of circumstances—and the bad news I had to deliver didn't make things any easier. But the squadron made special arrangements to get me back home for two days. No honeymoon, but at least we were able to have a wedding.

My ops officer in the 36th Tactical Fighter Squadron liked the way I flew and worked, and he turned out to be a great mentor. He was the kind of guy who worked hard, played hard, and demanded the best from everyone. While he had a rough exterior, he cared about his people and was well-respected throughout the squadron. Even though I was just a lieutenant, he took a personal interest in me. He challenged me and pushed me to upgrade to flight lead at the earliest opportunity.

CHANGING CAREER GOALS

As it turned out, my ops officer played a pivotal role in my follow-on assignment. As I was approaching the end of my tour at Osan, I got an assignment to George AFB in California to transition to the F-105 Weasel—a real change from the air-to-air mission I had been flying in Korea. Meanwhile, my ops officer had moved on to Hill AFB as a squadron commander. As I was preparing to return to the States, he gave me a call to ask about my next assignment. He must have really wanted to keep me in the air-to-air business because, when he heard I was headed for the Weasel community, he threw a fit. He finally said, "I'll get back to you," and hung up. He must have pulled some strings, because the next thing I knew, I had received orders to report to Holloman AFB in the F-4. That was a particularly great assignment, as Holloman had been selected to transition to the new F-15. I was thrilled beyond words.

Life's twists and turns, however, are rarely predictable. Once I arrived at Holloman, several unexpected factors prompted me to reconsider my career goals, and it was primarily a function of trying to achieve a healthy work-life balance. To begin with, I had hoped my new wife and I would have some much-needed stability in our next assignment. But, soon after arriving at Holloman, I found that wasn't going to be the case. The good news was that I was told I was being groomed to be one of the first weapons officers in the Eagle, even though I was only a first lieutenant. But the bad news was that I would transition to the F-15 at Luke AFB and then go straight to weapons school from there—which would mean the better part of a year away from home. Further complicating things, my wife was completing an internship in Criminal Justice as an up-and-coming probation officer, so she wouldn't be able to accompany me on my upgrade temporary tours of duty. Coming on the heels of my remote tour in Korea, the year of separation would be difficult for us both. Given the situation, I asked my flight commander whether I could delay my transition to the F-15 and settle in as a newlywed before moving on. The short answer was "absolutely not." That made no sense to me, because I could have easily moved from the 7th Tactical Fighter Squadron, which was the first to transition to the F-15, to the 9th Tactical Fighter Squadron, which wasn't due to make the transition until the following year. That would have given me the time my wife and I needed to settle into married life. But Holloman was dealing with some serious integrity issues that made for a toxic work environment—not the kind of place likely to support individual needs.

As I was considering my options, I learned that my parents had fallen on hard times on their farm in Nebraska and were getting a divorce, and

I felt compelled to get home to help pick up the pieces. So, with some regret, I left the "fast track" to Eagles by moving from the 7th Tactical Fighter Squadron to the 436th Tactical Fighter Training Squadron—also at Holloman—flying the AT-38 as an instructor pilot in the lead-in fighter training program. Knowing that move would put me out of the mainstream, I resigned myself to getting out of the Air Force once I had completed my initial commitment.

As it turned out, I spent two years helping UPT graduates transition to the fighter business. It was a wonderful assignment. I absolutely loved teaching and I loved the flying. Ironically, many of my fellow IPs didn't see it the same way. They were professional and did a great job, but their disappointment in being in what they considered a dead-end assignment was reflected in their attitudes.

THE AIR NATIONAL GUARD

About six months before completing my active-duty commitment, I heard about opportunities in the Air National Guard. A friend of mine who was leaving active duty about three months ahead of me offered some great advice: "Knowing how much you love to fly and serve, you ought to consider a Guard assignment." After giving that some thought, I dropped off a resume on my way back to the farm to help my parents. To my great delight, I was offered a slot with the Colorado Air National Guard, flying the A-7 at Buckley AFB in Denver. My situation couldn't have been better. Being stationed at Buckley in the Air National Guard meant my wife and I would have the predictable future we so desperately needed, while I'd be able to stay in the fighter business in Denver.

Eventually, the work-life balance reared its ugly head again. Things had been going well in my Guard unit but, in 1983, the farm economy had gone south, and I was getting pressure from my father to be more active on our struggling farm. Although he was proud that I went to the Academy and proud of my military career, he felt his economic situation was deteriorating because I was spending too much of my time doing Guard duty, even though it was only on the drill weekends during the farming season. From my perspective, I was juggling my responsibilities as best I could. On drill weekends, I'd get up at about three in the morning on Saturdays, hit the road, and arrive in Denver by 0630. Then I'd fly, sometimes on both Saturday and Sunday, then get back in my car and head back to the farm on Sunday evening. But, because my father didn't really understand my Guard responsibilities, he accused me of putting the Guard and my financial future ahead of family concerns. So, faced with a serious dilemma of how to maintain a work-life balance, I decided to discuss alternatives with my Guard unit.

I was really fortunate to have Wayne Schultz as my operations group commander. I sat down with him and explained to him what was going on. I outlined the dilemma I was facing, and he patiently listened to my rationale for taking some time off. I finished by saying, "You know, boss, I want you to remember this: if something pops, I expect you to recall me in a heartbeat because that's what I'm about." To my great relief, he approved my request for a leave of absence without hesitation and I returned to full-time work on the farm. Ironically, though, it quickly became apparent to me that even being there full time wasn't making an appreciable difference.

As it turned out, my service in the Guard wasn't over. One day, I was in a tractor plowing one of our fields. Our farm happened to lie right underneath one of Buckley's low-level routes. I happened to look up and saw what looked like a four-ship off in the distance. I quickly got out of my tractor and climbed up on top of the cab to wave at those guys. Four A-7s came screaming right over the top of me in the most beautiful diamond formation I'd ever seen. About two hours later, I finished my work and returned to the shop. As I was cleaning up, the phone rang. I picked it up and, to my surprise, it was my flight commander, Dick Tucker. All he said was, "I need you. It's time to come back." So, between the four-ship and Dick's call, I knew what I needed to do—I was going back to my unit as a traditional Guardsman.[115]

After a long talk, my dad finally understood my point of view and became supportive. I continued to farm with him until 1986, when he was forced to sell out. My wife and I continued farming on our own through 1991, when the farm economy forced us out as well. After harvest that year, I headed to F-16 training and was given the opportunity to become a full-time Guardsman, which proved to be very beneficial to our family.

The Guard gave me wonderful opportunities over the next several years. After our wing transitioned to the F-16 in the early 1990s, I was able to work through the different command levels, from flight commander to ops officer, to squadron commander, to group commander. I was honored to become the 140th Wing Commander in 2002 and served in that position until 2007, when I was appointed by then-Governor Bill Ritter as the adjutant general. This new position gave me the responsibility for more than 5,000 Army and Air National Guard members, as well as the Colorado Department of Military and Veterans Affairs. My command responsibility was for the Colorado National Guard's primary missions of national defense and state emergency response.

THE ADJUTANT GENERAL

The selection process for the TAG position was an interesting experience. When I walked in for the interview, I faced a table crowded with 20 people, all waiting to ask me questions. I sat down and the interrogation began. The very first question was actually a leading one: "As you well know, most senior leaders in the military tend to be conservative. And, in most cases, they're Republicans."

---

115 | Unlike full-time Guardsman positions, traditional Guardsmen positions only require service in their units for one weekend each month and two weeks during the year, thereby enabling the service member to pursue a civilian career while still serving in the Guard.

I thought, "The newly elected governor is Bill Ritter, and he's a Democrat. Wow, I can see where this is going."

The question continued: "As a senior officer, I have to assume you're a Republican and a conservative. How will you make a Democrat governor who has no military experience and no background with the military look good?"

Oh, boy. Well, I've never been afraid to give an honest answer, so I just kinda shook my head and said, "Well, I do happen to be a registered Republican. But nowhere in my oath does it say who I will support. As a Guardsman, my oath states that I will support and defend the Constitution of the United States, the constitution of the State of Colorado, and obey the orders of the governor of the state. Nowhere in my Guard oath does it say Republican governor or Democrat governor. It says 'governor.' I've sworn to obey those orders and I take that responsibility very, very seriously." Fortunately for me, from then on the questions became more focused on leadership and military issues. But that leading question made me think my chances of being selected as the next TAG were slim to none. To my amazement, I was notified of my appointment and sworn in by Governor Ritter as TAG in May 2007.

The transition to my new position required a fairly steep learning curve. To begin with, TAG positions in all states are filled by political appointees and, in the case of Colorado, TAG is a member of the governor's cabinet—so there's a significant political component to the job. Coming from the fighter community, that was an adjustment. Also, when I first came in as TAG, I didn't understand the Army units or culture very well. Particularly on the pilot side, Air Force officers really don't have much direct responsibility for people until later in our careers. On the other hand, an Army lieutenant has people under his or her direct command from the beginning, so there's a different leadership environment than what I was used to. Because I was now in charge of all Colorado National Guard units, I really had to expand my understanding of the total force. I quickly picked a command sergeant major from the Army Guard to be my senior enlisted leader. What a Godsend for helping me understand the Army Guard. Finally, as TAG, I was the executive director of the Department of Military and Veterans Affairs, so I had a responsibility to oversee issues affecting not just Guard members, but also those veterans living in our state who had served in the past. That was another education for me.

At the most fundamental level, a TAG's ultimate responsibilities are training and equipping—ensuring national guard members, both army and air, can respond to mission requirements, both at national as well as state levels. Guard units are the primary combat reserve for our active-duty forces, whereas reservists are in more of a supporting role. But I found that, to maintain the effectiveness of the force, my biggest responsibility was to develop leaders of character—very much in line with my Academy background.

Whether in the Guard or active duty, one of the primary jobs of any commander is to mentor people—to shape leaders of character. From that perspective, it's interesting to watch how we have evolved in this area. Whether it be the Army or the Air Force, responsibility for preparing future generations of leaders has been pushed down to lower levels. As an example, the Air Force inspection system now recognizes that the squadron commander has the direct responsibility to prepare his or her people to complete the mission of the United States Air Force. Toward that end, it's instructive to see our Air Force chief of staff embraces the principles to fly, fight, and win—the same principles we were all raised with at the Academy.

Looking back on our time at the Academy, we tended to view things in terms of black and white. But we quickly learned that the world is largely shades of gray, and I don't think we were well-prepared to deal with that. It takes a broader perspective to deal with the gray. Also, life is messy, and people are flawed. We don't always make the right decisions, but we can learn from our mistakes and become stronger as we move forward. From an organizational perspective, the challenge is to maintain a good balance of accounting for and dealing with human frailty, while at the same time adhering to our Core Values, which are absolutely essential in our Air Force and Army. Finally, if you don't have that strength of character, then you are basically going to fail more often than not, particularly when the pressure is on. I think that's what the Academy worked so hard to teach us: that even with really strong pressure on you, you have to have that character to do the right thing. To me, that's the enduring lesson from the Academy, and it's just as applicable in the Guard as it is in the active-duty Air Force and Army.

As TAG, I had a monthly meeting with my senior leaders and staff. Experience taught me that it was important to be well-informed and in touch with on-the-ground realities and, at the same time, to avoid micromanaging. Meeting once each month seemed to strike the right balance because I was able to avoid diving into the operational details while maintaining a clearer view of the overall health of the various organizations. Once the stand-up was over, I kept my senior leadership—the general officers and colonels serving in the equivalent of general officer positions in the full-time force—behind to go through specific challenges facing their organizations. I needed to be aware of specific issues that required top-level guidance and resources to help address issues such as suicide prevention and sexual harassment. It was also my opportunity to share TAG issues to prepare them for competing to become TAG following my tour of duty.

In working with my senior leaders, I found that it was important to recognize both the similarities and the differences between the services. Regardless of the branch of service, as officers reach the major/lieutenant colonel level in their careers, they're expected to deal with ambiguity and uncertainty, to examine the situation and figure out how best to execute with their organization and people. But this is where we begin to see cultural differences between the Army and the Air Force. In my experience, the Army has always tended to rely on centralized control, whereas the Air Force has always emphasized innovation. Our approach is to give organizations a clear task, and not to tell them exactly how to do it—to rely instead on people's creativity and understanding of mission requirements. In my experience, that's what we need to be successful in fighting for and defending our great Nation.

As I became more comfortable in my new position, I noticed that most senior leaders in the Army Guard tended to get too far into the weeds and, as a result, effectively discouraged innovation within their organizations. Because innovation requires an open mind and a willingness to consider different viewpoints, I wouldn't tolerate "yes" men and women; however, I didn't find that same attitude among some of my Army commanders. So I set out to explain my decision-making process to my senior leaders, and how essential open and honest debate was to achieving effective results. I also tried to teach my people that the world is not black and white, and that there are shades of gray that need to be considered, particularly before making a decision that alters a person's life or career. During my tenure as TAG, I sat on boards at the Pentagon with my active-duty counterparts to consider disciplinary measures for general officers. While not using names, I used these experiences as cautionary tales for my senior leaders in the Guard. I advised them that it's easy to get into trouble by convincing yourself that you're so right that there's no need to evaluate all the ramifications to be considered before you made a decision.

A CAUTIONARY NOTE

I've learned a great deal about leading people and organizations over the years, both on active duty and in the Guard. For instance, I've found that it's easy for leaders to become arrogant due to a variety of factors. People sometimes begin to believe their own officer performance reports, particularly when they're promoted early. If they don't have someone watching over them and reminding them to remain grounded, they inevitably develop hubris. Experience has taught me that it's important to remember where you came from, that everyone started out as a second lieutenant, and that everyone is a follower, to one extent or another. You don't know everything, regardless of your rank. Even if you're a recognized expert in your field, there's always more to learn. So the challenge is to stay grounded and remain humble. Once again, my old Ops Group Commander, Wayne Schultz, taught me a very valuable lesson that has served me well. Wayne is a very humble Iowa farm boy who graduated from Iowa State. He's a pretty quiet guy, despite being the Gunsmoke [Air Force aerial gunnery competition] champion in 1981. His advice to me was to be "humbly lethal." Go out there and kick ass—but never brag. If you're really that good, there's no need to tell others about it, because it'll be obvious to the people who count.

As I look back on my career, there's one thing that proved to be true time and time again: you never operate alone. For that reason, it's critical to know who you can rely on. I'll naturally gravitate to an Academy grad because I have a good understanding of their background and how they were brought up. The fact that they even graduated tells me one thing: that these are people with strength of character. For the same reason you'll tend to gravitate to your classmates—or even grads that are 20 years behind you—because we all share that common bond of the Long Blue Line. So take that responsibility seriously, and both you and the Air Force will prosper.

PART V

LEADERS OF CHARACTER IN MOMENTS OF CRISIS

We never know when our character will be tested. Sometimes tests appear dramatically, in the light of day; sometimes they creep in quietly, in the dark of night. Regardless, we need to be prepared to meet them and draw on every bit of character we have to overcome the unexpected. This harkens back to the basic lessons from doolie year, when we were pushed beyond what we thought were our limits. Years later, when time and circumstance put us in extraordinary situations, we were able to persevere.

The following chapters describe such situations. While other classmates have had analogous experiences, the selections here are intended to illustrate how character is tested in times of crises.

14

DESERT STORM AND SECRET SQUIRREL

by Colonel (Ret.) John H. Beard

Col. John "Jay" Beard, a B-52 squadron commander at Barksdale AFB in 1990, describes a highly classified mission he led that kicked off DESERT STORM, as well as the leadership challenges he encountered as he prepared his crews for a highly complex, dangerous, and unprecedented mission.

Jay Beard
CS-18

I had just become the 596th Bomb Squadron commander at Barksdale AFB in June of 1990. After having been in command of the B-52 squadron for just over one month, a special tasking came up involving the classified conversion of a nuclear AGM-86 Air-Launched Cruise Missile (ALCM) to a GPS-guided conventional munition.

I knew about the newly modified test weapon because I had been the wing director of training prior to taking command of the squadron. Our wing had been tasked by higher headquarters to run classified missions to test the conventional capabilities of our nuclear cruise missiles. So, as director of training, I was at least marginally read in on the program to help put those capabilities together. Soon after I became the squadron commander, I was told I needed to train crews to employ this new weapon in order to have a long-range strike capability to potentially counter Saddam Hussain's invasion of Kuwait.

I was asked how long it would take to get crews trained up on this system and be able to employ it in the Middle East. Given what was going on, the thought was that we could use this weapon against Saddam Hussein, but we'd have to do it from the States because we didn't have assets or capabilities in theater. I told the wing director of operations that I could have my crews ready in 24 hours. He looked at me incredulously, saying, "You know, I was expecting an answer like two weeks." I said, "I'll have them ready in 24 hours."

PUSHING TO THE LIMIT

It certainly wasn't an easy 24 hours—training the first three crews was pretty much an around-the-clock process. Eventually, I was able to expand it to seven crews with a few backups. That was also a real challenge, partly because my other crews (I had 18 complete six-man aircrews) weren't permitted to be read-in on the weapon and mission, but also because my squadron still had to maintain its full nuclear alert commitment. I had bombers on alert, as we were still in the midst of the Cold War, so the same crews I was using for this mission were also having to sit nuclear alert. Despite the heavy workload on my crews, I couldn't get relieved of the alert commitment for several months. After a few months, we were finally able to lessen our bomber alert commitment when other B-52 bases assumed some of our sorties, so I was able to ease up on my guys a bit. Still, we were having to continue with the nuclear certifications, bag study, etc.—all that continued non-stop. And, at the same time, we were having to train with the conventional ALCM, which at this point was still a test weapon.

WHERE DID THAT NAME COME FROM?

It quickly became obvious to the rest of the squadron that something was going on. The actual code name for our mission was SENIOR SUNRISE. However, even the code name was special-access only. So I designated training sorties and schedules for the mission crews as "SS." It didn't take long until one of my crewmembers took "SS" to the next level and came up with the moniker of "Secret Squirrel," which has stuck to this day.

Once we had completed the initial training, we had aircraft that some of my people couldn't get access to because these aircraft were loaded with the highly classified GPS-guided conventional ALCMs. I also had designated crews coming in for early morning briefings because, when the order came, our planned launch window was to be somewhere between 11:00 at night and 6:00 in the morning, due to the limited number of GPS satellites that had been deployed by 1990. After the briefings, I'd release those crews, but their day was far from over. They had to put in a full day with the rest of the crews, preparing for their nuclear commitment.

Maintaining a constant state of readiness was a real challenge for all of us. It wasn't easy to maintain a calm demeanor, given the pressure we were all under. I was the designated mission commander. Because of the middle-of-the-night briefings, I was surviving on about four to five hours of sleep. In addition to that, I had my regular squadron commander duties. It was pretty stressful. As the situation in the Middle East continued to develop and tensions built, we knew we were getting closer to launch. But a great deal of the stress was never knowing whether this day would be the day we'd get the order to launch.

Obviously, there were a lot of leadership challenges during this period. I was losing guys from stress and fatigue. I had to pull a couple of my men off the mission because they were being worked beyond their physical and emotional capability. For instance, I had one guy whose wife was terminally ill. Another crewmember took out the stress on his wife, so I had to take action on a domestic abuse situation. A third crew-member started spending himself and his family deep into debt, so I had to take action on that. So the intense pressure was presenting a number of personnel issues, in addition to challenges inherent in the technical aspects of the mission.

THE LONG-AWAITED LAUNCH

When the order finally came to launch, it was a genuine relief after more than six months of intense preparation. We launched seven aircraft at maximum gross weight starting at 6:30 in the morning in total darkness and strict radio silence.

The mission got off to a rough start. We were all radio silent when we took off, but we had a scheduled check-in about 30 minutes after launch. When I called for a formation check, I got a terse "Standby" from one of my crews. I let him go for a bit, thinking he was just task-saturated, then called for another check-in. I got another "Standby." Finally, once we had passed the go/no-go point, he checked in with me. As fate would have it, he had lost an engine on climb-out and didn't want to be left behind, so he waited until we were past the go/no-go point before checking in. He ended up flying the entire mission with one engine shut down. In fact, engines were a real problem for us, primarily because of the long mission duration. Before this mission was complete, I had aircraft in my formation with multiple engines shut down and retained external stores [weapons that failed to launch].

Engines weren't the only problem, though. One crew lost its auto-pilot 12 hours after launch, so they had to "hand-fly" the aircraft for the remainder of the 35-hour mission. Four other crews ended up retaining missiles due to maintenance issues, which upped their fuel consumption dramatically. That forced them to take on more fuel at air refueling points than we had planned. Further complicating the fuel situation, we ran into unforecasted 190-knot headwinds on our return. Additionally, one of our 14-ship tanker formations couldn't get airborne for the fourth planned refueling due to severe winds at their launch base, so we had to scramble three KC-10s out of France to take their place. Ultimately, we ended up taking on so much of their fuel that all three tankers were near emergency fuel when we finished—they couldn't give us another drop of gas. I personally took on 265,000 pounds of fuel and I authorized my bomber crews to take on fuel above the peace-time gross weight limit of 488,000 pounds.

We also had significant mission-threatening communication problems. For instance, the Navy was supposed to talk to us over the Red Sea via a "trusted agent" on-board one of their ships who was read-in on the mission. His job was to make sure the U.S. Navy didn't shoot us down. The communications plan was to verify our identity with a code-word challenge, but there was no answer response. Further complicating things, an aircraft we assumed was Libyan launched against us. Fortunately, the aircraft just came up and took a look, then ran off. But it was a pretty tense situation for a while.

We thought we had planned for all contingencies, but there are always unknowns that crop up on a mission as complex as that one. We didn't really expect to have that many retained stores. We anticipated losing some engines on such a long mission due to loss of oil, but we didn't anticipate losing so many.

You never know whether you've made the right decisions until you can look back with the benefit of hindsight. No matter—decisions must be made. I can look back and think there were a few things I could have done differently, but knowing what I knew then, I'm comfortable with the decisions I made.

We put six months of hard preparation into that mission—really hard preparation. And, due to the courage and dedication of our aircrews, we struck all assigned targets, completed the longest-ever combat mission, and set the stage for one of the most successful air campaigns in aerial history.

Although I could not have imagined it on the day I first arrived at the Academy, the discipline, education, and determination to succeed was preparing me to serve as a leader when the moment came. It was rewarding to successfully put that skillset to the task in combat and lead the longest combat mission in aviation history and the first-ever operational use of a GPS guided munition.

15

CRISIS AT THE EDGE OF SPACE

by Lieutenant Colonel (Ret.) Larry E. Faber

In 1985 Capt. Larry Faber was the pilot of a TR-1 (an updated version of the high-altitude U-2 reconnaissance aircraft). Based at RAF Alconbury, United Kingdom, he flew a fateful mission that earned him the prestigious Jabara Award. Tested under unique and harrowing circumstances, Larry describes what it took to successfully recover the damaged aircraft.

Larry Faber
CS-05

I almost didn't get to fly the U-2.

I was stationed at Mather AFB, flying KC-135s. I had seen something in the *Air Force Times* about the Air Force needing U-2 pilots. As I read through the requirements, I realized that, while I had hours in a couple of different types of aircraft (F-105, T-37), I didn't have enough total flying time. But I thought, "Why not just throw an application in? What do I have to lose?" So I did.

Next thing I knew I got a call from the wing director of operations (DO). He told me the Military Personnel Center (MPC) had rejected my application because I didn't meet the requirement of being qualified in two different aircraft. I pointed out that I had flown the T-37 at Mather in the Accelerated Copilot Enrichment program, as well as the KC-135. I had also gotten about 50 hours in the F-105 after UPT. So my DO said he'd see what he could do. He called the assignments folks at MPC and explained the situation. They agreed to forward my application to Beale AFB, where the U-2s were based.

Shortly thereafter, I got a call from Beale, and they said they'd like to interview me. They said the whole process would last about two weeks, starting with interviews with the squadron operations officer, the squadron commander, the director of operations, the vice wing commander, and the wing commander. If I passed those interviews, I'd get three low-altitude orientation rides in the two-seat U-2 with an IP. So, I went out to Beale to go through the process.

My first interview was with the ops officer. When he looked at my records, he said, "First of all, you're only 29 years old. Second, you don't have 1,500 hours of total flying time (I had around 1,100). We've never taken anyone with that limited amount of experience, so your prospects don't look good."

I wasn't sure how to respond—all I could think of to say was, "Give me a shot. Maybe I can surprise you."

I guess that was a good enough response, because he let me continue with the interview process. As it turned out, I passed the other interviews and ended up flying the three orientation sorties. The first two were with squadron IPs. But the third was with that same ops officer who had said my prospects didn't look good.

That flight was a real challenge. The ops officer didn't say a word to me during the entire flight, other than answer challenge responses on checklist items. We landed, shut down, filled out the forms, walked into the squadron without a single word.

Finally, he said, "Just have a seat here in my office. I've got to go talk to the commander." After what seemed like an eternity, he came back and told me the squadron commander wanted to see me. I walked into the squadron commander's office and saw him sitting behind his desk with my grade book open in front of him, studying it. And he was not looking at me. I was standing at attention in his doorway.

Finally, without looking up at me, he said, "So you want to fly the U-2. You really think you can fly this aircraft?"

"Yes, Sir," I responded.

He kind of flipped the pages and, still not looking up, he said, "Okay." With that, I was accepted into the U-2 program.

NO EASY TASK

Flying the U-2 is extremely demanding. You're typically thousands of miles from friendlies. There's no contact with anybody. You're not under air traffic control. There's no way to talk to anybody. So there's a tremendous amount of trust required. Judgment is absolutely critical, because you could easily end up causing an international incident. And, as I quickly learned, having a high degree of discipline is essential—you have to do the right thing in all situations.

I also found that teamwork was an important part of the job. In a pressure suit, we couldn't do the walk-around. We couldn't set up the cockpit—about all we could do was sit in the van that drove us to the aircraft and review the forms and not much else. Every high flight in the U-2 required two pilots—a primary mission pilot and a back-up pilot. The back-up pre-flighted the aircraft and set up the cockpit. After engine start, the back-up pilot monitored taxi operations and kept a close eye on take-off conditions, particularly forecasted winds. The U-2's crosswind limit was only 15 knots, so that was a critical aspect.

Needless to say, you needed to have a tremendous amount of faith in your fellow pilots—you had to be certain that your back-up pilot was doing exactly the right things for you. That faith resulted in a special bond between pilots because your life was literally in their hands. Most of the time, the U-2 missions were pretty uneventful. But there were other times when things went wrong. That was when you realized why it was so critical to have the maturity and the discipline to fly that airplane. And I don't think any of us really grew into that until we had several years under our belt flying the U-2.

THE ULTIMATE TEST

This particular mission was in August of '85, and I was stationed at RAF Alconbury in England, flying the TR-1. We had been flying flight plans along Warsaw Pact borders, designed to "elicit a response" from ground-based radars in enemy territory. During the pre-mission brief, our intel guys told me there were no known surface-to-air missile threats for the area we'd be flying into on this particular mission, so the task was to look for early warning responses from ground radar.

As was the normal routine, after the pre-mission brief with the intel folks, I got my flight physical and got into the pressure suit. We had to be on oxygen an hour prior to the mission, so there was a lot of sitting around. Then they took me out to the aircraft in the van and loaded me into the cockpit. As was always the case, I was strapped in by the life support guys. I started the engine and taxied out to the active runway. After a 2,000-foot take-off roll, I pulled the nose up to 60 degrees and began the climb to operational altitude. As I passed 52,000 feet, I could see the layers in the atmosphere and the darkening sky above me turning from dark blue to deep indigo. It was very quiet without the usual radio chatter on London Military frequency. The only sound I could hear was my own breathing in my headset.

Everything was ops-normal for the first four-and-a-half hours. I had been flying a course perpendicular to the Czech border, then turning away from the border at the last minute to check out the ground-based radar responses. As I flew the pre-planned route, the only thing I noted was that I was getting defensive systems activations, indicating that ground-based radars were scanning the sky, looking for threats. But, at that point, they weren't locked onto me.

As was always the case, I was in a constant climb as I burned off fuel. As my altitude increased, I noticed that my Exhaust Gas Temperature [EGT, a measure of engine thrust] was decreasing just a little bit. We had a small wheel mechanism below the throttle in the TR-1 that enabled us to make fine adjustments to the EGT. I kept rolling the wheel forward as I climbed, but the EGT was still creeping down. It finally dawned on me that there must be something else going on here. Over time, my EGT dropped a couple of hundred degrees centigrade, so I knew something was definitely up.

I turned away from the border and thought, "No need to rush here. Not at all." But the next thing I knew, I started having hydraulic problems. Then the generator dropped off the line. I started shutting things down because I thought, "Well, the transformer rectifier can pick up the DC load and I'll be okay." As it turned out, the transformer rectifier didn't pick up the electrical load, so I had to shut more and more systems down. At this point, I had all my mission equipment turned off and I was descending.

Because I had also lost my inertial navigation system (INS), I picked up my chart to see exactly where I was. I knew my location when the INS fell off-line, so I did a bit of dead-reckoning navigation, took my pencil, and drew a circle where I was. Then I looked on the chart to see what alternative landing spots would be. At this point, I was still at a pretty high altitude, so my thought was that at some point I could pick up a heading to Ramstein Air Base in West Germany. That was still a good ways away, but by flying L/D max airspeed[116] I should be able to make it.

Needless to say, there were a lot of things going through my mind as I considered my options. My father spent 33 years in the Air Force flying fighters and a variety of test aircraft. I can remember his advice going through my head: "If you ever get in a bad situation, remember that the

116 | "L/D max speed" refers to the airspeed at which the aircraft generates the greatest amount of lift and the lowest amount of drag, thereby enabling the aircraft to glide the greatest possible distance.

government put an ejection seat in that aircraft for a reason." That was in the back of my mind as I was thinking through the worst-case scenario.

It was a busy time, trying to make sure I had gone through the checklist and completed all actions. But there were also some unusual things happening that I couldn't quite figure out—some things just weren't adding up. For instance, based on my estimated position, it appeared that I was losing altitude more quickly than I should have been, despite the fact that I was flying the prescribed L/D max airspeed from the chart in my checklist. What kept going through my mind was that I must have missed something or somehow miscalculated. I was still pretty heavy, given that I was only about half-way through my mission duration; still, aircraft weight, by itself, wouldn't account for the increased loss of altitude. Then I wondered if I was experiencing additional drag that wasn't accounted for in the L/D max chart. (As it turned out, a subsequent investigation discovered that the L/D max chart hadn't been updated to reflect the addition of modified mission equipment.) Then there was the added pressure from thinking that I was the chief of standardization/ evaluation in my unit at RAF Alconbury and, if anyone should be able to figure things out, it should be me.

As I looked below me, I could see a broken cloud layer, but it didn't look like there were too many holes I could get through. My instinctive reaction was to give up some altitude if I could find a good hole in the clouds. On the other hand, I knew if I couldn't find a suitable landing runway, I'd have given up altitude that I'd need for a safe recovery later. And, as I was talking myself through this, I also realized that if I couldn't find a suitable landing runway, I'd have to pull the handles and get out [eject]. That would have to be my ultimate back-up plan.

When I finally got down to the low 30,000-foot range, I decided it was time to see if I could get the engine re-lit. It started coming up and my spirits came up with it, thinking, "Hey, this is great." Suddenly I heard this loud "boom," and my head violently bounced off the canopy as the engine seized. Wow. Later, after an investigation by the engine manufacturer, Pratt and Whitney, they found that the gearbox had failed. Part of that gearbox had gone into the number seven turbine bearing, and that's why the engine seized.

I was down around 20,000 feet at this point and realized I needed to find a place to land as soon as possible. Without an engine, electrical systems, or navigation equipment, my only chance would be to find a hole in the clouds. So, I ignored my L/D max speed and pushed over toward the cloud deck to pick up some airspeed. My thinking at this point was that any piece of concrete or asphalt has got to be better than nothing.

When I broke out of the clouds, I saw a German helicopter base. It had a very short runway—I think about 1,800 or 2,000 feet, not long at all. My first thought was that I might be able to handle it, but then I remembered I'd have to make a no-flap landing, which meant I'd be carrying extra airspeed. In the TR-1, every knot above normal landing speed requires an additional thousand feet of runway. So, that idea wasn't going to work.

Now that I was below the cloud deck, I could search out ahead of me to see where I was going. That's when I saw Ramstein AB, way off in the distance. So I set up my L/D max again and hoped I'd be able to get overhead Ramstein, right about my high key altitude. Hopefully I'd be able to make one turn and land. But when I was about six miles from Ramstein, I realized I wouldn't be able to hit the high key. My only option was to just to do a straight-in approach and hope I could stretch it out enough to make the runway. I lowered the gear manually and pushed the nose over again a little bit, because I needed additional airspeed to try to lock the gear in place. Fortunately, I had just enough altitude so I was able to land at Ramstein safely. Needless to say, it created a lot of attention when a black airplane landed unannounced at Ramstein, so the security police were out there to meet me when I came to a stop on the runway.

My airplane stayed at Ramstein for quite a while. I went through a lengthy maintenance debrief that lasted three days because our maintenance team needed to know exactly what happened. They determined that the engine had, in fact, frozen up. They could turn it manually a few degrees and that was all—it would just bounce back and forth. They flew another engine over from Alconbury. After three days at Ramstein and full debriefings, they sent me back to Alconbury and sent another guy over to do a Functional Check Flight and fly the airplane back.

THE AFTERMATH

I had no idea that I had been submitted for an award for that mission. I left Alconbury and went to the Armed Forces Staff College. One day, in the middle of a class period, our section leader made the announcement that I had been awarded the Jabara Award. That was the first I'd heard of it.

When I look back on the whole experience, I've often thought about when I first came to the U-2 program. As a new pilot, I was handed a stack of manuals and told to read them. The Dash One[117] came in three volumes, so there was a lot to absorb. Unfortunately, there was no syllabus or formal training program per se. What I had to do was read the manuals, talk to experienced instructor pilots, and ask lots of questions. In the end, that's what enabled me to get out of a very bad situation in the TR-1.

So here's an important lesson from my experience: regardless of what job you're in, whether it's flying or personnel, or whatever, there's always someone in your organization who knows more than you. Don't be afraid to seek them out. Ask lots of questions and take advantage of their knowledge and experience—that's how you'll gain the expertise

---

117 | The "Dash One" is a term used by Air Force pilots referring to the operator's manual for a particular aircraft. Dash One contents depend on the particular aircraft, but typically include extensive details on aircraft systems, operating limitations, normal and emergency procedures, flight characteristics, and performance data. Depending on the aircraft type, the Dash One can consist of multiple volumes.

you'll need to make major contributions to the mission. And, ultimately, that may make the difference between success and failure under extraordinary and high-pressure situations. It may also save your life.

16

PEERING BEHIND THE IRON CURTAIN

by Lieutenant Colonel (Ret.) Herbert A. Harrison

Herb Harrison
CS-25

As a young captain, Lt. Col. Herb Harrison found himself behind the front lines of the Cold War, working for a small, little-known U.S. organization reporting on Soviet military activity in East Germany. Herb's critical work with the U.S. Military Liaison Mission (MLM), while a little-known chapter in the Cold War, is a story of personal sacrifice, courage, and devotion to duty.

At first glance, the Glienecke Bridge looked like an ordinary two-lane structure stretching across the river, much like the old ones I remember seeing on the East Coast in my childhood. Old gray-green steel trusses, large rivets, twin arches. But, unlike the bridges in the States, this one was manned by heavily armed Soviet guards and was our entry point into East Germany. After years of study as a tactical intelligence officer, I was about to get a real, on-the-ground look at Soviet equipment, tactics, and troop formations as a newly assigned member of the U.S. Military Liaison Mission

THE INAUGURAL TOUR: CONFRONTING REALITY

I wasn't sure what to expect on my first mission, but I remember being both exhilarated and apprehensive. Even though I was an experienced intelligence officer and photo interpreter, I remember thinking this was something hard to imagine.

We stopped at the Soviet checkpoint halfway across the bridge where two armed Soviet soldiers waited to inspect our MLM credentials. To my relief, they waved us through without hesitation. We drove to the Potsdam House, which served as our MLM Headquarters in the Eastern Zone. After an update and a quick breakfast, we climbed into our Mercedes sedan and my driver—known as a "tour NCO"—routed us through the streets of Potsdam. As he drove, he explained the basic protocols and the dos and don'ts when approaching a military installation or convoy.

As I gazed out of the window, I saw that the environment was a stark contrast to the West Germany I was familiar with. Painted in shades of gray and brown, the landscape was as lifeless as the people who silently stared at our car as we drove through the small villages. My first impression was that everything around me was dark—it was as if I had stepped into a black-and-white movie. Although it was late summer, there were no window boxes with beautiful flowers spilling down over apartment walls as I was used to seeing in West Germany. People dressed in drab clothes, and their moods matched their appearance. The East Germans we passed just stared at us with no reaction whatsoever—they silently watched us drive by, then turned away to go about their business. No one smiled, no one waved. Later, I found out that the people on the streets weren't allowed to speak to us or interact in any way.

As we wound our way through the small villages, I began to understand how destitute and hopeless it really was for the East German people. Although it was around five in the morning, I could already see incredibly long lines of people waiting for food. By six o'clock, people were being turned away, as shelves had quickly emptied out. As it turned out, that same process was repeated every single day. In fact, on another occasion I went into a shoe store and, although there was a nice display of shoes in the window, inside the store there were only ten pairs on the shelves. While the outside impression was one of affluence, the reality behind the show window was completely different. I couldn't help thinking about the stark contrast between what I was seeing here and the smallest convenience store in America.

I had expected my inaugural tour would be emotionally exhilarating and non-eventful, and that proved to be the case until we saw a Soviet military convoy heading toward us on the opposite side of the street. I was with a highly experienced tour NCO, who cautioned me to remain calm and to keep our equipment out of sight. It was a surreal moment. Although I'd been studying the Soviet order of battle for years, here I was face to face with the real thing.

As the convoy approached, I saw that their equipment was heavily concealed under a camouflaged tarp. Several approaching trucks were loaded with what appeared to be a sophisticated anti-aircraft weapon not known to be in the zone of occupation. Although it was hidden under the tarp, I was sure of what it was. I pointed it out to the tour NCO, who said I must be mistaken and, besides, because of the tarp, there was no way we could confirm the sighting. Realizing that no one would believe a rookie tour officer, I took a chance and quickly snapped several pictures of the equipment as it passed. One of the Soviets saw what I was doing and sounded the alarm. The tour NCO reacted quickly, swerving onto a side road and accelerating away from the convoy to avoid being detained.

Fortunately, the rest of our tour was uneventful. Upon returning to Berlin, I reported what we saw in the convoy we passed. At first, everyone was skeptical of the sighting but, once the film had been developed and studied, several experts confirmed what I had seen. When asked how I knew, I explained my photo interpretation training included identifying equipment under camouflage from aerial photography. I used the same technique from a ground perspective, and it proved to be effective. Air Force guys are not known to be well-versed in ground equipment, so my sighting gave me instant credibility, particularly with the Army contingent. To my great relief, my time in the MLM appeared to be off to a good start.

ORIGINS OF THE MLM

Military Liaison Missions were formed as part of a quadripartite agreement shortly after WWII between the Allied Powers (U.S., UK, France) and the Soviet Union. Each of the Allied Powers signed a separate bilateral agreement with the Soviet Union allowing for the mutual existence of military personal to be stationed within each other's Zone of Occupation. The U.S. signed the Huebner-Malinin agreement with the USSR in April 1947. The agreement established a Soviet Military Liaison Mission, accredited to the commander-in-chief, U.S. Army Europe, and the U.S. Military Liaison Mission, accredited to commander-in-chief Group of Soviet Forces Germany. The terms of the agreement authorized each mission to have 14 accredited members and guaranteed right of free travel for accredited members throughout the other's zone of responsibility without escort or supervision "except in places of disposition of military units."

The purpose of the liaison missions was to monitor each other's forces and improve relationships between the Soviet Union and the Western occupation forces. The missions were initially tasked with implementing the agreements made at the Potsdam Conference, which included disarming and demilitarizing German forces; however, that task grew to include establishing official communication between the supreme commanders, estimating troop strengths, military troop movements, and point of contact for exchange of each other's agents/spies.

From the U.S. perspective, the primary task of the MLM became surveillance and reconnaissance of Soviet forces on the ground and in the air.

SELECTION

Like many things in my Air Force career, my selection for the MLM was totally unexpected. I was the squadron section chief of a photo interpretation section at RAF Alconbury when my squadron commander summoned me to the conference room to speak to an Air Force colonel from Berlin. This meeting was the first time I heard about the United States Military Liaison Mission. The colonel briefed me on the organization and what it did behind the Iron Curtain. As I listened to the unit presentation, I couldn't help wondering why the Air Force participated in a high-risk, clandestine mission like this, and why I'd be qualified to be a member. As the colonel explained, my expertise in Soviet military equipment and installations, my fluency in French, and my recent stint as an exchange officer with the French Air Force made me a viable candidate to fly with the French Air Force to identify Soviet equipment and movement around Berlin. After hearing the presentation, I politely informed the colonel that I had already decided to leave the service at the completion of my six-year commitment to the Air Force. He gave me his card and said if I changed my mind to contact him.

As with many times in the past, the hand of fate reached in to change everything. The U.S. and Russian Cold War was intensifying, and intelligence gathering was now a higher priority in Washington. Within weeks of my turning down the MLM assignment, a freeze was implemented to keep intelligence officers in place. Needless to say, I was frustrated that my future was being placed on hold by events that were totally beyond my control. Not wanting to remain in the same job at Alconbury, I pulled out the colonel's number and gave him a call, saying I would accept the assignment if he could get me moved immediately. Due to the recently announced freeze-in-place announcement, I had little confidence he'd be able to get me out of my current assignment at Alconbury. To my surprise, I received orders for the USMLM a few weeks later. Although I didn't know it at the time, the circumstances behind my selection were highly unusual.

I arrived in Berlin in the morning and was directed to the MLM facility. The building was nestled in a residential area and surrounded by a high wall with barbed wire. The colonel who recruited me wasted no time giving me some bad news: The position I had been hired to fill—as an airborne observer with the French Air Force—was actually a U.S. Army position. I remember thinking, "What's that got to do with me?" He continued: the Army had not been able to fill the billet and had therefore offered it to the Air Force, which is why he had come to Alconbury to talk to me about the position. But, between the time I had gotten my orders and arrived in Berlin, the Army had found a suitable candidate and took back their airborne observer position, leaving me without an assignment. Making things worse, I needed to speak either German or Russian to be eligible to fill a ground observer position in the MLM. Because my only other language fluency was French, I was ineligible; therefore, the Air Force was going to have to come up with another assignment for me. Needless to say, I was stunned. The music had stopped, and I was left without a chair.

Once again, fate intervened. As it turned out, the Air Force was authorized five officer positions in the MLM. Only four positions were filled when I arrived, and one of those officers was due to depart in a few months, which would leave the Air component in a critical manning shortage. The unit deliberated my situation and, to my surprise and relief, a day later I got some welcome news: the unit requested and got a waiver for me to stay based on my knowledge of Soviet equipment, my exceptionally high score on the Defense Language Aptitude Battery test and, most important, the critical shortage of tour officers. The one caveat was that I had to begin independent language study while waiting for a slot at the Defense Language Institute in Monterrey, California.

I agreed and chose German, believing it would be better to communicate with the Soviets in a third language rather than to give them the advantage of speaking in their native tongue. I immediately bought a beginner German Berlitz book, started independent self-study, and took private lessons between tours. Within six months, the unit evaluated my proficiency and decided that my German was at an acceptable level without going to formal language training. In fact, thanks to my private lessons, I was able to pick up a local dialect that few in the unit knew. It looked like things were back on track.

COMING UP TO SPEED

Learning how to be an effective tour officer was challenging and fun, but there were no instruction manuals. Training was through word of mouth and by absorbing lessons learned from those who came before you. One lesson passed on to me in my very first tour was to follow my instincts—if a situation raised the hair on the back of my neck, danger was imminent, and I should leave immediately. I also learned that life in the MLM was exceptionally stressful. You'd think that, with specially equipped vehicles, top-quality equipment, and quasi-diplomatic status, traveling around East Germany as observers wouldn't be particularly dangerous, but the absolute opposite was true. From the moment we crossed the Glienecke Bridge, we were under constant surveillance by *Stasi* (East German Secret Police) and Soviet agents, and endured constant physical and psychological harassment. We couldn't let down our guard for a moment—even in our official residence in Potsdam, we had to assume the house was bugged and had hidden cameras. But the real cat-and-mouse game began once a tour departed the Potsdam House. *Stasi* agents tailed us constantly and reported our whereabouts to the Soviets. On very successful missions, we'd lose the tail, penetrate the target area unnoticed, acquire the target/information, and return to Berlin without incident. But there were always missions that weren't as successful. In some cases, MLM members were detected and chased off before achieving their collection objectives. In the worst cases, members were detected, captured, and detained by the Soviets. There were also instances where members had their vehicles rammed, were shot at, and were beaten by Soviet troops. In the most infamous and tragic case, Army Major Arthur D. Nicholson was shot by a Soviet sentry and left by his captors to bleed to death on the perimeter of a Soviet installation.

Despite the risks, the mission continued. Just when our Air Force component was about to achieve full strength, our commander and the deputy commander departed unexpectedly, due to a scandal believed to be orchestrated by the Soviets. That, plus one additional planned transfer, left two of us to do the job of five. I was designated as the interim commander in charge of one untrained second lieutenant tour officer, three tour NCOs, and our administrative support personnel and photo lab. Knowing the critical nature of our mission, our team pulled together. We all believed we were making a difference. We could not allow the Soviets to win. Most important, we wouldn't allow our support to our unit and country to suffer. We now had two tour teams to perform the same mission and schedule of five. A tour team was typically out for two to four days, followed by a three-day break back in the MLM area in Berlin. Those three days were crucial, not only to give us time to write reports but, just as important, to enable us to recover both physically and emotionally from the time in East Germany. Given that schedule, our personnel shortage posed a real challenge.

The manning constraints and compressed schedule added to what was already a stressful situation. While touring, we ate sandwiches and drank a ton of coffee. We slept in camouflaged locations in forests, either on the ground or in the car. The tour officer and tour NCO slept in shifts, taking turns keeping watch. With our traditional five-team manning, we had been able to keep a team in East Germany every day of the week, with one team in reserve to avoid burnout. However, our new schedule pushed us to the limit. I recorded many weeks where I worked up to 107 hours, coming in just long enough to write a report, plan a new mission, get a few hours of sleep, change drivers, and head back out. This went on for several months. On some occasions, I volunteered to assist my Army colleagues with night missions to help ease the manning and scheduling issues. The good news was that we were able to maintain our schedule and the missions were successful. The bad news was that it took a very heavy toll on our health and wellbeing.

Teamwork was the absolute bedrock of our operation. I quickly learned to rely on my tour NCOs for their in-depth knowledge of the terrain, superb driving skills, and unquestioned ability to maintain their composure in dangerous and stressful situations. I also had absolute confidence in knowing my teammates were reliable in their word. I never worried about whether the vehicle was prepared or that the perimeter was secured—if they said it was done, it was done. The absolute trust and faith we had in one another saved us from many bad situations. For instance, on one occasion we had positioned our vehicle to observe what we suspected to be training activity on a new aircraft system. We had to remain in an open area near a steep drop-off to get a clear view of the heavily guarded installation. I left the car while my tour NCO stood guard. Once in position, an uneasy feeling swept over me—something just didn't seem right. I hustled back to the car and told my tour NCO to start the car and drive as fast as possible back down the narrow road along the cliff. He didn't hesitate. As we sped off, I still wasn't sure exactly what the threat was until I until I looked out the side window and saw military men in black uniforms coming up the cliff. They appeared to be *Spetsnaz* (Soviet Special Forces). Had I waited ten seconds later, and had my tour NCO not taken immediate action, we would have been trapped by some very bad people. That one lesson served me well, and I passed it on to all who followed me.

THE VALUE OF THE ACADEMY EXPERIENCE

Looking back on my time at the Academy, there were several crucial lessons that served me well during in my time in the MLM. I had entered the Academy with some degree of skepticism because my high school in Long Island was decidedly anti-war and anti-military; however, the Academy changed my views about the military and its mission. The fourth-class system taught us teamwork and courage and instilled a strong sense of duty. We learned to face challenges calmly—to assess, plan, and execute as a team. While I was still not convinced we should have gone into Vietnam, I graduated with a much clearer understanding of the military's role and determination to take my place in it. We had to be ready when duty called, and the Academy training prepared me for what needed to be done. I'm convinced that was a key factor in any success I may have had in our MLM operations.

I was fortunate to have had a fascinating and rewarding career as an intelligence professional in the Air Force, but my time in the MLM was particularly satisfying. By necessity, we were a very low-profile organization on the front lines of the Cold War. However, through our reporting on the constantly changing environment in East Germany, we were able to identify events that could potentially affect the balance of power between East and West and passed crucial information to decision makers at the highest levels of government.

17

RESCUE FROM THE FRIGID WATERS

by Mr. William T. Gillin

Bill Gillin
CS-16

Duty and sacrifice are not only demonstrated in combat. Capt. William Gillin, a rescue helicopter pilot based at Elmendorf AFB, Alaska, was awarded the Jabara Award for Outstanding Airmanship in 1981 for his heroic actions in rescuing passengers and crew from a cruise ship in the Gulf of Alaska.

It was October 4th, 1980, early on a Saturday morning. I happened to be on call that weekend. About 3:00 am, my home phone rang, rousing me from a deep sleep. The caller from the Air Force Rescue Coordination Center at Elmendorf AFB said, "Captain Gillin, we have a mission for you. There's a cruise ship in the Gulf of Alaska, about 120 miles out to sea, south of Yakutat. They've caught fire and are abandoning ship. There are 519 people on board, many of them elderly."

Now I was wide awake! I had a map of Alaska on the wall, and I looked at the area he was talking about. When I saw the location, I thought, "Wow, they're sending us out there? It's going to be a long day!"

My wife jumped up and made some sandwiches for us as I donned my flight suit and gathered my gear. I hurried out to the base, met the crew, briefed up, and we launched out at about 0430. It was dark, but fortunately the visibility was still pretty good at that point.

We navigated over Portage Pass under a low overcast and rendez-voused with our HC-130 just off the coast. We conducted an air-to-air refueling, made a brief stop at Yakutat to pick up blankets for the survivors, then headed out to sea. Our HC-130 had to lead us, as our HH-3E didn't have much in the way of navigation aids, particularly at low level and far out at sea.

When we arrived on scene, we could see the cruise ship *Prinsendam* in the distance, with smoke coming out of it. Beyond the *Prinsendam,* we saw a string of lifeboats stretching out for several miles. The large oil tanker *Williamsburgh*, nearly 1,100 feet long, was nearby to lend assistance. We made our first shipboard landing on it, something we had never trained for. We unloaded the blankets, then began our rescue operations.

The Coast Guard helicopters were arriving on scene and were later joined by two Canadian helicopters. Because our HH-3 was the only air-refuellable helicopter on scene, we decided that it would be best if we took the lifeboat farthest out. We put our pararescue guys (PJs for short) down into the frigid water next to the boat. They got into the lifeboat and started helping the passengers. Each lifeboat probably had more than 60 people on board. I remember being astounded, wondering how we'd be able to hoist all these people up one at a time. I thought, "This is going to be a long operation." But that was the only choice we had.

The rescue process required a great deal of teamwork. The AC was in the right seat, which is where the AC flies in a helicopter. The main door is on the right side with the hoist, which enabled the AC to look down where we were hovering as the flight engineer (FE) lowered the hoist. The hoist we were using had a jungle penetrator with flotation collar, a strap, and paddles that folded down. The passenger sat on the paddles, hugged the collar, and the PJ secured them with a strap that went around their back. The whole process was slowed down somewhat because of the condition of the elderly passengers who, by this time, had been in open lifeboats for several hours and were cold and exhausted.

The AC was doing the hover work while I monitored the engine instruments. Our FE was alone in the cargo compartment because our two PJs were down in the boat. The FE was struggling as he hoisted the passengers up one by one, getting them to the door, pulling them in, and buckling them into a troop seat. He would then run the hoist back down for the next one to be rescued. It was an arduous process. After struggling to bring several passengers into the cargo compartment, he asked for some help.

This was something we hadn't trained for—we're not supposed to leave our crew positions, so this was totally unscripted. Since I couldn't see the boat from my seat, we decided the best thing I could do was go back and help the FE. So I scrambled back, strapped on a gunner's belt, and started pulling people into the chopper. That sped things up quite a bit. After taking on 8 to 12 people, depending on our fuel state, I'd jump back into my seat in the cockpit and take over the flying. We'd then fly them to the *Williamsburgh*, where I made most of the landings to give the AC a break.

Because it was impractical to lower passengers one at a time to the *Williamsburgh*, we'd land on the tanker and help our passengers out of the aircraft. Then we'd fly back to the waiting lifeboats and repeat the process. The only thing that interrupted our trips from lifeboats to the tanker were two more aerial refuelings. We'd top off from our HC-130 and then go back and rescue more people. That went on for several hours, until we were notified to head for the *Prinsendam*—the fire was now out of control and she was dead in the water. The captain had given the order to abandon ship and the crew needed to be evacuated. While the AC hovered over the stern of the ship, the FE and I pulled the crew-members in. The captain was the last one up. We flew the crew to the *Williamsburgh*, let them off, then flew back out to "our" lifeboat to continue loading passengers.

As the day wore on, we learned that a powerful storm, the remains of a typhoon, was moving in. We could see the seas were getting higher. The ceiling fell to about 300 feet, it was raining, visibility was down to one-half mile and seas were running high. Wind and turbulence made it difficult to hover over the lifeboats and get the passengers aboard. I remember an elderly lady they had just strapped onto the jungle penetrator. She was ready to be hoisted up when suddenly a huge wave about 30 feet high hit the boat. Our FE was running the hoist and immediately recognized the danger as the hoist cable got tangled underneath the boat's rudder. He released as much of the cable as he could to give it some slack, but when the boat dropped down the back side of the wave, the cable snapped. At that point, we were out of commission and couldn't help anyone else. Fortunately, that elderly passenger was okay. She didn't get jerked out of the boat, but it was a pretty tense situation.

We radioed our HC-130 to update him on our situation. We told him that we were now out of commission, low on fuel, and asked him to lead us back to Yakutat. He said, "Sorry, we're involved in something else." That "something else" turned out to be the rescue of a Canadian helicopter that had an emergency due to smoke in the cockpit and loss of cockpit instruments. Our HC-130 ended up making two attempts to join up on him, coming in from underneath the clouds at about 200 feet. They joined up, and our HC-130 led them back to Yakutat, flying just above stall speed.

Meanwhile, we were informed that another oil tanker, the 850-foot *Sohio Intrepid*, smaller than the *Williamsburgh*, had arrived in the area, and was going to stay to assist. The tanker had been enroute to Valdez, north of our position, to load up with oil from the pipeline. Our HC-130 recommended that we land on the *Sohio Intrepid* and wait for them to lead the ailing Canadian helicopter to Yakutat. Then they'd return to the tanker, where we'd take off, join up and refuel, and follow them back to shore. That sounded like a reasonable plan.

We began to search for the *Sohio Intrepid*, but the visibility was falling rapidly in the rain. The tanker was reported to be about ten miles from our position, and we'd been given a heading to rendezvous with her. But, after flying that heading for more than five minutes, we still couldn't spot her. Fortunately for us, a Coast Guard cutter had also arrived in the area by that time. We contacted them and asked if they could identify us on their surface radar. They said if we could descend to 50 feet above the water, they should be able to locate us and give us an updated heading to the tanker. The crosswind was pretty strong, so we turned to the heading the Coast Guard cutter gave us and put in a five-degree correction to account for the winds. After several minutes, we were able to spot the *Sohio Intrepid*.

Because the tanker was empty, she was riding high in the water and was rolling and pitching in the 30-foot seas—not very favorable for landing on their deck. Furthermore, we wondered how well the deck would hold our HH-3. Our AC was able to communicate through the Coast Guard to the tanker crew to learn that the deck would support our helicopter. As we closed on the tanker, we could see that there was no helipad and there were pipes running down the middle of the deck, so the approach would be tight. We would have to land sideways to the ship with our refueling probe over the pipes and our tail over the side. Because the tanker was pitching, I was struggling to time my landing with the rising and falling of the ship. I was just about to touch down on my first approach when the deck suddenly fell away. I went around, made another approach and, after some maneuvering, was able to touch down safely. We sat on the deck with engines at idle, waiting on our HC-130 to rejoin and lead us back to shore in the deteriorating weather.

After about an hour, our HC-130 gave us an update from Yakutat: they'd arrived safely but were waiting in line to get refueled. So we sat on the tanker's deck with engines at idle, waiting for our HC-130 to return. By the time they arrived, it was after five in the afternoon, getting dark, with low clouds, rain, and strong winds. They asked us for our fuel state, which at that point was pretty low. Given the turbulence, our HC-130 crew recommended against air refueling and suggested we shut down and remain onboard the tanker for the night. The ship's crew helped us secure our aircraft with tiedowns and cables. The captain took us inside, where we were greeted with a good meal and bunks to sleep in. Our crew had flown 11.2 hours, made 9 shipboard landings, three inflight refuelings, and hoisted 61 survivors to safety.

We breathed a huge sigh of relief, but our part in the rescue wasn't quite finished. When we left our lifeboat for the last time, we notified the Coast Guard on-scene commander of the boat's location. We learned later that a Coast Guard helicopter had picked up some more passengers from that boat, then returned to Yakutat for fuel. But, somehow, in all the activity, the PJs and 20 passengers were still adrift after dark and unaccounted for. During the night, I was roused from my bunk and asked to come to the tanker's bridge. The Air Force Rescue Center asked for our last known position of the lifeboat. I referred to the log I had been keeping and gave them the heading and distance from the *Williamsburgh* at the time we left them. The Coast Guard used that information, along with wind and sea currents, to set up a search pattern. A Coast Guard cutter found and recovered them in rough seas at 1:50 a.m. Our two PJs were truly heroes.

In the end, 519 people were rescued through a massive, coordinated effort, with no fatalities. While I was recognized with the Jabara Award, the rescue mission would never have been successful without a tremendous team effort. All our crewmembers, including the HC-130 crew, did an outstanding job, as did our maintenance folks, an Air Force flight surgeon, other PJs who had been airlifted to the *Williamsburgh*, the other aircrews involved, and the Coast Guard cutters and oil tankers that were so essential in supporting the airborne effort.

Speaking as an Academy grad, it's important to note that you'll never know when and if you'll find yourself in such a position, where challenging circumstances can test your mettle. But, even if you don't encounter such dramatic situations as ours, the values that guided all of us on this mission—integrity, service, and excellence—are just as important in everyday life as they are in moments of crisis.

18

FROM FIGHTER PILOT TO INFANTRY PLATOON SERGEANT

by Major (Ret.) Rowe P. Stayton

Maj. Rowe Stayton is unique among our classmates. In 1981, he separated from the Air Force as an F-15 fighter pilot to pursue a law degree. Then came 9/11. Like many of us, Rowe tried to get back into the fight to defend his country; however, the Air Force Military Personnel Center said that he was too old for the fight. Rather than giving up, he enlisted in the Army National Guard in Arkansas, and later  *deployed to Iraq as an infantry soldier and platoon sergeant. This is his story.*

Rowe Stayton
CS-36

243

My Air Force career started out like that of many other classmates. I went to pilot training at Williams AFB. My first assignment after graduation was as a T-37 instructor, and I served at Williams for three years. After finishing my tour at Williams, I was fortunate enough to get an F-15 as my first operational assignment. I spent three years in the 27th Tactical Fighter Squadron at Langley AFB, flying the air-to-air mission. It was a great opportunity and I loved both the mission and the people I flew with.

As time went on though, my career goals changed, and I decided I wanted to become an attorney. I applied for and was accepted to law school at the University of Denver. Because I still loved flying, I decided to join an Air National Guard unit in Des Moines, Iowa while I pursued a legal career. What a great life—I commuted every weekend from Denver to fly the A-7 in Iowa. I'd only flown air-to-air in the F-15, so this was a great opportunity to learn the air-to-ground mission. I got to work with some outstanding Air National Guard officers for the next seven years. As time went on, though, it became apparent that I wouldn't be able to keep the level of proficiency I wanted in the A-7 because of my growing law practice in Denver. It was a difficult decision, but I felt it was best to step aside after eight years of active duty and seven years with my Guard unit.

Looking back, I know that was the right decision to make. Still, I really missed the people I'd served with. So, when DESERT SHIELD and DESERT STORM kicked off, I tried to get into the C-130 reserve unit in Colorado Springs. They actually accepted me, but the war was over before I could get to upgrade training, so I had to put that on hold.

GETTING BACK INTO THE FIGHT

Then came 9/11. At that time, I was 50 years old, but I just felt I had to get back in the fight. I decided to call a classmate of mine who I worked closely with at the Academy, Nort Schwartz. At the time he was working for the secretary of defense. Given the circumstances, Nort was pretty busy, to say the least. Still, he took my call, and I told him what I wanted to do. He laughed and said, "There's no need for a 50-year-old fighter pilot in the active-duty Air Force. Why don't you look for a Guard unit?" So that's what I did.

After looking around, I managed to work a deal with the Air National Guard unit in Denver. I was told they'd bring me in as a lawyer and then, after some period of time, would let me transition to an F-16 position. I was thrilled, because this was really what I wanted to do. Unfortunately, I discovered there was a regulation that prohibited me from coming back in as a judge advocate general unless I was forty-five years or younger. I questioned the age limit, thinking, "How tough can it be to work in a courtroom in the Air Force?" But, despite my best efforts, I was told I was ineligible to serve.

Needless to say, I was pretty disappointed. But, if the Academy taught me anything, it was to never give up. After considering my options, I decided to try to get back into the fight through another branch of service, the Army. I managed to locate an Army National Guard unit in Arkansas where I had a hunting and fishing cabin. So I started the application process. It wasn't any easier than it had been with the Air National Guard—in fact, they "lost" my paperwork on two separate occasions. But it was finally approved, and I was called up. I drove to Arkansas, was sworn in as an E-5 (sergeant) and joined the Arkansas Army National Guard in an infantry unit.

ADAPTING TO THE ARMY

The transition wasn't an easy one, as I was an ex-Air Force major having to adapt to a new position as an infantry sergeant in the Army. It was also a challenge because I found that, as I aged a bit, I didn't process things as quickly as I used to. That's what Nort was getting at when I asked him about getting back in the fight—he recognized that a 50-year-old fighter pilot probably doesn't process the air combat arena as quickly as a 28-year-old fighter pilot does. So it was an uphill climb in many respects.

For me to get back into the fight as an infantryman, there were two things I had to learn right off the bat. First, I had to learn the enlisted rank structure. As an ex-fighter pilot, I really didn't understand the enlisted side of things. Although the actual rank structure was pretty straightforward, there were certain protocols and cultural aspects I didn't understand. For instance, at the Academy, we had some of the finest NCOs in the Air Force serving as our group sergeant majors. They helped tutor and mentor us. As a matter of fact, most of us on group staff probably spent more time talking to the sergeant majors about being good officers than we did our AOCs. To a man, they really wanted the cadets to succeed. By contrast, when I came into the Army, it wasn't like that at all.

To begin with, the enlisted corps in the Army is extremely rank-oriented and, as a result, there are very clear divisions. Due to the demands in the combat environment, they put a very high priority on physical performance—much more so than in the Air Force. So here was a 50-some year-old man coming into a team with 18, 19, and 20-year olds—you can imagine the reaction. On the one hand, the soldiers thought it was really cool that I decided to come back in, particularly given that I had been an Air Force major, a fighter pilot, and a lawyer. On the other hand, my previous achievements meant nothing when we went out in the sector. So, to gain respect from my people, I knew had to step up my game to operate in the very physical manner that my position required.

I started lifting weights and running. That was a great start. But, ironically, one of the things that helped me gain the most respect stemmed from having been the Wing Open boxing champ at the Academy. As I said, in the Army enlisted corps, you have to perform physically—and sometimes that requires getting physical. There were always a couple of guys who wanted to call me out. I had brought my gloves with me, so if anyone wanted to try me on for size or didn't want to follow my lead, we boxed. Now, I may not be a good wrestler, but I can certainly box.

So I did pretty well and, in the process, I earned their respect. Earning their respect made a world of difference when it came to being a successful team leader, squad leader, and then, later on, a platoon sergeant. The importance of earning your peoples' respect was another one of the important lessons I learned at the Academy.

There were other significant cultural differences I had to deal with as I transitioned to my new role in the infantry. I can honestly say that, as a flight lead, I knew that everyone on my wing was highly competent in all circumstances. In the Army, on the other hand, I quickly learned that you can't make that assumption. That's not my service parochialism speaking; it's just the nature of the beast. In the active-duty Army, for example, when they test people to see which military occupation specialty they're best suited for, the lower-scoring individuals tend to be assigned to the infantry, whereas the higher-scoring people are put into the more technical career fields, such as cyber warfare or air and missile defense. Consequently, infantry training is based on the lowest common denominator and involves constant repetition. People are watched very closely and there's very little room for creativity. To be fair, in the fighter community, there were a few pilots who weren't well-suited for the mission, either because of the way they processed information or because they weren't sufficiently aggressive. But those pilots were weeded out of the community on an informal basis and ended up going to other jobs. As a result, the line fighter pilots, particularly the weapons officers, were highly talented and people you knew you could count on in a fight. On the other hand, the demographics and selection process in the Army meant you really had to watch the infantry troops carefully. My unit in Arkansas was a bit more of a mixed bag. I had older schoolteachers and police officers who were always great soldiers. But I also had guys who were right out of high school and required more "hands-on" supervision. In the fighter world, I could give a pre-flight brief and be confident the mission would either be executed the way I briefed or, if not, any errors would be corrected after a debrief. I didn't have that confidence in my Army unit.

One of the first things I learned at the Academy was the importance of doing your duty. That was a foundational principle in everything we did. By contrast, one's concept of duty in the Army wasn't always as well-formed or as intuitive as I would have expected. It certainly wasn't something I could take for granted. For instance, I was deployed to Iraq in 2004. Six months into my tour, I was assigned to a new squad and stayed with that unit for another seven months. The squad leader was a good friend of mine and, at that point, had seen a lot more combat that I had. Toward the end of our tour, our squad was tasked with clearing five houses that were a hotbed of insurgent activity on Haifa Street—sardonically named "Purple Heart Boulevard" by the troops—in Baghdad. My squad leader gathered us together and, to my amazement, told us, "We're not going to do it. I'm not going to get anybody hurt." I couldn't believe it. I pulled him aside and called him out on that—not because I was heroic or suicidal, but because I just felt I had to remind him of what our duty was.

Don't get me wrong, I was scared. I was scared every time I went out. Initially, I thought there was something wrong with me for feeling that way, but the longer I was in the combat zone, the more I realized that everyone was scared. So I adopted an attitude that it's normal to be scared. Matter of fact, it's not normal to not be scared. But you do your duty anyway. You've got to do your job. From that perspective, I would never have forgiven myself for not challenging the squad leader. Had we not cleared those houses, we would have endangered a large troop movement that was due to move along Haifa Street. Our job was to ensure they didn't get attacked or shot at. After some discussion, my squad leader actually saw it my way. Having said that, I understood why he wanted to stand down. It was his squad, and there were ten soldiers counting on him to get them home safely. But that didn't matter because we had an obligation to do our duty. So, we did. Fortunately, no one got hurt, but it was something we needed to do. The teaching point for me was that it's critical in the profession of arms that we prop each other up and support each other in doing our duty.

EATING CROW

Not all conversations I had with superiors had such a happy ending.

We'd been in Baghdad about six weeks, and I had been observing some leadership failures I considered to be unforced errors. For instance, I was on a mission to an outpost in Baghdad and was standing in line with all the other enlisted guys to get some food. Suddenly our company commander walked in with members of his staff and personal security. They looked at the long line, cut right in front of us, and got fed first. I remember thinking, "Wow, I don't think that would have flown well at the Academy." You should always take care of your people first. That was just one trivial—but very visible—instance I saw of a lack of leadership by example during my tour in Iraq, but it was indicative of larger failures I'd seen.

While I was in Iraq, I had been communicating with Nort Schwartz and another classmate, Bruce Wright. So, when I came back from this particular mission, I sent Nort an email and in the subject line I put "For Your Eyes Only." I said to Nort, "I don't know what you're being told but, from my viewpoint as an E-5 team leader, there are some leadership problems over here."

In all fairness, I don't know that I was seeing the big picture. And, being an Academy grad, a former major fighter pilot, there was probably some ego on my part. But I was trying to let Nort know about some problems I was seeing from the ground level.

After sending that email, I left on a three-day mission. When I got back, I had a return email from Nort. I thought, "This is cool." I opened it. And, to my horror, Nort said, "Look, Rowe, I just read your email. It was too good. I had to send it up. But don't worry, we've sanitized all the aspects of it so there's no way they could identify who wrote this."

Three days later, I was out in sector driving a Humvee. Over the radio from the command post, I heard, "Is Sergeant Stayton in that vehicle?" My squad leader said, "Yeah, he's here." Command post said, "Well, tell him to be at the chow hall at Camp Warrior at seventeen hundred hours." Needless to say, I was pretty curious. I was able to get a bit of intel before the meeting—turned out they wanted to talk about the email I had sent.

As directed, I showed up at 1700. I was only guy in my unit to go, but the rest of the battalion was there—probably 200 to 250 soldiers. Then our battalion commander walked in. He started by talking about things that had happened in sector—pretty routine stuff. I thought I had dodged a bullet since my name hadn't come up by then. But, after about 30 minutes, he said, "Well, that's enough of that." Then he turned to his staff and said, "Okay, pass out the email." Well, he passed out a copy of my email to everyone in the room. Fortunately, names were blacked out. But then he started talking about insubordination, that he disagreed with the author's viewpoint, and that the author was dead wrong in his allegations.

They knew it was me; I was sure of it. That's why they had me come in. So I raised my hand to let the battalion commander know it was me. And he just glared at me and said, "No." So I put my hand back down and listened to about 20 minutes of what was probably well-deserved criticism for me going around him and not bringing up the issue with him directly. Finally, he dismissed us by saying, "Well, we're not going to prosecute this guy. We don't know who it is but if we find out or if he does it again"—and he was looking at me as he said this—"there will be consequences." Then he dismissed everyone.

As everyone was leaving, I went up and said, "Colonel, it was me. I wrote that email." He glared at me and said, "We knew it was you. You're the only guy in the whole battalion that could write a letter like this. That's because the subject and the verb actually agreed with each other."

I tried to talk to him about leadership based on what I had been seeing at my level. I said, "Well, this is my viewpoint. I haven't seen a whole lot of what I'd consider to be leadership by example. Your subordinate commanders aren't taking care of their soldiers." Those kinds of things. And, after about five minutes into the conversation, he started calling me "sergeant."

Now, I did learn very quickly in the Army that when you begin every sentence with a person's rank, the exchange is over—there's no more give and take. It's no longer a two-way conversation; it's now just a monologue. Finally, he turned away and walked off.

I went back and sent Nort another email, asking him if they had a job for a gate guard at the Pentagon. I figured I was finished in Iraq. But, as it turned out, nothing happened to me. However, the company commander I complained about was replaced within four weeks. We got a West Pointer in, and the difference was night and day.

The first thing the new company commander did was what we call a show-up inspection. The Army's very equipment-oriented. You're given certain tasks. You've got to have a compass. You've got to have bandages. You've got to have all the right kind of equipment, otherwise you can't do the job. So the first thing our new company commander wanted to do was a show-up inspection, because he wasn't about to have his soldiers tasked to do something they weren't properly equipped to handle. And I was sitting there watching this and thinking, "Yeah, yeah. This is what it's about."

It was just amazing watching that change in leadership. I watched the way he took care of his soldiers. So, while I suffered some short-term difficulty in the battalion's eyes, over the long term I think it helped.

I really appreciate what Nort did. But, oh, man!

19

PROFESSIONAL COMPETENCE AND THE UNEXPECTED

by Captain Chesley "Sully" Sullenberger, III

Sully Sullenberger
CS-18

The term "Miracle on the Hudson" was unknown until the breaking news report on January 15, 2009: an Airbus A320 had hit a flock of birds shortly after takeoff from LaGuardia Airport and safely ditched in the Hudson River, saving 155 passengers and crew. This is Captain Sully Sullenberger's account of the lessons he learned, and the role character played in avoiding a tragedy of epic proportions.

It has now been more than 50 years since I entered the United States Air Force Academy on Monday, June 23, 1969, during the Vietnam War. Yet I still clearly recall that first day. There were 1,406 of us new cadets who, if we were successful, would graduate four years later as the 15th class, the Class of 1973. 844 of us would graduate. Once my classmates and I had our hair cut and been handed a stack of uniforms and the training began, it was obvious to us that we had encountered a system designed to change us, to challenge us, to tear us away from the comfortable, the easy, the familiar. It was intended to convince us that, if we worked hard and worked together, we could accomplish things we did not know we could. We were going to discover inner reserves of strength we did not know we had. We would soon know it could no longer be about "me." Instead, it was going to be about "us."

We took an oath of office that first day to be sworn in as cadets, the same oath we would take upon graduation as we were commissioned officers in the United States Air Force. Those words made quite an impression on me. I remember them still.

We said, "I,…, do solemnly swear that I will support and defend the Constitution of the United States against all enemies, foreign and domestic; that I will bear true faith and allegiance to the same; that I take this obligation freely, without any mental reservation or purpose of evasion; and that I will well and faithfully discharge the duties of the office on which I am about to enter. So help me God."

This was not just a promise that one can decide whether or not to keep. It was a sacred, solemn vow that I swore to uphold, at the cost of my life, if necessary.

So, we embarked on a life of purpose, of service, and for some, of sacrifice.

INSTILLED VALUES

My parents were of what we now call the Greatest Generation, I think with good reason. They grew up during a previous huge financial upheaval, the Great Depression of the 1930s and, like many of his contemporaries, my father served as a naval officer in World War II. They described themselves as ordinary people who found themselves in extraordinary circumstances. They said they were just doing their jobs.

But, as we now know, with the benefit of hindsight, through the long lens of history, by just doing their jobs, they saved the world from fascism and autocratic rule. It is estimated that 75 million died in that titanic global struggle.

They had certain clearly articulated values that they passed on to me and that my wife and I have passed on to our now adult daughters: a sense of civic duty, not entitlement; of service above self; and a willingness to share our society's many sacrifices—all of them, even the really inconvenient ones.

Given the many distractions in our popular culture, sometimes it seems as though these important civic virtues have gotten lost in the noise. They don't seem as apparent as they once did. Some may even wonder if they still exist. But they do.

These concepts were familiar to me before I entered the Academy, but at the Academy I learned them in earnest.

We learned values that some seem to feel they have the luxury of thinking of only as abstractions. As if to say, "How often in our everyday lives are we ever called upon to demonstrate integrity, courage, or compassion as if someone's life or livelihood depended on it?" The answer is— more often than we think. For these values are not just abstractions. They are real, and they have real meaning in real life with real consequences.

I also learned at the Academy and since the importance of and the power of leadership by personal example, by trying to embody these traits. I'm reminded that one of my Academy classmates, a fellow fighter pilot and later fellow airline pilot, a dozen years ago finally lost his battle with cancer. His widow asked me to speak at his memorial service which, of course, I was honored to do. One of the things I said about Chris was that he was one of those exceptional people who lived his life in such a way that his values were apparent. He didn't have to tell you what he believed, or have a sign on his desk, or a poster on the wall, or wear a t-shirt emblazoned with a slogan. If you spent enough time around him and, if you paid attention, you knew everything about him that you needed to know. He not only had real core values, but he tried to make them real on a daily basis. I've been trying to live up to Chris's example.

The Air Force Core Values and corresponding virtues clearly define our aspirations and expectations for ourselves and for each other. From my perspective as a former Air Force officer and fighter pilot, and former airline pilot and captain, l can tell you how they resonate with me and my experience.

THE ULTIMATE TEST

In my 54 years of flying, I learned not only the kind of leadership that is necessary in a crisis, but that leadership is what makes the difference between success and failure, life and death.

From my father I learned about the awesome responsibilities of command—that a commander, a leader, must take responsibility for and ultimately is responsible for every aspect of the welfare of those in his or her care. And woe be to any commander who through some lack of foresight or carelessness causes someone to be harmed. In other words, with great authority comes great responsibility.

I felt those obligations deeply on the day when I had to meet my most difficult challenge on Flight 1549 on January 15, 2009. I knew I had to find a way to save the lives of everyone on board. After our emergency forced landing in the Hudson River, I could not let anyone die for any reason if I could possibly help it, so I went through the aircraft cabin twice to make sure no one was left behind. Then I made it a point to be the last one off the airplane and into a raft, and made sure I was the last one out of our raft and onto the ferry that rescued us. I knew that my job was literally to save everyone else before myself. We weren't trained to do that. It was just obvious that was what should happen. A leader should be the first to face the threat and the last to safety.

As is always the case after an aircraft mishap, our flight was investigated by the National Transportation Safety Board and was under the microscope for 15 months, where the investigators' job was to follow the truth wherever it led, to interview everyone involved, to analyze the data from all the recorders, to do an analysis of the airplane and its systems. And, since I was captain, I was pilot in command, and everything that happened on our flight was ultimately my responsibility, their job was to scrutinize every thought I had, every choice I made, every syllable I uttered, every action I took or did not take. But that's how we learn. That's what we owe all our passengers and crews.

Fear is a normal human reaction to threat. I have long known that courage is not the absence of fear; it is doing what is required in spite of it. But, because I had done the hard work, attained the knowledge, skill, experience and judgment over many years, I had the confidence and realistic optimism to take what I did know, adapt it, and apply it in a new way to solve a problem I had never seen before. I had the mental discipline to compartmentalize my mind and achieve a kind of practiced professional calm, even in this existential crisis. When I made the one announcement to our passengers and crew right before our landing, I made it a point to sound confident, not agitated. I knew that courage can be contagious. A leader sets the tone. You get what you project, whether it is confidence and courage, or fear, anger, and hatred. We must model the attitudes and behavior that we need to see in others.

Master your craft and then master yourself. That means mastering your ego to unleash the power of your team. While ego can be a powerful driving force, left unchecked it can isolate you from the communication, collaboration, and innovation of others you may need to avert disaster. We have to be able to check our egos at the door. I have gotten to know and talked at length with Gene Kranz, one of the NASA flight directors famous for leading the mission control efforts that safely guided Apollo 13 home after its service module exploded, who told me once that his proudest moment during that crisis was when his team brought him the solution to a problem he had not even asked about. "A leader builds leaders," he said.

One of the most fundamental responsibilities of leadership is to create an environment, a culture, in which we all are able and willing to do our best work. Visit work areas, listen to those on the front line, learn their issues and concerns. Remove the obstacles and barriers to excellence and success. Empower your team by investing in their learning and growth. Let your team members know it is not only their right but their responsibility to speak up and make it psychologically safe to do so.

After graduate school, I became an Air Force fighter pilot. Suffice it to say we're trained to a very high professional standard, our skill honed to a razor's edge. We brief our missions in great detail but, as with any endeavor, once we begin the flight and our plan meets reality, we must adapt. But it's after the flight in the debriefing where the learning really occurs, where we, leaders and followers alike, hold ourselves accountable to the same high standards and, in brutally honest exchanges talk about what worked, what didn't, and why. We should not just fly the same hour 20,000 times, but always be trying to make the next hour, the next flight, better than the previous one.

And that's what I call the fighter pilot ethos: continuous learning, constantly striving for excellence. It is a deep and abiding understanding that, in critical domains like aviation and others, just good enough isn't.

So don't pressure your team to cut corners; inspire them to excel. Create an environment in which everyone knows that excellence is the standard, and they should not let themselves be pressured to do just what is most expedient, cheapest, or easiest. Be sure they know that only they can rush themselves by feeling pressure, whether real or perceived, and they should not let that happen.

I also have made it a priority to have a deeper understanding of my profession, the world, and life to learn more than just what to do and how to do it; in other words, the "what" and the "how." I began to learn the "why" of what we do. And the "why" is critically important for at least two reasons. First, it helps to motivate ourselves and others. Why must we do this? Why is it important? What happens if we don't? And, second, it helps us chart a course in terra incognita, like our flight—a novel event for which we'd never trained. But, because I understood the "why" of my profession, as well as the "what" and the "how," even in this novel event I could set clear priorities.

LESSONS LEARNED

I have had my struggles and failures, times that I haven't lived up to the highest standards and didn't always find a clear path forward. We all have. But we must be resilient, learning from our successes and failures. Our imperfections do not define us. Our character does.

Act on your values to help you navigate uncertainty. When dealing with imperfect information, ambiguity, high workloads, and extreme time pressure, it is important to keep in mind the shared values of your organization that define not only what you do, but why you do it, and for whom. Thinking about doing the right thing at the right time for the right reasons provides a sense of direction to align your values with true north and establishes the guardrails that protect you and your organization from making egregious mistakes.

Do not misunderstand the nature of loyalty. Our highest duties are to our Nation's values and ideals, to the common good, not just to any individual. We and our Nation are most successful and respected when we are truest to our ideals.

I've been asked—are great leaders born or made? I believe they're made—and that's true for any profession. These are skills that can be taught. We can all learn to be better in whatever we do.

It can start with something as simple as knowing the names of people you depend on. I have always made it a point to do that. It is a sign of respect, of mutual respect. It is a way of acknowledging them as a person, worthy of respect. You can often tell what kind of leader a person is by how they treat the people around them, especially people who do not have a lot of status. And, if you lead well, build the team well, and treat them with respect, making that kind of human investment pays great dividends. As the late Warren Bennis, a great leadership expert and long-time University of Southern California professor said, "When leaders treat followers with respect, followers respond with trust." If they know that you've got their back and you're not just looking out for yourself, they will follow you to hell and back. Professor Bennis also said that while you can manage things, people deserve to be led; and there is, in fact, no difference between becoming an effective leader and becoming a fully integrated human being.

LEAVE A LEGACY

In the weeks and months after the famous flight, I began to hear from air-line colleagues of mine, people I'd flown with years, sometimes decades before, and they began to tell me about long-ago events that I'd forgotten, but that they had not, because something I had said, something I'd done, some situation we'd faced and the way we'd handled it, had resonated with them, and they shared them with me.

It turns out my reputation had been built one interaction, one person, one day at a time. I think that's true in each of our lives. In every encounter with another person, there is inherently an opportunity: for good, for ill, or for indifference. We just have to choose which it's going to be. At the end of our lives, I think it's unlikely that we're going to be counting our money, or cataloguing our successes, or the things that we managed to accumulate. I think it's much more likely that we may simply ask ourselves questions: "Did I live well? Did I serve a cause greater than myself? Did I make a difference?"

PART VI

A LIFETIME
OF SERVICE

Service doesn't stop when you leave active duty. The following chapters describe how our classmates have channeled their Academy experiences and the Air Force Core Values into business, civil service, the law, medicine, the priesthood, community service, and education. The examples here demonstrate the larger commitment to lead in all circumstances, regardless of profession or organization.

20

FROM THE ACADEMY TO THE BOARDROOM

by Mr. William M. Harris

Academy graduates have been highly successful in the business world, as well as in their military careers. Bill Harris describes how the leadership lessons he learned at the Academy contributed to his success as president of one of the world's largest real estate investment firms.

Bill Harris
CS-26

The primary mission of the United States Air Force Academy is to educate, train, and inspire young men and women to become leaders of character. The essence of the Academy is to produce leaders who are exceptionally well-prepared to lead in a complex, challenging, and technically sophisticated environment. Unlike any other institution of higher learning, the Air Force Academy provides an environment to learn and to apply leadership techniques that will effectively advance the goals and objectives of the organization. As a leader in training at the Academy, I learned to establish clear, challenging goals and objectives for my organization. Moreover, I learned respect for my team members while guiding them to attain common goals.

"GUTS" SQUADRON

During my first-class summer in 1972, I was selected to be the squadron commander of "Guts" Squadron during Basic Cadet Training. During the end of my second-class academic year, I was able to hand-pick my staff to facilitate the training of the basic cadets. Following Operation Third Lieutenant in Taiwan, I returned to start the second session of BCT. This opportunity presented exciting challenges as I prepared to transition from following orders as a team member to being the one leading the team.

My arrival a few days early to observe the training was extremely dis-heartening. Guts Squadron was dead last in the squadron competition. There was clear frustration on the faces of both the upper-class staff and the basic cadets. Rooms were tossed, mattresses dumped on the floor and mass special inspections conducted each evening. These basic cadets were not ready to enter the Cadet Wing at the start of the academic year. Clearly, dramatic changes were in order. More yelling and abuse were not the answer to the problem. At that point, I decided to change how my staff would interact with the basic cadets. Life at Guts Squadron was going to be very different from the traditional BCT experience. Respect and teamwork would become key! I met with my staff prior to taking command of the squadron and gave them an assessment of the situation. I told them it was our mission to train these basic cadets so they were ready to enter the Wing and take on the academic year. I wanted to be tough on the basics but I wanted to use a positive approach—no yelling for the sake of yelling. It's easy to make life difficult for the basics. It's difficult to earn their respect and to obtain positive results. The upper-class understood the leadership approach and the primary objectives. As was tradition, the new staff takes over command of the basic cadets at the evening meal formation. All participants and many tourists are waiting for the command "Fall out and make corrections!" As previously agreed, my staff did not move and did not say a word following the command. The basics immediately knew that things had changed. I'm sure they were waiting for the proverbial shoe to drop.

Following the evening formation, I met with the basics of Guts Squadron. I told them I respected them for their commitment to the United States Air Force Academy. I also told them I hated to lose and I knew there wasn't anyone in the room who wanted to be in last place. I assured them that, if they worked hard, I would recognize the effort. We were going to start with the basics—shoes, uniform and room. We would grow from there. Finally, I told them my staff was waiting for them in the squadron area ready to start the process that would breed success for Guts Squadron and each basic cadet—no verbal abuse but lots of hard work. The environment at Guts Squadron changed immediately. Both staff and basics tackled each day's objectives with great enthusiasm. That spirit transferred to the athletic fields where Guts started to win—a lot! We never asked the basics to do something we wouldn't do. Each upperclass cadet was right there with them (myself included—always). The basics knew I was their squadron commander and not their friend. I knew their names and praised each effort. At the end of three weeks, the Guts basics were ready to enter the Wing and to tackle academics. Their efforts took them from last place to second place. With their momentum, a little more time would have put them in first place. I was very proud of their accomplishments.

CEMENTING LEADERSHIP PRINCIPLES

Following BCT and the start of academics, I was the squadron commander of the 26th Squadron Red Barons as well as the wing operations and training officer. During this time period, I was able to hone the tenets of leadership that would guide my actions during the balance of my professional career.

- Lead by example.
- Establish clear, challenging goals and objectives for the team and each team member.
- Clearly articulate the roles and responsibilities for each member of the team.
- Respect each member of the team. Do not lead through intimidation.
- Admit your mistakes. Learn from them and move on.
- Make the difficult decisions. Procrastinating won't make them any easier.
- Constantly revisit your goals and objectives. Adjust where appropriate.
- Identify and promote your high performing team members. Never stop recruiting top talent.

APPLYING LESSONS LEARNED

After separating from the Air Force in 1979, I enrolled in the School of Law at Boston University. Following graduation in 1982, I became a member of the Connecticut Bar and accepted a position with Aetna Realty as a real estate attorney. During my time at Aetna, I transferred to the Real Estate Investment Group as a businessperson and real estate investment professional. I have never forgotten the leadership lessons I learned that summer as the squadron commander of Guts. The Air Force Academy gave me a rare opportunity to learn a very valuable leadership lesson. This is the essence of the Academy mission. As a real estate investment professional, I have repeatedly used those skills to rescue flailing organizations.

In 1992, I became the regional president of a real estate firm in northern California that was losing clients and money. I left my old job on a Friday and I was at the office for my new job early on Saturday morning. I took the organization back to the basics. I built a solid business plan with clear objectives. I established roles and responsibilities for each member of the organization. I created a policy and procedures manual to guide the actions of the team (think Dash One and checklist). I identified the key members of the team and delegated responsibilities to those individuals. I terminated the employment of sub-par performers and replaced them with high-performing team members. Applying the principles of objectives, discipline, and teamwork, I turned a profit within six months and never had a monthly loss from that point forward.

In 1998, I became the president and chief operating officer of a U.S.-based real estate investment firm. Once again, I went back to my Air Force Academy experiences and applied the principles of leadership I learned as a cadet. My new company was an amalgamation of two organizations. The two disparate organizations never blended. The company had $3 billion of assets under management (all in the United States) and most of their clients were so dissatisfied with their organization they wanted their money back. As with my previous experiences, I initially focused my efforts on rebuilding the leadership team. How they previously conducted business and ran their organization were irrelevant. Business plans, policies and procedures, and roles and responsibilities were the primary focus to establish a solid working foundation.

I sold the firm's existing real estate assets and returned the funds to the dissatisfied clients. The leadership team then established new investment programs and marketed our services to new pension fund clients. Also, the leadership team committed investment of its own capital in each investment fund along with the clients' capital. This obligation focused the efforts of the investment professionals, knowing their money was at risk along with that of our clients.

The personal integrity of the team members was critical to the success of the organization. The firm invested pension fund money in commercial real estate properties on behalf of individual teachers and public state workers. We had a fiduciary responsibility to protect the retirement funds of the individual pension fund participants. Any breach in the integrity of the organization would be detrimental to our ability to grow our firm and capture new sources of capital.

During my rebuilding effort, I was in the process of hiring a young man for a real estate analyst position. During the vetting process, and contrary to the content of his resume, I learned that he did not have an undergraduate degree as was required for the position. He told me that he needed to complete a foreign language requirement before receiving his undergraduate degree. I told him that, if he had explained his situation to me, I would have hired him subject to completing the course work and obtaining his undergraduate degree; however, the misstatement on his resume removed him from consideration. In addition to superior real estate skills, the personal integrity of each team member was critical to our business and clients, without exception.

Upon my retirement, my company had become one of the largest real estate investment firms in the world, with 400 employees, $43 billion of assets under management, and offices in the United States, Europe, and Asia. The success of the organization can be attributed to the leadership skills I learned and practiced at the Air Force Academy.

Way to go, Guts!

21

THE ROAD TO SENIOR EXECUTIVE SERVICE

by Lieutenant General (Ret.) John L. Hudson

Lt. Gen. Jack Hudson served in key positions, both as a general officer and later as a Civil Service-equivalent in the Senior Executive Service. Upon his retirement from the Air Force, Jack continued his distinguished service as Director of the National Museum of the Air Force at Wright-Patterson AFB, Ohio. He reflects on the role character has played in the wide variety of organizations he has led, as well as the exemplars who inspired him.

Jack Hudson
CS-25

There are certain attributes that are in the DNA of a leader of character. I base this assertion on people I've worked for and with over 36 years of active duty, from second lieutenant to lieutenant general;

nearly nine years in the Civil Service; and as a member of the Senior Executive Service.

My first exposure to leaders of character came with my first operational assignment as an A-10 pilot with the 510th Tactical Fighter Squadron (TFS) at Royal Air Force Bentwaters, UK. For most of my time in the 510th, the commander was Lt. Col. Howard Moss, an experienced F-4 pilot and Vietnam combat veteran. Because the squadron had been recently reactivated after 12 years of inactive status, newly assigned pilots came from a wide variety of backgrounds: a few transitioned from the F-4; some had previous time in a variety of aircraft like the OV-10, O-2, T-28, A-7, F-104, F-86, and Cobra helicopters; a few young instructor pilots were from Air Training Command, and there were a handful of second lieutenants fresh out of pilot training. This was the first squadron commander tour for Lt. Col. Moss. At a 510th reunion in Las Vegas in 2018, he told the dinner crowd that, after he first looked at the roster and background of the pilots he would soon lead, his comment to the ops officer was, "Boy, are we in trouble." He and the ops officer would have to figure out how to knit this diverse group into a combat-ready fighting unit, ready to take on the forces of the Warsaw Pact if major conventional war broke out in Europe.

SETTING HIGH STANDARDS

Lt. Col. Moss was tough and demanding, both in the air and on the ground. He set high expectations for how we flew and what he wanted to see on the bombing and gunnery ranges. On every range sortie, we were required to fill out a sheet with our bombing and strafing scores, and he reviewed every score sheet from every pilot on a daily basis. We were expected to do well and, if one of us had issues on a range sortie, he or the ops officer would follow up with the pilot. On the ground, he gave us every bit of responsibility he thought we could handle; if it was too much, he backed off until we were ready. Although he told us in no uncertain terms what our job was, he didn't tell us how do it. Instead, he tasked experienced fighter pilots to mentor the less-experienced pilots. He also built a sense of ownership: he told us all it was not his squadron, but ours. In all things, he motivated us to do our best. He said he never saw people with our kind of background respond with our kind of backbone. He talked about how much of a privilege it was to work with people like us every day. As a result of his strong, hands-on leadership, the squadron quickly came together and became a tight-knit combat-ready unit. In fact, the squadron posted the best overall bombing and strafing scores in the wing for five consecutive six-month periods.

KEYS TO OPERATIONAL SUCCESS

Lt. Col. Moss and his operations officers knew the fighter business stone cold, and they knew how to get the most out of the experience their pilots had. For instance, they put experienced fighter pilots in charge of each of the three flights within the squadron. They also paired up other experienced pilots with the lesser-experienced pilots and had them fly together as much as possible, which resulted in a great mentoring program. My combat partner was Major Rich Ambrose, another experienced combat veteran. Although I was younger and less-experienced, Maj. Ambrose had me fly as flight lead, which enabled me to learn from him and to gain valuable experience more quickly than I would have in another unit.

Why was the newly formed 510th so successful? First and foremost, Lt. Col. Moss was a leader of character: He was tough and demanding, he set high expectations, he gave us lots of responsibility and held us accountable, and he kicked our butts when we needed it. At all times, we knew he had our backs. He and his ops officer owned whatever happened in the squadron—they gave credit whenever something good happened and they took the blame whenever something bad happened. As a result, we bonded as a unit. My experience in the 510th TFS gave me a bedrock foundation for the rest of my time in our USAF. I keep in touch with all these leaders of character to this day.

LEADERSHIP LESSONS IN
THE FLIGHT TEST BUSINESS

Following my assignment to the 510th, I began the one-year course at the USAF Test Pilot School (TPS) at Edwards AFB. During my time in the A-10 Combined Test Force, the USAF Flight Test Center commander was Major General Peter "Peet" Odgers, a highly experienced pilot, test pilot, and combat veteran from Southeast Asia. Gen. Odgers was a Naval Academy grad, Class of 1955, and turned out to be an inspirational role model and mentor in my career.

After completing the TPS, I was assigned to the A-10 Combined Test Force and participated in the Single Seat Night Attack (SSNA) test program with the only two-seat A-10 in existence, the YA-10B. The objective of the SSNA program was to measure front-seat pilot workload while flying representative close air support and interdiction missions at night, at very low level, with the front-seat pilot doing all the mission work and the back-seat pilot functioning as the safety observer. The aircraft was equipped with some equipment not present in the A-10A: a forward-looking infrared pod, a ground-mapping radar pod, a laser designator, a wide-field heads-up display, and an imaging infrared Maverick training missile. Between the additional equipment, night conditions, and low altitude, the pilot's workload was quite high.

As the commander of the Flight Test Center, Gen. Odgers was the senior officer in charge of a vast and complex flight test operation. A highly experienced operational and test pilot, he knew the business from the inside out and set high expectations for our performance. He gave us a lot of leeway to get the flight test missions accomplished, but he also expected we would do this safely and responsibly, in a manner that we were trained to do as TPS graduates. He spent time with us to see how we were doing; however, while he was detail-oriented in terms of understanding and following test missions, he stayed out of our way and trusted us to get things right by using our TPS training to stay safe and successfully execute the test program. On the personal side, he demonstrated a complete commitment to his people and kept track of those he had led and mentored along the way. When I was selected for brigadier, major, and lieutenant general, he sent me a hand-written note each time.

LEARNING TO READ MINDS AND SEE THE FUTURE

From summer 1987 to summer 1990, I was a program element monitor (PEM) in the office of the assistant secretary of the Air Force (Acquisition), an office that worked classified programs. In very early 1989, as a new lieutenant colonel and PEM, I was assigned to the Tri-Service Standoff Attack Missile. Shortly thereafter, I was tasked to build a briefing for the assistant secretary, Mr. Jack Welch, and his military deputy, Lt. Gen. Ronald Yates. The briefing was critical in that it would be used for upcoming testimony to the four congressional authorizations and appropriations committees.

I worked hard on this briefing and was really pleased with it. The time came for me to present the brief to Mr. Welch and Gen. Yates, along with several other PEMs on a Saturday morning. During my brief, Mr. Welch didn't say too much; neither did Gen. Yates—until the end of the briefing when he told me to get out and not come back until I had a briefing that he and Mr. Welch could use, rather than one that was for my personal use. The implication was clear: I had failed to put myself in their shoes and was speaking from my own narrow perspective.

I'd never been thrown out of a briefing before. I trudged back to our office space with our division chief. I felt terrible, but he gave me some helpful guidance and directed me to get back to work. I spent the next week-and-a-half redoing a 20-chart briefing. In retrospect, it was obvious I hadn't considered the fact that they were responsible for hundreds of programs, not just mine; that they needed concise, plain English messages for congressional testimony; and that they depended on me for required charts and back-up material. This second time around, I did everything I could to put myself in the shoes of Mr. Welch and Gen. Yates.

I was rescheduled for my revised presentation, along with all the others who failed the first time through. I gave the briefing and again Mr. Welch did not say much, and neither did Gen. Yates. At the end of the brief, Gen. Yates told me, "Get out of here. Go back and tell all the other PEMs what you did to put together a briefing we can actually use for congressional testimony."

Gen. Yates taught me an extremely valuable lesson: how to read minds and see the future. As impossible as that may seem, he taught me how to put myself in my boss's shoes, as well as my boss's boss's shoes. By looking at the issue from their perspective, I'd be able to understand the breadth of their responsibility. That would help me make the connection between what I knew as the program expert, and what they needed as the Air Force spokespersons for congressional testimony. Although Gen. Yates never spelled it out in explicit terms, his one comment at the end of that disastrous first briefing made me realize what I needed to do. But, just as important, his one comment at the end of my redo fully restored my confidence. He was truly a leader of character.

DEVELOPING FUTURE LEADERS

From early summer 1993 to early summer 1994, I had the privilege of serving as the executive officer to Air Force Vice Chief of Staff General Michael Carns, USAFA Class of '59. Assignments like this are tremendous learning opportunities; I was able to learn up close from a very highly experienced leader at the top of the USAF. As Gen. Carns' executive officer, I was able to sit in on meetings with general officers and civilian equivalents to discuss a variety of issues, all from a variety of Air Staff perspectives.

First and foremost, Gen. Carns was a mentor. For instance, he was an absolute operational expert. Whenever he came across issues regarding operational requirements, he would meet with the experts, from three-stars down to action officers, and ask them what they thought the requirements were. Then he'd lead them through the process of "peeling the onion back" to identify what the essential requirements were, as opposed to what they wanted to have. By doing that, he was able to help these officers make a distinction between the acceptable and perfect solutions. As a result, they left with a better understanding of the true requirements.

Throughout the learning process, Gen. Carns treated his people with dignity and respect. Witnessing his deep experience and keen intellect was one thing, but watching the way he schooled and mentored his people was an even more valuable learning experience for me. This leader of character knew he was training the future senior leadership of our Air Force and took that responsibility very seriously.

LEADERS OF CHARACTER IN ACTION

On August 15th, 2005, I began what would be my last active-duty assignment, as a lieutenant general and commander of the Aeronautical Systems Center (ASC) at Wright-Patterson AFB Ohio. During my time as ASC commander, I was very fortunate to have leaders of character throughout my organization. A mix of military and civilian leaders, some were in place when I began as commander; some I hired during my four-year tenure.

I've often reflected on why these people were so good at what they did and why they worked together so well. My conclusion is that, while they came from various backgrounds, they all shared three attributes I highly valued: integrity, truth telling, and full engagement. For example, my chief of financial management (FM) was Ms. Ann McDermott, a member of the SES. As ASC's FM, she teamed well with our acquisition wing leaders, our program managers, and the staffs in the offices of the assistant secretary of the Air Force (Acquisition) and the assistant secretary of the Air Force (Financial Management). With Ann in charge, I had no worries about our budget execution because she knew the business so well. Her integrity was rock-solid: during our periodic budget reviews with the Pentagon staff, our program managers, and warfighter customers, we consistently justified the funds we needed and turned back funds we knew we couldn't execute. As a result, the Air Force knew we were honest and truthful regarding what money we needed, and what we could turn back. Ann was also superb at "truth telling" with respect to budget execution—there were no hidden agendas. As a result, she was highly trusted by all and gave our organization great credibility.

LEARNING FROM FAILURE

As I was approaching retirement in August 2009, I heard that the position of deputy director of the National Museum of the USAF was opening up. I applied for it, was offered the job, and took it. After serving as the deputy for a year, I assumed the position of director for the next eight years. In that role, I was responsible for 96 civilian Air Force employees, 600 volunteers, the USAF historical collection, and more than one million square feet of museum space. In addition, we had about one million visitors per year. It was a great opportunity, and I thoroughly enjoyed the challenge.

Soon after I became the director, the inspector general for the Air Force Materiel Command informed me that the museum had not had a thorough IG inspection for 20+ years, and that we could expect one very soon. While no one welcomes the thought of an IG inspection, I knew from experience that it's a good way to review practices and procedures. The IG came and did a very thorough inspection of the entire museum. We did well on most everything except for the Logistics Capability Assessment Program, which we failed. The primary shortcomings were in the Restoration Division, which got failing grades in seven of ten areas. Our Exhibits Division took some major hits as well, based on shortfalls in shop equipment maintenance. This was all my responsibility. I owned it. Now what to do?

The easy part was publicly recognizing all the people who did well in the inspection: the outstanding performers and the outstanding teams.

For the areas that did not do well, I sat down with the division chiefs, my GS-13 direct reports in Restoration and Exhibits, and we talked through the content of the IG report and where our shortfalls were. My approach was not to fix the blame, but to fix the problem. I emphasized at every opportunity that this was a learning opportunity for us, that we'd take every IG recommendation seriously, act on it, move forward, and get better. We'd keep what we did well, and fix what needed to be fixed. I involved them in the solution by asking them what they thought we needed to answer the IG recommendations and improve going forward. I talked with the entire museum team at our director's calls as well.

In Restoration, we peeled back every one of the seven areas we failed and came up with a plan to get ready for the reinspection that would come in about nine months. Our Restoration Division chief, GS-13 Mr. Roger Deere, led his people well. He took ownership of the issues, was fully engaged, and got all the shortfalls fixed with great integrity. I also sat down with Exhibits and went through their IG write-ups. It turned out that some of our highly experienced employees were maintaining the heavy machinery without consulting manuals. In some cases, these machines were hand-me-downs from other units on base, and didn't come with owner manuals. But rather than make excuses, we used this as an opportunity to do a hard analysis on what we really needed to get the work done. As a result, we got rid of unneeded machines, found manuals for the machines we really needed, and made them part of the safety and maintenance routines. As a result, the Exhibits Division work area became safer, cleaner, and more open.

Looking back, what made us successful was taking full ownership of the shortfalls, viewing our failures as learning and improvement opportunities, and avoiding playing the blame game. The fact that our leaders were willing to step up and own the problems with a positive learning attitude was key to enabling our people at the working level to successfully correct the deficiencies and move forward.

MANAGING WORKLOAD

The museum was open every day of the year except for major holidays. However, we also held events on weekends, particularly for educational outreach programs to tell the USAF story to the public and to inspire young people toward the Air Force and build their interest in science, technology, engineering, and math. While our special events earned rave reviews, they came at the cost of significant overtime hours for our Special Events Division and our Operations Division. Then, Headquarters Air Force Materiel Command cut the number of people on our staff. Obviously, something had to give.

I tasked our chief of special events, GS-13 Teresa Montgomery, to pull together a team to develop a set of recommendations for prioritizing after-hour and weekend events to provide the best benefit to the mission, while minimizing resources. I knew this would be a big job, particularly since it would be hard to say "no" to after-hour and weekend event requests we had previously said "yes" to. But I knew that, of all my nine division chiefs, Teresa could develop a new policy that would fit our needs. She was and is a leader of character.

Teresa built a small team of division chiefs most affected by after-hour and weekend events, to include Public Affairs. She inventoried all the special events we did after hours, on weekends, and during normal operating hours. She broke them down into tiers of value for the mission and tiers of cost to resources (labor hours on our people). She did this in a way that fully involved her team members. She came back to me periodically for heading checks. Eventually she worked her draft policy proposal with all the museum division chiefs, took inputs, and came up with a final draft. She briefed the plan at a meeting of all division chiefs, our deputy director, and me. After going around the table and getting a head nod from everyone there, I accepted the proposal and we made it museum policy. This became a major improvement in how we processed event requests; it gave us a means to say "yes" or "no" when it came time to make decisions about what to do with these requests.

What did Teresa have that made her and her team successful? She knew the special events business extremely well; she had a great background in planning and executing events and in the protocol world, too. She was tough when she needed to be and was always approachable when someone needed help. She knew how to be a great teammate, how to listen, and when to listen. Ms. Teresa Montgomery is a leader of character.

THE MEMPHIS BELLE: MATCHING REQUIREMENTS AGAINST RESOURCES

In the 2014-2015 timeframe, our museum team began plan a 75-year commemoration of the *Memphis Belle* and her crew. We would commemorate the B-17's 25th mission by restoring and displaying the original aircraft, along with constructing many exhibits to tell the story of the *Memphis Belle* and strategic bombardment in WW II. Our team recommended placing the fully restored aircraft on an elevated platform, with exhibits around the walking area, so that the visiting public could get a good view of the ball turret and the bomb bay. The restoration was a difficult challenge, given the requirement to design, construct, and install the exhibits for the grand opening by 17 May 2018. Our original goal was to get the aircraft to look exactly like it did on 17 May 1943, on both the inside and the outside. For example, we went to great lengths to ensure that the flight control cables in the aircraft were the correct configuration for the aircraft in May 1943, even though no one could see them from the outside when viewing the display.

About a year out from the grand opening of the *Memphis Belle* exhibit, it became apparent that our Restoration team wouldn't be able to complete the full exterior and interior work prior to the grand opening. Our Restoration division chief, GS-13 Mr. Roger Deere, and his team and other members of the *Memphis Belle* team developed a very sensible alternative: make the exterior restoration the baseline requirement and complete the interior restoration over time, once the aircraft was on display. By rephasing our requirements against our limited resources,

Roger enabled us to remain within budget and avoid running people into the ground. The key was to make a distinction between the real operational requirements and the desired requirements—much like Gen. Carns taught me years ago. As a result, we were able to restore the exterior safely and accurately, while still meeting our deadline.

The second major part of the exhibit was envisioned to be the large number of exhibit display cases that contained, for example, photos of the crew, their uniforms, and other memorabilia that were donated to the museum: maps; a Norden bombsight; and many other items and wall boards with text that would tell the story. All these had to be designed, built, and installed. As with the aircraft restoration, it quickly became obvious that it would take large amounts of overtime and stress to get all these done. Some in the museum said we had to do this. Others (me included) believed it was too much. I tasked the team to come up with a prioritized list of exhibits and to estimate what the resources were to do each one. We met weekly with the project manager and our division chiefs to review progress and work to go. Our exhibits division chief, GS-13 Mr. Greg Hassler, did a superb job of working with his employees to optimize the normal work hours with some overtime to get the Block 1 cases designed, built, and installed safely, with no serious injuries or accidents, and on time.

We had an immensely successful grand opening. The aircraft looked terrific, as did the exhibit cases. Thousands of people saw the *Memphis Belle* and the exhibits firsthand. By prioritizing requirements for exhibits, and deferring the "nice to haves," we got the most important ones done, we optimized overtime, and did it all safely. Mr. Deere and Mr. Hassler were leaders of character in the way they presented viable alternatives, worked with their people, and got the baseline work done safely and accurately.

THE DNA IN LEADERS OF CHARACTER

Leaders of character are needed in all organizations, regardless of size or scope of responsibility. Everyone from the lowest ranking airman and civil service member to the chief of staff and the highest civil service member can and must be a leader of character.

Leaders of character own whatever happens in his/her unit. They don't blame others or shirk responsibility. They give credit to their people for all the things that go well, while taking the blame for things that do not go well. Furthermore, leaders of character are willing to publicly acknowledge organizational shortcomings. By doing that, unit members know their commander/boss is shouldering the responsibility, will take action to fix the problems, and make things better moving forward.

Leaders of character are teachers and mentors. They know their business and know it well. They know they must grow their replacements and take that responsibility seriously.

Leaders of character set clear expectations for unit performance and hold people accountable.

Leaders of character are great teammates and a joy to work with.

Leaders of character have open and transparent agendas. There's nothing hidden. They work toward the greater good.

Leaders of character listen well, especially to subject matter experts. They know how much or how little to get into the details, and how much leeway to give those who work for them.

Leaders of character match resources with what they are asking their people to do. What A-10 squadron commander would ask his/her pilots to go into battle without bullets in the ammo drum? The commander is there to serve the people in the unit, not the other way around.

OWN YOUR FUTURE

For the Class of 2023: every second lieutenant should strive to be a leader of character. A second lieutenant in UPT, for example, is not in command of a unit but nonetheless owns his/her performance in UPT, including how he/she works with others. No one is alone in UPT; students must work together to succeed. In the formation phase, students get together well ahead of the flight briefing, talk things through, and then plan for how they'll meet mission requirements when they brief with the instructor pilot(s). The second lieutenants own their own performance—there's no room to blame others or weather conditions for their own shortcomings.

I congratulate the Class of 2023 upon their graduation and commissioning. I wish each the best in their journey as leaders of character, in all facets of their lives, during their active-duty career and beyond.

22

FROM AIR FORCE OFFICER TO CATHOLIC PRIEST

by Monsignor Stephen J. Rossetti

*Following his service in the Air Force, Steve Ros-
setti devoted his life to attending to spiritual needs
and leading his congregants. He contemplated the
parallels between his service as an Air Force leader
and as a priest in the Catholic Church, as well as
the importance and role of character development
at the Academy.*

Steve Rossetti
CS-37

Years ago, before I became a priest, I remember speaking to an
old military chaplain who said that service academy training is
a lot like the old seminary formation, just without the God part. His
thought stuck with me these 40-plus years. There were indeed a lot of
similarities between our training at USAFA and the former regimented
seminary program.

Both have a heavily structured daily regimen. Such a regimen does
not allow for significant personal problems. One could not have major

problems and survive the system. There is no time for it. When we were cadets, I don't even recall knowing that there was a counseling center. I suppose there was, but it sure wasn't highlighted. If you had a problem, you were expected to suck it up, stop whining, and move forward.

I don't think that was all bad. It didn't allow for a lot of the narcissism that I see so much of in today's society. There are several research studies suggesting that narcissism is rising today. At USAFA, there was simply no time to do a lot of self-focusing. We had a structured regimen to follow, a mission to accomplish, and we were expected to follow it and to contribute. As they said, "Lead, follow, or get out of the way." Perhaps that's why only slightly more than half of our entering class ended up graduating. The rigorous training weeded out many.

My mother, God rest her, said of my brother (Class of 1970) and myself that there was something different about us. She meant it in a positive way. To this day, my brother Paul and I share a bond of being part of the "Short Blue Line." He loved his time at the Academy and went on to become a fighter pilot, flying missions in Vietnam and testing the F-16. I did well at the Academy but always wondered about the whole discipline thing, the military mentality, and what seemed to me a lack of willingness to look more deeply into ideas and issues. I recall being on Operation Third Lieutenant and our host junior officer looking at me quizzically and saying, "You're a thinker." I don't think he meant it as a compliment.

It's going on 50 years later and I am now a happy attendee at the annual NCLS, held each February on site at the Academy. I love it. The quality of speakers and the inspiring messages delivered by such heroic people are truly a gift.

Some of the very best memories I have of my time at the Academy and in the Air Force are the truly outstanding people I came to know. Who does not know Mal Wakin, Irv Rokke, Norty Schwartz, and many others? Their inspiration and example taught us what ethics and leadership were supposed to look like. Courses are fine, but it was the example of such stellar people that taught us what we needed to know.

I have been fortunate on two occasions in the last decade to spend some time on the "Ice," i.e., Antarctica, as the chaplain. I was even weathered in at the South Pole, a not-uncommon experience, and spent Christmas at the end of the earth. It was a privilege to celebrate Christmas Mass and actually baptize an adult at the Mass, a very unusual set of circumstances, to be sure.

But, during my nearly two months on the Ice, I found myself gravitating toward and hanging out with the military folks. I was the chaplain to all and made my rounds diligently, but I especially enjoyed hanging out with the men and women of the Air Force and Navy detachments. I found them to be a cut above. They were dedicated, kind, professional, and worked together as a harmonious team. It reminded me what I missed after having left the Air Force some years before that. I missed the people, their teamwork, and their sense of mission. They were just fine people.

I was also privileged to return to USAFA a few years ago and to be one of the invited speakers at NCLS. Never did I imagine that I would be standing in one of the large lecture halls addressing a roomful of cadets. It was a thrill, to be sure. I even enjoyed being presented with the "plaque" in appreciation.

I began my talk by saying that I was a proud member of the Class of 1973, and I am a life-time member of the Association of Graduates. As is typical when I write my presentations, I try to imagine what it must be like to be in the audience during one of my talks. What must a cadet think to look up and see a graduate in a Roman Collar, an ordained Catholic priest? I was indeed the first USAFA graduate to become a Catholic priest, although there have been a number since.

So I began my talk by admitting it might seem a little odd to transition from being an Air Force officer to the Catholic priesthood. However,

I don't think it really was. Many of our priestly vocations come from the ranks of the military. I said it wasn't such a big jump between selflessly serving one's country to serving a higher power, the living God. It wasn't such a big jump between holding up values of dedication, service, professionalism, and teamwork of the military and the values of Christian ministry. I thought, "A good soldier makes a good Christian."

In fact, I have noticed over the years that there is a common undercurrent among many of the talks at the leadership seminar. Many of the speakers imply, likely unconsciously, that they serve their country as a type of spiritual "calling." They may or may not invoke their God, but the implication is that they will serve the cause of freedom and the people of their country, even if it means sacrificing their lives. This is very much the spirit of the Christian martyrs.

At this year's NCLS, I had a few spare moments and enjoyed chatting with a third classman and a doolie in Arnold Hall. We got onto the subject of service and calling. Both of them spoke of being at USAFA as a call from God. I found it edifying.

After all, what is the difference between a mercenary and a professional soldier? The line can be razor-thin, but it is a critical line not to cross. Yes, the soldier is paid and yes, he or she hopes to be rewarded for his/her service. But the true professional soldier ought to be dedicated to a higher cause, a cause worth dying for. Some of them will make the ultimate sacrifice.

This is especially true in the USA. I believe this country has a special calling from God to promote human dignity, freedom, and our democratic values. We fight tyranny in all its forms and have come to the aid of beleaguered people around the globe. We have not always been faithful to that calling, as failings in such places as My Lai and Abu Ghraib testify. But the organization continues to self-correct and moves on.

The Academy's NCLS is an example of the military trying to learn from its mistakes and to instill in its members a sense of service, mission, and ethical leadership. It is the nature of our lives always to be in danger of crossing the razor-thin line and devolving into mercenaries. Thus, we need constantly to hold up a sense of mission and service to a higher cause.

America is that higher cause. I believe it has a divine calling. We are to be a beacon of freedom and a force to promote the innate dignity of all people. We do not always live up to our calling, but we keep trying.

In recent years, there has been a rallying cry of "America First." It is true that we cannot serve others if our country has been rendered impotent and ethically adrift. But part of what America is, and what makes America great, is precisely a sense of service to others outside of ourselves and beyond our borders. Our country will not truly be America if we do not assist those in need, whether it is those suffering from tyranny, natural disasters, or from any force that would threaten their human worth.

The values I learned at USAFA and from my brothers and sisters in the military were values of service, mission, teamwork, humility, and kindness. From the perspective of a Catholic priest, the foundation for a solid priestly life rests on such values. I received good training from USAFA for a life of dedicated service, first serving my country and then serving my Lord. I told the cadets in my presentation that service as a priest and service as an Air Force officer are not so different.

But back to the old Catholic priest who said a service academy training was like the old, disciplined seminary without God. I would suggest that, for many of us, God was an important part of our lives from day one when they shaved our heads. I happily attended daily Mass at the Academy and, providentially, my squadron CS-37 was very close to the chapel. It was a very short walk at 5:50 a.m. up the little ramp and into the downstairs chapel. As those two young cadets in Arnold Hall told me a few months ago, they were at the Academy because they believed God called them to serve. Looking back, there is no doubt in my mind that that is why I was there as well.

I have grown in gratitude for this "vocation" as a cadet and as an AF military officer. If I had to do it again, I would be in Jack's Valley sucking dirt rather than in Woodstock smoking dope. I treasure the friendships I made. I am grateful for the examples of great leadership and upright living that so many officers and enlisted showed me. I am grateful for the formation I received at the expense of the dedication and service of many others. And this grateful graduate expects to be in the front row at next year's NCLS. I am anxious to sit among the cadets once again and to be inspired by the heroes of our day.

23

RELATIONSHIPS MATTER

by The Honorable Denny J. Merideth

The bonds we share in the profession of arms are unique. The relationships we establish with peers, subordinates, and superiors are critical in accomplishing the mission, regardless of specialty. From that perspective, relationships are at the heart of the military ethos. Denny Merideth gave a real-world example of the importance of one particular relationship, and how it motivated him to become part of a rescue from the chaos of Afghanistan.

Denny Merideth
CS-08

The members of the Class of 1973 were raised and cultivated by the "Greatest Generation." Shaped by the Great Depression and the ravages of World War II, our parents were instrumental in molding the character of their sons who walked up the "Bring Me Men" Ramp in June of 1969.

The life lessons my father handed down were constantly on display in my youth. There was no flash of brilliance, but rather a daily example of moral character and leadership tackling the challenges of raising a family, building a business, forming a community, and making his part of the world a better place. He had a dynamic impact on everyone he met, and his depth of character was unmistakable. Of all the traits he inspired, building relationships was the most memorable. He always brought out the best in those around him through a sincere respect for the individual. Perhaps this was rooted somewhat in the way he dealt with the losses of fellow airmen when he was a B-17 pilot. Regardless of the motivation, his respect for others was unmistakable and, in return, he was given a level of respect that was humbling.

The Academy built upon the foundation laid by my parents and reinforced the tenets of leadership demonstrated by my father. The Academy was the first step in a long, fascinating, and varied career in government service. My Air Force career was fairly typical of those of my classmates, but I was also fortunate enough to serve in the Missouri Legislature as a state representative, as well as a diplomat in the U.S. State Department. Along the way, there was time dedicated to service on school boards, hospital boards, and in community development organizations where forming relationships were critical to success. Although farming and coaching rugby were lifelong passions, spending time with my family has undoubtedly been the most rewarding.

Setting your sights on a goal is crucial to moving forward, but effectively adapting to change leads to opportunities never imagined. I had always wanted to be a fighter pilot but ended up as a first assignment IP at Laughlin AFB. To say I was disappointed belies what I perceived to be a devasting setback. But, while I could not have known it at the time, that assignment was not only a great learning experience, but it also led me into the international arena: after three great years at Laughlin, I was offered the opportunity to go to the American Embassy in Amman, Jordan as an instructor with the Jordanian Air Force. So, as a young captain, I found myself assigned to the Military Assistance Program in the embassy. The opportunity to interact directly with combat-experienced

Jordanian leaders was invaluable. The flying was as exhilarating as the environment challenging and the relationships delicate.

The positive impact of building trusting relationships soon became apparent in what would normally be considered a mundane aspect of the job. The International Military Education and Training (IMET) program had become a path for funneling favors within the Jordanian military services and failure of trainees was truly epidemic. The waste of time and resources adversely impacted the growth of capabilities and damaged the reputation of the Jordanians within the U.S. military communities. The solution was not complicated, but instilling the proper attitude among testers and eliminating the propensity for senior officers to dole out favors required gaining the support of officers who previously were not prone to change the status quo. Establishing a level of mutual trust and respect led to adapting the process that moved the Jordanians from an appalling failure rate to one of the highest success rates within the IMET programs. Relationships mattered in building bridges and success.

Flying fighters soon became a reality. Following the "Outstanding F-15 Graduate Award" at Luke, I was assigned to Holloman AFB and enjoyed the benefits of flying fighters in the 1980s. A follow-on assignment as an IP at Luke AFB ensued, but soon the harsh reality of life intervened—my father was killed in a tractor accident on his farm in Missouri. I submitted paperwork to get out of the Air Force to help my family but, at that time, the Air Force was not letting fighter pilots separate from the service due to the pilot shortage. Again, adapting to the conditions, an air liaison officer job at Fort Campbell, Kentucky presented itself as a workable alternative. Driving back and forth to the farm in Missouri every weekend for two years permitted me to contribute to the family farm in a tangible fashion. As it turned out, I was fortunate, in that I could not have asked for more fantastic leadership and mentoring than I got at Fort Campbell. I had a chance to build relationships across services and view different organizational perspectives, leading to development in both military and personal growth. Some of the best mentoring came from senior NCOs, people who were deeply committed to their troops, their organizations, and their country. They were great patriots.

Following flying assignments to Iceland and Saudi Arabia, retirement provided the opportunity to move back to Missouri and settle into farming. A few months later. the state representative for the district resigned, which generated a special election to fill the empty seat. My father had been active in local politics and had defeated a corrupt consortium of individuals who were poised to slide into the vacated seat. To preserve my father's legacy, I felt the right thing to do was to oppose this same group and run for the open position as an independent. This was a significant challenge, as there had not been an independent elected to the Missouri House of Representatives in more than a hundred years. It was indeed an uphill battle. In the run-up to the election, consideration was given to the principal issues: what were the needs of 30,000 constituents? What resources were available to bring to bear to address those needs? How could the lives of all the constituents be improved? Winning the election with only 52% of the vote was simply the first challenge. There was a great deal of work to be done on all fronts, not the least of which was to build constructive relationships with people who could help me be the best possible representative.

Doing an honest job as an elected representative is challenging enough in itself, but being an independent in an equally divided chamber presents another level of trials. The true job consisted of two principal responsibilities. The first was as a legislator. Because the legislative process is a well-defined one, that was relatively straightforward—it was time-consuming but obvious; sponsoring legislation, opposing legislation, debating, and voting in House sessions. The second responsibility was to serve as a representative of the people in the district. Although a bit more nuanced, the essence was to really get to know the people, their concerns, promote their issues, and help solve their problems. I quickly discovered that, even at the state level, I had an amazing degree of access to people and resources to help my constituents. Building a great network of people required sincerity in relationships with a level of trust that could help on a wide range of issues, including honest feedback.

I also feel fortunate that, during my tenure in the House, the idea of working together in pursuit of good governance was everyone's primary objective, regardless of party. The partisan divide experienced in today's arena was only beginning and serious debate among colleagues was still possible. Regardless of how heated the debates were in committee hearings and on the floor, we could still relate to each other as human beings and build constructive relationships in the pursuit of good governance.

As in the Air Force, in elected office I found that one's ability to build trusting relationships—the ones that help you get things done for the common good—rests upon personal credibility, and that is largely a function of integrity. While integrity is one of our Air and Space Force Core Values, it is sometimes more difficult to find in other arenas. But, while it may be more difficult to find, I saw that when you go into any job with integrity, people are very quick to recognize that aspect of your personality. That is when they want to work with you because they know they can trust you. Building relationships mattered.

As with many of our classmates, 9/11 fundamentally changed my outlook. I began to consider questions like "What can I do? Should I be doing something different? Is there a way I can become part of a larger team that can have an impact in these difficult times?" Having a degree in international affairs and serving in Jordan with the U.S. Embassy in the late-'70s, the possibility of joining the State Department was something that piqued my interest. So one day I literally jumped off a combine on the farm and went to take the Foreign Service exam.

The whole application process was onerous, but you have to respect the State Department for the thoroughness of their selection and training. While I was going through the application process with State, I was still serving in the Missouri House, as well as being heavily involved on the farm. But even with 20/20 hindsight I would not have done anything different, even though I ended up starting on the bottom rung in the Foreign Service. I found myself immersed in a fascinating career that was different from anything I could have imagined.

As with all incoming Foreign Service Officers, my initial assignment was in the Consular Section. A willingness to get involved led to a myriad of opportunities for speaking engagements, representative events throughout the areas of assignments, and direct support to embassy leadership. While the technical aspects of the job were new, I quickly discovered that, as in the Air Force and in the Missouri Legislature, relationships were the key to getting things done, and that integrity and technical competence were the keys to building those trusting relationships. For me, as a political officer with additional responsibilities in the political-military arena, the opportunities were endless.

I have heard it said that "only 20 percent of the job is substance. The other 80 percent is relationships." While that may be a bit overstated, there is an important truth there. It's not that intelligence and technical competence aren't important, because they are. But, in terms of getting things done, you cannot do it on your own, particularly in the diplomatic arena. From that perspective, trusting relationships are truly a force multiplier. For example, one of my State Department jobs entailed working with our NATO allies on the development and operational deployment of the F-35. A great deal of time and effort had been spent building a high level of trust with both those supporting the program and those in opposition. These relationships proved extremely valuable, as during parliamentary debates on the F-35 in the Netherlands, I received a series of late-night texts from parliamentarians asking for my views on everything from system capabilities to sustainability. I clearly was not the foremost technical expert on the weapon system, but I was viewed as a reliable partner who would provide an honest assessment.

Relationships mattered and, in a close debate, were critical to any success I may have had.

In 2009, I spent time in Uruzgan Province of Afghanistan with the Dutch. In 2010, I began a year assigned as the senior political officer in the British-run Provincial Reconstruction Team (PRT) in Helmand Province, Afghanistan. PRTs are multi-national offices staffed by military officers, diplomats, and subject matter experts supporting reconstruction efforts, in this case located in Lashkargah, in the southwestern region. It was during my service in the PRT that I forged one of the most meaningful and consequential relationships of my career.

At that time, Helmand was one of the most politically and militarily unsettled areas in the entire country. It was the poppy growing capital of Afghanistan, and with Pakistan on the border and numerous transportation routes, there was a great deal of opium production. And, of course, along with the opium production came a great deal of money and corruption. As the senior U.S. representative and head of the political section, it was important for me to be out in the countryside, meeting with a variety of local officials, understanding the situation on the ground, and coming up with viable reconstruction strategies. One of the primary responsibilities was also to mentor the provincial governor. I was able to build a special trusting relationship with the governor and travel through the majority of the province, with the exception of the areas controlled by the Taliban. But none of that would have been possible without my Afghan interpreter, Arif.

Arif was a young man who was highly experienced, having also served as my predecessor's interpreter. He was highly educated, graduating from Herat University in western Afghanistan. At one point, he had shown an interest in running for the parliament, because he was a very patriotic man and dedicated to improving conditions within his country. Arif was not only articulate and highly fluent in English, but he also knew the regional politics and had his own relationships with local leaders, which enabled me to reach out in ways that I never would have been able to do with a less-qualified interpreter. Trust and honesty were also extremely important to him. These were not only fundamental values we shared, but they also gave him insights into whom I could meet with to make a difference in people's lives. I'm reluctant to call Arif an interpreter because he was more like a co-equal partner.

In all of the third-world countries I have been in, I have found that people are universally astute in deciding with whom they can build a trusting and constructive relationship. They do not need to spend a great deal of time with you to decide whether you are sincere and can be trusted. In fact, most of the people from these areas I have met are able to read you in a matter of minutes, not days. They are able to read your tone and body language and will decide very quickly whether you are someone they want to deal with. That really came into play in Afghanistan when Arif and I met with all manner of contacts, including local officials, community leaders, Taliban, and drug traffickers. Seeing problems was easy, and finding solutions was complex and difficult. Paths often were dependent upon our ability to establish a constructive dialogue. For instance, there was one village in the northwest part of the province that was controlled by the Taliban. It was pretty isolated and well outside of provincial influence. But we constantly met with two of the leaders and had success in improving conditions in the village. It was through their influence that we were able to reopen the road so goods and services could begin flowing into the village. That was due to the kind of relationship we were able to establish and coming across as a trustworthy interlocutor was a critical prerequisite.

During my time in the PRT we went out on a variety of missions, lasting anywhere from a few days to a few weeks. Arif and I lived side by side, sometimes sleeping on cots in the same room. Of course, when we were not out on a mission, he lived downtown with his family, but we were together much of the time. Our bonds were not only based on common interests, but on genuine friendship.

Every morning we began the day going over our reports and our plans in a nearby area that was full of beautiful flowers, and we would just talk—we called it our "garden time." We would cover local developments, national directions, communications that were driven by the coalition, the Afghans, the Taliban, and the Pakistanis to prepare for what was taking place that day. Garden time was a great education for me. But, more important, our garden time helped deepen our relationship. Arif's openness and genuine friendship went well beyond what you would expect of a normal interpreter. When I left Afghanistan in June of 2012, I knew I was leaving behind not only a trusted colleague, but a close friend. We stayed in touch only occasionally after I left. Leaving one job, my focus has always been on the next, with serious reflection on lessons learned but an eye to what is ahead.

Adapting to events with the illness of my mother-in-law, we retired from State to live in Colorado Springs, putting together a couple of businesses and coaching rugby as a volunteer at the Academy.

When the provinces began to fall to the Taliban in the summer of 2021, my concern for Arif and his family grew. I reached out to both Arif and Naeem, another one of my interpreters from the PRT. Naeem had moved from the PRT to the U.S. Embassy in Kabul and had worked directly with the State Department, so I hoped he would have some useful information to share.

Naeem got back to me right away. He and his family received their Special Immigrant Visas only a few months prior to the chaos and had already settled in Philadelphia. Naeem was able to get me Arif's WhatsApp contact information and we began a stream of communication as he was struggling to stay one step ahead of the Taliban. Arif was a high-priority target for the Taliban due to his work with the coalition in Kandahar and Helmand provinces, as well as his work with the government. He and his family had been constantly moving to evade capture. I was not able to learn much more because, given the threat, I needed to limit our communication to the bare essentials: where he was and what he needed. But I also wanted to give him an avenue of hope, to know that somebody was caring for him and doing what they could to help him and his family.

The chaos in Afghanistan was complicated by the lack of information available through our own civilian and military resources. To find a way to assist Arif, I began contacting a long list of offices and individuals. Through contacts across civilian, military, political, Non-Governmental Organizations, and allied officials, a picture began to evolve on the entire situation. It was literally only through relationships that this became possible. Senators and congressmen listened with an honest desire to assist but were not able to provide any insight at all. An ambassador from the UK was extremely responsive and helpful as the Brits were escorting high-risk Afghans to the airport. A Danish ambassador was on the ground at the airport and was the ultimate solution to getting Arif and his family safely on a plane to Copenhagen. Upon contacting an individual in a certain agency, he advised that the awareness I had was better than anything they had been able to put together, which did not make me feel any better. It was a frustrating time with a few weeks of sleepless nights, a lot of time on the phone, and a lot of time communicating through calls, emails, and messaging.

Keeping hope alive during this ordeal was imperative as the eventual outcome was never a guarantee. Primary contacts in State were instrumental, along with other agencies and allies in getting Arif and his family out. Still, it quickly became apparent that simply going through official channels was not going to get the results needed, so unofficial contacts were imperative. Looking back, connecting the dots would have never happened without an extensive network of great people stepping up. The conversations generally ran along these lines: "Hey, I know Joe who is doing this, and Bill is over there as well, he might be able to help." So, it was not just the people I knew who were working Arif's situation, but the people in their networks as well. Each of these individuals were able to contribute one or two pieces of information that could help build a bigger picture.

It is one thing to understand difficulties people are experiencing, but it is another thing to recognize the highs and lows they are going through. The first day or so I was communicating with Arif I sensed a relative fatalism that seemed to be dampening his spirits. But then there was a day that it was obvious that his hope had been revived. I could feel in his communication that he felt he was going to get out and that his family was going to be safe. But the next day he told me he had just gotten word that 800 Taliban had come to Kabul from Helmand and 3,000 more from Kandahar. Their primary mission was to go house to house and search for people the Taliban considered to be high-value targets. I could see that he was convinced that, if they did not get out of there soon, they had no hope for survival. Having somebody that you were so close to for so long go through that was absolutely heartbreaking. It was also incredibly frustrating not to be able to put my arms around him, give him a hug of encouragement, or take the family by the hand and lead them out of there myself. All credit goes to the Danes who helped get the family through the chaos and on a plane to Denmark.

The next ten months for Arif, his wife Zia, and their seven children were spent in refugee camps and housing. Even though he was in the special immigrant visa process, the wheels seemed to move slowly. However, they were safe and had a destination. My wife, Heidi, and I had video calls with Arif and his family on a weekly basis. We were preparing our home for them to stay as they transitioned into the States. On July 4th, 2022, Heidi and I picked up Arif, Zia and the children at Denver International Airport and brought them to our home. Tears were plentiful as they began to describe their journey and disbelief of the welcoming in our home. The children range from 2 to 16 and are amazingly strong. Their future is now bright as they look to become doctors, lawyers, and engineers. They have a vision, they have confidence, and they are unique survivors who will add to the mosaic of American families.

As I look back on a long and varied career, I would say the key to any success I may have had was due to relationships—not just the relationships I built within my own organization, but in other organizations as well. As it turns out, building relationships within your own community is fairly easy to do. For instance, if you are in a squadron or even in the fighter community at large, you have a great deal in common with the people around you. But to accomplish almost any mission, you need to collaborate with other communities that you are not be familiar with. My first exposure to that was my assignment to Jordan, and it was particularly important, due to the international nature of the job. But the same principles apply, regardless of where you are working.

There are many factors today that make it difficult to form meaningful relationships, from an overreliance on electronic communication to the very nature of social media. The reality is that it is much easier and simpler to communicate via text, emails, and PowerPoint slides than it is to actively seek out other people and engage in face-to-face conversations. Whether you are dealing with another young lieutenant, an airman or even someone of higher rank, it is easier to retreat behind a computer and send an email, rather than relying on face-to-face dialogue. In my experience, that's how organizations become stovepiped and unable to work across organizational boundaries. From that perspective, the most successful organizations understand that working outside the community is sometimes more important than working inside the community. So I would encourage anyone starting out in their career to never overlook the importance of building strong, trusting, relationships. Relationships matter; respect, sincerity, and trust are essential.

24

MEDICINE AND LEADERSHIP

by Dr. William J. Drury, MD

Dr. Bill Drury describes how his experiences at the Academy were fundamental in his becoming a leader in the medical community. His call for wise and compassionate decision-making goes to the heart of character-based leadership. Note his ironic—and prophetic—observation that COVID-19 "may be turn out to be the deadliest infectious disease outbreak of our lives."

Bill Drury
CS-32

Shortly after graduating from USAFA with the Class of 1973, I was fortunate enough to be admitted to medical school at Creighton University. In due course, I graduated and had a satisfying career in both the military and civilian worlds as an orthopedic surgeon.

As I write this, the world remains in the throes of what may be the deadliest infectious disease outbreak of our lives. In a very short time, the COVID-19 coronavirus has infected more than 550 million people worldwide and resulted in more than 6 million deaths. The origins of the disease are unclear. While vaccines seem to be minimizing symptoms for many, newer strains of the virus are likely to evolve, requiring additional vaccinations, perhaps as often as every nine months.

This is a time for our political and medical leaders to make wise and compassionate decisions on our behalf, and to provide us honest and accurate information during a period of great uncertainty. But, from my perspective, we're also sorely in need of leadership from the medical community to minimize anxiety and help us make appropriate changes in our daily activities to allow us to remain safe while living with this disease.

What form should this leadership take? How do we recognize real leadership in our medical professionals? The American Association for Physician Leadership has outlined several characteristics that define a health-care leader. In addition, my time in the medical field has suggested a few others. A review of some of these traits provides a basis for observing and evaluating the performance of physician leaders. More significantly, I believe my time at the Academy provided a strong foundation for the development of these traits in my own character.

First of all, an authentic physician leader must demonstrate a clear and strong ethical code of conduct. It must be obvious that all medical and policy decisions are based first and foremost on a profound respect for the welfare of patients and the community rather than self-interest. Medical ethicists insist that, as treating physicians, we act with concern for patient autonomy and an honest intent to do what is best for the patient. A leader must go further and demonstrate that non-medical personnel and policy decisions, as well as his or her personal actions, are honorable, mature, free from prejudice, and consistent with the overall mission. Training in, and service to, the Academy's Honor Code provides a baseline for ethical behavior that dovetails nicely with this requirement. The addition of the Honor Oath in 1984 (…I resolve to do my duty and live honorably…) as part of the Acceptance Day ceremony is meant to highlight a cadet's commitment to an ethical life on both a personal and professional level.

Next, our physician leaders must be adaptable. While ethical foundations must be rock-solid and unchanging, science is always in flux and reactions to medical problems change as our collective knowledge base grows. It is not a sign of weakness nor indecision that medical recommendations change over time; rather, it is an acknowledgement that new information requires new strategies. As an example, for a time, physicians ridiculed the idea that hand washing and removal of blood-stained clothing when examining patients was contributing to the spread of infectious diseases. Such an attitude would be horrifying today. Our physician leaders cannot be apologetic for changing recommendations based on new data. I believe that living through the wildly changing environments at USAFA (transition from civilian high school student to basic cadet, shift to Jack's Valley, initiation of academic year, evolution from harassed doolie to upper-class mentor and, in my case, advancement from student glider pilot to cadet instructor pilot) all contributed to an ability to successfully adapt in a rapidly evolving world.

Another characteristic of the modern physician leader is the ability to collaborate with others across organizational lines. In the past, many physicians worked in near isolation, often having little interaction with others who were not involved in direct patient care. Within their narrow universe, they often had what were essentially dictatorial powers. Today, physicians are part of large organizations, including hospitals, multi-specialty groups and health insurance corporations. In the case of our national healthcare leaders, that organization extends to our federal bureaucracy, and indeed the entire population of the United States. While individual physicians may have less direct control over personnel and policy matters than before, the organizations in which they function have a much wider and more powerful influence. As a result, leaders must be able to align their goals and objectives with those of these organizations and work together with non-physicians to create processes for implementation of complex objectives. Instead of ordering a small group of subordinates to perform in a specific manner, as in the past, modern leaders must function more like a General Dwight Eisenhower in the run-up to D-Day. His genius lay in getting military personnel, civilian manufacturers, and international supply chains to work together collaboratively to accomplish the largest and most complex amphibious assault in history.

My introduction to the concept of collaboration toward a common goal took place during the Leadership Reaction Course during Doolie Summer. We were divided into small groups, rotating through multiple stations, each station having some physical problem to solve. Success depended on selecting a leader, encouraging input from all team members, selecting one plan of action, and organizing the team to perform the tasks required to correctly solve the problem. I have been involved with many hospital committees over the years that functioned in essentially the same fashion, and my time at the Academy prepared me well for success in these projects.

A real leader must be visionary. He or she must have a clear idea of what success looks like and must be able to work backward from that vision and understand the steps required to make that goal a reality. Leaders must be able to draw, from their own experience, lessons of history and the wisdom of others in similar and disparate fields to see a pathway to realization of that success. A leader must be able to transmit that vision to others to form a dedicated and goal-oriented team to accomplish the mission. As a glider instructor pilot, I was given a taste of these requirements when I took on the responsibility of training cadets who had never flown before and advancing them to the point of taking a glider up solo. This task weighed heavily on me, especially as I watched them from the ground when they first went up by themselves.

An effective leader must be inspirational. He or she must motivate his or her team through a clear vision, by his or her personal behavior and work ethic, respect for subordinates, courage in the face of adversity, and personal commitment to the mission. While providing inspiration personally, he or she must also be open to inspiration from others, listening to and honestly evaluating advice from teammates in service to the goal. I recall a speech by the legendary Robin Olds when an F-4 fighter was dedicated on the Terrazzo. He described the aircraft in almost human terms, thanking it for helping him complete many dangerous combat missions and getting him home safely, even when it was "wounded." After that speech, the entire Cadet Wing would have eagerly followed him into combat.

Finally, as a means of demonstrating all of the traits I have discussed so far, a physician leader must be a great communicator. A leader must be able to speak, write, and behave in a manner that consistently projects commitment, honesty, professionalism, and courage. Having all of the other positive characteristics of leadership will be useless if our leaders are unable to connect with us on a human level. The many cadet leadership positions provided during our time at the Academy certainly helped to hone these skills. For me, being named captain of our intramural lacrosse team was an experience that helped me in my ability to lead and work with others.

It's no coincidence that many experiences at the Academy are designed to instill within cadets the very qualities described above. After all, the mission of the Academy is to develop leaders of character for the Air Force. But, as I've seen in the medical community, leaders of character are sorely needed throughout our society.

25

CHOOSING THE HARDER RIGHT

by Lieutenant Colonel (Ret.) Christopher A. Taravella, Esq.

Chris Taravella
CS-21

Following his retirement from the Air Force as a judge advocate, Chris Taravella joined Chrysler Corporation in 1985, where he worked as the head of the litigation department under Lee Iacocca. In 1997, he became general counsel of the merged Chrysler Financial Corporation and Mercedes-Benz Credit Corporation, where he served for nine years. As Chris explains, the higher one goes in any organization, the more complex decisions become and the greater the consequences for any missteps. He draws upon his Academy experiences and the role of character in choosing the "harder right," as opposed to the "easier wrong."

You are on a journey.

You have set off from Base Camp in Nepal at 17,598 feet. It has been a life-long goal to summit the world's highest mountain, Mt. Everest, at 29,035 feet. You are an achiever: you set goals, go after them, and achieve them. You are an Air Force Academy graduate. No small feat just getting in, let alone graduating.

For years you've prepared for the climb, and are in excellent mental, spiritual, and physical health. Your physical preparation and conditioning included walking across ladder rungs on ladders placed horizontally and parallel to the ground, propped up by sawhorses in the back yard with a full 75 pounds of gear and wearing climbing boots/crampons to prepare for the constantly shifting, very dangerous Khumbu Icefall. You've paid $65,000 to hire an experienced guide and a Sherpa porter team to increase the 29% odds that you will summit. You've chosen the South Col route, named after the col lying between Mount Everest and Lhotse.

More than 300 people have died attempting the climb, and only about 4,500 people have summited. The Death Zone is littered with bodies that likely will never be recovered because it is too expensive and too dangerous to recover them.

After a six-week stay at Base Camp that allows you to acclimatize yourself to altitude, you set off with your guide, Sherpa team, and porters through the unstable Khumbu Icefall. You successfully negotiate the Icefall and the 2,000-foot climb in elevation by walking over aluminum ladders placed over the ever-shifting crevices. You arrive at Camp 1, altitude 19,500 feet, where you spend the night.

The route from Camp 1 to Camp 2 is extremely hot; the temperature reaches 100 degrees Fahrenheit.

Camp 2 is at 21,000 feet, crossing through a narrow passage dubbed "Nuptse Corner." Next is the ascent of the Lhotse face, using ropes set by your guide team, after which you arrive at Camp 3 (23,500 feet), which occupies the Lhotse Face. The climb is steep and very icy and you're digging your crampons into the ice. You are clipped into a rope to stop as much as a two-mile fall that otherwise most certainly would kill you. You arrive at Camp 3.

From Camp 3 you negotiate the "Geneva Spur" and the "Yellow Band." You are using oxygen now as the air truly is thin. You are breathing harder and faster. You finally arrive at Camp 4, which lies on the South Col at 26,300 feet. You are now in the Death Zone.

You're now ready for the summit "gun lap." You do not tarry here as the altitude is wearing you down and the weather constantly changes. The summit leg is to start at 2000 hours local time and the goal is to summit within 10 to 12 hours. The weather is perfect: clear and not very windy. But the weather forecast provides for a one-day window of opportunity, after which low visibility and high winds are expected. You're ready to go. It's before midnight when you start out. You reach the Balcony at 27,500 feet and turn west.

You climb from the Balcony to the South Summit at 28,500 feet. On the way up at the Hillary Step (28,750 feet), your team runs into a climber who was left behind by a team climbing ahead of you. The climber is in trouble, shivering and barely breathing. Although for the most part incoherent, he is clearly asking for help. He needs oxygen and obviously needs to get down as soon as possible to lower altitude.

You're exhausted, but the adrenaline is pumping and your heart beats fast in anticipation. Your breath is short and you remain on oxygen bottles because the air is so thin here. "If you can force your heart and nerve and sinew, to serve your turn long after they are gone, and so hold on where there is nothing in you, except the will that says to them: 'Hold on!'"[118]

Your guide looks at you and the team and points out that the climber likely will die if immediate help is not provided. That means escorting/carrying him back to camp. It also means providing him with one of the few remaining oxygen bottles that you have. And it means helping the climber descend—abandoning the venture and your lifelong ambition. What to do?

118 | "If" by Rudyard Kipling.

You go through a mental checklist: weather closing in; opportunity knocks; what are the rules of the mountain? Are there such rules? Am I expected to help rescue a climber who finds himself in a position, maybe even placed himself in a position, that he needs to be rescued? You ask your guide, "What are the rules of the mountain?" Your guide reports that there is no rule that requires rescue. Hmmmmm. No legal rule. Or maybe whether there is a legal rule governing this situation never even occurs to you? This is not a technical, legal issue; or is it?

You go through a moral checklist—from your head to your heart. What to do? "Gee—I really want to summit—right here, right now, today. And I can do it. I'll catch him on the way down—if he's still there and alive—and help him out then. What does your brain tell you to do? What does your heart tell you to do? What does your soul tell you to do?[119]

Are you a "head person," a "heart person," or "soul person," or a little bit of all three? What do you do? This is gut check, isn't it? Who are you?

THE HERE AND NOW: "WHO'S GOING RIGHT?"

From time to time, we find ourselves in a situation that poses a moral, ethical, perhaps even spiritual dilemma. It is those situations that tell others and ourselves who we are. Sometimes there is clear guidance, the North Star "Polaris" that provides us clear direction. Perhaps there are written rules governing what to do in a given situation. But what if there aren't clear written rules that set forth the path to follow? Then what? Do you lead with your mind? Do you lead with your heart? Do you lead with your soul? Are they in conflict? If so, how do you balance

119 | *See* the ethical dilemma posed in "The Parable of the Sadhu" by Bowen H. McCoy, Harvard Business Review, May-June 1997.
   "How do you feel about contributing to the death of a fellow man?"
   "Where, in your opinion," I asked, "is the limit of our responsibility in a situation like this? We had our own well-being to worry about. Our Sherpa guides were unwilling to jeopardize us or the porters for the sadhu. No one else on the mountain was willing to commit himself beyond certain self-imposed limits."
   "We do not know if the sadhu lived or died."

them and arrive at a decision with which you can live; a decision that you can look back on and say with pride, "Even with 20/20 hindsight, I did the right thing. I can live with myself. I can look at myself in the mirror and say, 'Well done!'"

As a judge advocate (JAG, or Judge Advocate General) in the United States Air Force and in the United States Air Force Reserve, I was provided guidance with rules and regulations that set forth minimum standards that lawyers were to follow. These rules and regulations were provided by the state licensing authority. They provided minimum standards by which all lawyers, military and civilian, must govern themselves.

Lawyers, including JAGs who serve as lawyers in the military community, are licensed by state. Each state has rules of professional conduct that prescribe the minimum ethical expectations that lawyers are required to meet.[120] These rules form a sort of honor code by which lawyers must abide. They require honesty, courage, and accountability. Lawyers who fail to abide by the rules are subject to discipline, including, without limitation, permanent revocation of a license to practice law in the licensing state.[121]

The minimum standards are just that: minimums. They are somewhat akin to FAA regulations prescribing for airplane pilots minimum visibility and ceiling requirements for an Instrument Landing System (ILS) landing approach. The requirements vary by category of aircraft. For example, a 200' ceiling may be required for a given ILS approach at an airport. But a pilot may not be comfortable with a 200' ceiling. The pilot's own minimum standard may be a 300' ceiling. The pilot must know who she is, what her capabilities are, and what her comfort level is in different conditions.

---

120 | *See*, e.g., the Colorado Rules of Professional Conduct, Wyoming's Rules of Professional Conduct for Attorneys at Law, and the Michigan Rules of Professional Conduct. While each state has its own version of rules guiding lawyers in the ethical arena, for illustration purposes, the Colorado Rules of Professional Conduct will be referred to herein.

121 | *See*, e.g., Colorado's Office of Attorney Regulation.

At the end of the day, lawyers must make judgment calls but are not left to their own devices. They may reach out for assistance and secure advice with respect to the resolution of ethical issues that inevitably come up in the practice of law. Is that so different from business? From life?

There are not always clear-cut rules and regulations governing the conduct of a lawyer. Sometimes the gut/heart/soul must enter the internal fray and provide input.

One of my more challenging moments as a JAG prosecutor was during a trial before a full panel (in essence, a jury trial) at Hanscom Air Force Base, Massachusetts. During pre-trial preparation, I had interviewed the government's star witness, an informant in a drug trial. So I knew what the witness would say, the "truth" according to the witness.[122] At trial, perhaps in an effort to ingratiate himself with the government, the witness told a story that implicated the accused but was different from the story he had told me before trial during trial preparation.

What to do? The convening authority had charged me to represent the United States Air Force. A prosecutor's job is to get a conviction, right? Maybe, maybe not. But here, while I believed the accused airman was guilty of the drug charges brought to trial by the convening authority, I did not believe that justice was being done in that I believed that the witness had perjured himself.

Having made that conclusion, my heart, mind, and soul were aligned. I told the military judge that I needed to recall the witness/informant at the end of the trial. Interestingly, the recall of the witness/informant was over a defense objection. The military judge pointed out that he was not going to stop me from impeaching my own witness. When the witness/informant was recalled, I proceeded to impeach him in front of the jury, pointing out the discrepancies in his testimony. This task, of course, is normally reserved for the defense counsel, a rather inexperienced JAG.

122 | "Truth!" said Pilate. "What does that mean?" The Bible, John 18:38.

The predictable result was an acquittal.[123] I felt good about that and look back on the decision with 20/20 hindsight as the right thing to do.

In addition, while it may seem anomalous, there are rules and laws governing the conduct of war, referred to as the Laws of Armed Conflict.[124] The Geneva Convention of 1929 adopted, among other things, the Humanitarian Law of Armed Conflicts. Senior German military officers were prosecuted in the Nuremburg war trials held from 1945-1949. American military officers and personnel as well have been held accountable for war crimes.[125]

The war in Vietnam posed particular challenges for American military forces. From rice paddy to rice paddy, village to village, it was unclear exactly who the enemy was. The enemy did not wear uniforms as required by the Geneva Convention. A person working in a rice paddy by day may be on patrol at night, in a search-and-destroy mission aimed right at your life. The take-away from these events that applies today as well: one cannot plead in defense of a war crime that one was "just following orders." There is such a thing as an unlawful order, which upon being followed can result in severe consequences.

How such rules play out in the various challenges that society and the world face today can pose challenging moral dilemmas. For example, on September 11, 2001, if air traffic controllers had sufficient information to vector scrambled Air Force fighters to intercept any of flights American Airlines #11, American Airlines #77, United Airlines #175, or United Airlines #93, what would have been the right thing to do—intercept and destroy a hijacked civilian airliner with innocent passengers before it could harm others, or allow it to run its course? There are persuasive arguments for either option that never were ripe because the

---

123 | *See* CO RPC 3.3(a)(3).

124 | Contrary to John Lyly's "Euphues": "All is fair in love and war."

125 | Captain Ernest Medina and Lt. William Calley were court-martialed for alleged killings of civilian non-combatants at My Lai, Viet Nam in 1968.

fighters were unable to locate the civilian airliners, in part because the planes' transponders had been turned off by the hijackers.

In attempting to zealously represent one's client, a lawyer unfortunately may cross the line. When the lawyer does cross the line, discipline may very well be the result.[126]

Teamwork plays an essential role in the practice of law, just as it does at USAFA. Our class's unofficial motto was "cooperate and graduate." In early morning squadron runs, it was not at all unusual to carry a classmate to the finish line.

The discipline ingrained in our class continued to serve us in our military and civilian careers. We learned that we were capable of achieving things that we previously thought were beyond our limits. We learned not to give up in the face of adversity. While we may have questioned the mission, we nevertheless did our best to achieve it.[127] We learned to "take the hit" for our classmates rather than throw them under the bus in order to make ourselves look better. The response was, "No excuse," even when there was, in fact, an underlying excuse for whatever the accusation might be.

The concepts of discipline and teamwork apply in our lives today as it seldom is possible to accomplish something of significance without teamwork, especially as various facets of careers are becoming increasingly specialized and, quite often, the expertise required to deal with a problem can require various specialists enrolled in a common cause.

It is very valuable for lawyers to be afforded the opportunity to confer with another. "No man [or woman] is an island entirely of itself."[128] Col-

126 | *See*, e.g., *Misbehaving Attorneys, Angry Judges, and the Need for a Balanced Approach to the Reviewability of Findings of Misconduct* by Robert B. Tannebaum, The University of Chicago Law Review, 75:1857.

127 | "Forward, the Light Brigade!" "Was there a man dismayed? Not though the soldier knew someone had blundered. Theirs not to make reply, Theirs not to reason why, Theirs but to do and die. Into the valley of Death rode the six hundred." *The Charge of the Light Brigade*, Alfred Lord Tennyson.

128 | *No man is an Island* by John Donne.

laboration in the legal field is important if not essential in today's world. Such collaboration has advantages of providing different perspectives, support, accountability, and perhaps most important, such collaboration can help to prevent one from making a mistake. Teamwork in the legal career field not only involves teamwork among lawyers. Members of a legal team often include administrative assistants and paralegals. Division of tasks that may overlap is very helpful in getting the job done. Teamwork in business and in life, as well, can pay handsome dividends.

In summary, it may not be clear to others who we are. It may not even be clear to ourselves who we are. How we react to situations we face tells others and ourselves who we are. And how we react will help to define who we are. As graduates, we have taken "the road less traveled by. And that has made all the difference."[129] Our USAFA experience helped us explore and learn our outer limits of faith, hope, tolerance, endurance, and courage. But there was a price to be paid for that: blood, sweat, and even tears. For the most part, had we known what we were getting into in the first place when we were fresh out of high school, then perhaps some of us would never have done it. But, looking back, we are glad that we did it. That has made all the difference.

---

129 | *The Road Less Traveled* by Robert Frost.

26

COMMUNITY LEADERSHIP

by Colonel (Ret.) Robert A. Munson, MD

Duty, while a fundamental component of the military ethos, is not unique to the Military Services—volunteer organizations across the country depend on it. Col. Bob Munson served in the Air Force for nearly 30 years. His varied career began as a pilot. Followed by medical school and qualification as an internal medicine physician, Bob became one of only a handful of rated "pilot-physicians" in the Air Force. Since his retirement, he has been a bedrock in a host of volunteer efforts, from deploying overseas with the American Red Cross, to supporting natural disaster relief efforts, to fundraising for the Academy, and serving on the AOG's Board of Directors. In response to the COVID crisis, he organized the local Academy graduate community to help with mass COVID vaccination events, for which he was recognized with the 2021 Air Force Academy Distinguished Service Award. He talked about how he channeled his sense of duty from the Air Force—Service Before Self—into the betterment of his community.

Bob Munson
CS-34

All of us entering the Academy did so voluntarily. We all agreed to enter the service and take on that "obligation freely, without any mental reservation or purpose of evasion." I certainly did so, but I wasn't happy about it. I had wanted to go to a "party" school, like Tufts University in Boston. My family was economically challenged, so I got an ROTC scholarship so I could afford a "party" school. But, late in my senior year, all the party schools I had been accepted to dropped ROTC. That was their way of protesting the government's war in Vietnam.

So, yes, I was a volunteer to enter the Air Force Academy. But, as I quickly learned, at the Academy the word "party" had a different meaning. A "shower party" did not involve drinking beer in togas with friends while the stereo blared out the Rolling Stones. Nope, I learned firsthand that a shower "party" involved me screaming out, verbatim, Maj. John M. Schofield's address to the Graduating Class of 1879 at West Point, in a dorm hallway, dressed only in issued "whitie tighties," all while an upper classman was screaming "LOUDER, SMACK, I CAN'T HEAR YOU!"

Was I the only one who saw the irony in using Maj. Gen. Schofield's address at a shower party? Suffice that I wasn't an enthusiastic USAF Academy volunteer, nor did the "cadet development program" techniques used in those days help my attitude. So I adopted the "fly below the radar" method of getting by. I didn't raise my hand, stayed within the mean, and avoided senior cadet positions. I was critical of cadets who volunteered to serve; in my view, they were currying favor from the officer leadership by working as their tools.

Slowly, ever so slowly, my clue light started flickering. Notably, it was the exemplars all around the Academy who lit it my clue light: classmates, roommates, upperclassmen, officers, and NCOs. My roommates were all exemplars. Most grew into leadership positions as cadets. They didn't get extra pay and they got no benefits to speak of. I began to realize how they served on behalf of their classmates. All went on to an Air Force career; five are deservedly profiled in this book and a sixth is the author.

From them I learned that the fundamental reward of service is intrinsic: the sense of satisfaction from doing well for others. I call it "psychic pay."

I also got to experience the slap-in-the-face method for learning the meaning of service. My AOC had offered me the job of cadet squadron commander, only if I wanted to volunteer. I didn't. To my surprise, I found myself the next day at rigid attention in front of the well-respected vice-commandant of cadets, Col. "Steady" Eddie Levell. He hammered me, working me up one side and down the other. His stated regret: had he the power, he would have tossed me out of the Academy because, "You NEVER turn down a command responsibility." I was profoundly shamed and embarrassed. Fifty years later, I still feel my cheeks flush with the memory. While I lost that opportunity to serve, it was a great learning experience.

VOLUNTEERISM AND THE AIR FORCE

On active duty, I was no different from most successful officers in that I looked for ways to volunteer. It didn't take me long to learn that the tasks no one wants to do often present the best opportunities. When the manpower folks at Randolph AFB were forcing fighter pilots into the prop-driven OV-10, I was glad to help (though I never had a fighter pilot thank me for taking his slot). Once I was assigned to a flying squadron, I discovered that no one wanted to be the snack bar officer (derisively referred to as the "snacko"), an extra duty so low it was typically assigned to brand-new second lieutenants—of which there were none in the squadron. I did it for two years, and the extra responsibility and resulting visibility gave me the chance to be a flight commander and later chief of training. Looking back, I'm convinced that those years as the "snacko" contributed to my having the choice of either an F-15 fighter assignment or attending medical school.

I ended up going to medical school, but again volunteerism played a role in shaping my career. Following med school, I was slated to go into a gastroenterology fellowship. A few months prior to starting the fellowship, I was asked to volunteer to fill a pilot-physician opening at the Human Systems Program Office. Very few pilots and certainly no physicians would ever volunteer to switch into the Acquisitions field, and there was nothing that required me to do so, given that I'd been accepted for the gastroenterology fellowship. It was a difficult decision. After serving the short commitment, I could have retired from the Air Force into a well-compensated specialty and lived the good life. But there were no other pilot-physicians who could fill the position, so I volunteered to drop the dream fellowship and return to what I had once been so slow to learn: service before self. It turned out great. Serving with the hidden teams that are the real backbone of the Air Force is an experience everyone should have.

THE NATURE OF VOLUNTEERISM

In retirement, my wife Pam and I have chosen to serve without pay. We're not unique; government statistics recently reported 67 million Americans—25.9 percent of the population—do volunteer work. So our Core Value "Service Before Self" isn't unique to the military—it's a strong motivator in the civilian sector as well. In fact, service is truly a part of the American fabric.

Nevertheless, there's a difference between being a military volunteer and a volunteer in any other profession or organization. In 1972, Gen. Bernard Rogers made it clear as speaker at our ring dining-in when he walked us through the difference between our profession and every other. His message, paraphrased, was that, "In the military, you can be ordered to die for your country; in every other profession, you can walk away at any time."

Volunteers to benefit the public would uniformly balk at dying for their favorite cause. And that leads to the subject of effective leadership. The authoritative style of leadership doesn't hack it in the volunteer community. You can't order a volunteer to do something that they don't feel comfortable with, that they feel isn't in line with the organizational mission, or that they don't particularly want to do. The collaborative form of leadership, on the other hand, works well in the volunteer world. It values diversity of ideas and promotes inclusiveness. This approach tends to make everyone feel a sense of ownership in the organizational mission.

THE AMERICAN RED CROSS

The most organized civilian volunteer organization I've worked for is the Red Cross. When my wife Pam and I deploy to a disaster, the Red Cross gets us there in less than 24 hours. Their volunteers are led by supervisors and managers who are also volunteers. But, as it is a volunteer organization, the supervisors are limited in their means of getting their volunteers to execute. In complicated teams, the best technique is collaborative leadership. Allow me to provide a couple of examples of how collaborative leadership worked for me.

The first involved setting up a "clean" Red Cross shelter at the Gridley County Fairgrounds in California. We were tasked with preventing incursion of epidemic norovirus (aka "cruise ship diarrhea") into a new shelter during the response to the 2018 Paradise Fire that Pam and I deployed to. Seven Red Cross shelters had already been infected when our team was directed to set up this shelter, and my Health Services role was to keep it "clean." The environment was not promising: three shelters within 200 yards were infected, as were the campgrounds. There was no restriction on "clients" (aka "evacuees") from free movement within the complex and our clients had use the toilets and showers within these common areas.

As Health Services lead at the first day's organizational meeting prior to admitting clients, I provided an explanation of how norovirus was spread (contaminated hands and surfaces). I then walked the shelter team through prevention measures; no one allowed to enter the shelter without washing hands first, no one in the shelter but clients and staff, Red Cross staff and state officials not allowed in if they had come from a contaminated shelter, no person-to-person contact, all surfaces cleaned after being used, etc. Then I asked the staff to ask questions and make suggestions. Almost every suggestion was workable and got buy-in from the staff. They started owning it and more suggestions followed. The volunteers modified their work area processes to prevent the spread, which often broke with Red Cross practices. For example, the staff changed all client-self-service practices to staff-full-service; so instead of clients picking through of a bowl of fruit bars or examining soft drink choices themselves, a staff member served the clients. Staff rolled in with more ideas and innovations; one good example was Pam's idea for constructing a coffee stirrer dispenser that a staff member would shake to get one to pop out to a client. As our processes improved, the clients got involved. They were particularly effective at pointing out violations by other clients and, yes, sometimes by staff. Controlling the entry point was key, and again clients helped by diverting folks who had not washed their hands. With confidence came ownership; staff "owners" turned away the county public health inspectors who had just inspected an infected shelter. Those inspectors were embarrassed because they knew better. Days later, the team turned away the California chief of public health, with reporter and cameraman, for the very same reason.

How well did it work? Very well. Norovirus is one of the most, if not the most, infectious viral agent around. But, for a week, not one resident or staff member got infected, despite being in the middle of that norovirus swamp where, at one point, as much as 20% of an adjacent shelter's population were infected. Only when the Red Cross sent in clients from other infected shelters, as part of the sheltering draw-down, was there finally an outbreak in our shelter.

COVID AND THE ACADEMY

A final example of using collaborative leadership involved volunteers in the COVID pandemic era, right at the USAF Academy. Challenge: how best to get 16,000 shots into arms. In January 2021, the USAF Academy clinic started getting intermittent shipments of the first approved vaccine from Pfizer. At this point, 340,000 Americans had died. I was a long-time physician volunteer on staff with the 10th Medical Group and was asked to help with vaccinations. After two vaccination clinics, it was clear that a lot more manpower was needed. Doing the vaccinations and getting data into a computer is straightforward but could only be done by the military. What takes more manpower is crowd control: greeting patients, providing education, handing out questionnaires, filling out vaccine records, shuttling patients through in-processing and to the vaccinators, manning the observation area, and out-processing. Crowd management requires the most manpower and takes up 90% of the time the clients are in the vaccination process.

I recommended getting volunteers to help, and the immunization chief was only too happy to put me in charge of making that happen. At first, I turned to friends, classmates, and spouses, but the vaccination deliveries picked up. I then went to the Red Cross. Astonishingly, their leadership decided the Red Cross had no role in the pandemic, and restricted local chapters from providing support. That turned out to be for the good, as the graduate community was only too happy to get into the fight. How happy? One email to the local AOG Ramparts Range chapter brought 144 graduate/spouse volunteers on the first day, and we totaled more than 240 after two weeks. Almost all were retired, so until they were fully vaccinated, they were at some risk for severe disease. Yet no one balked at helping. This was a great example that their commitment to service before self is still strong, long after their military service had ended.

The mass vaccination events became weekly, and the volunteers were welcomed by the medical staff. Without volunteers and having too few military augmentees, the clinic's best effort had been 500 shots in eight hours. In the first volunteer-supported mass vaccination event, 752 personnel were vaccinated in eight hours. At the second event, both the volunteers and staff had moved up the learning curve and 1,302 were vaccinated. From then on, our numbers were only limited by the number of vaccine doses and the availability of arms.

In the first months, I had been one-man leader-supervisor scheduling volunteers, organizing shift rosters, coordinating with staff, managing the forms and supplies, briefing the volunteers, and supervising during each POD (Point of Distribution). But grads were used to taking charge, and their spouses were used to taking charge of their grads. So it came as no surprise that they were all "owning" their work areas, starting with POD #1. And these same volunteers were free with feedback and suggestions. It was a setting ripe for collaborative leadership. For every good idea offered, I gave the volunteer the freedom to implement it. By the second POD, I started naming shift supervisors to oversee all their volunteers, subsequently spreading the supervisor roles to others at successive PODs. By the sixth POD, five of these supervisors stepped up and agreed to be POD leads, sharing what I had been doing. I then went out of town for two weeks; when I returned, the new POD leads had improved the volunteer operation in my absence. The supplies had been put in a wheeled cart and the forms organized into folders, the processing line had been diagrammed with volunteer positions identified, the volunteers were now in orange vests, and shift leads were in yellow vests so they could be identified within the crowd of patients and personnel working the vaccination lines. The volunteers had taken ownership. The organization had matured.

LEVERAGING LEADERSHIP
SKILLS AND KNOWLEDGE

In my post-retirement years of volunteering for non-profit organizations, I've seen the whole spectrum of leadership, from inspirational to truly horrible leaders. Volunteers in those organizations get no leadership training to speak of—they just come in off the street. Inevitably, the leaders had learned leadership in a previous profession, while the horrible leaders had no training and no clue. Community volunteer opportunities have given me the chance to apply the leadership lessons from the Academy and my Air Force career to very worthwhile causes. For instance, adapting one's leadership style to the task and to the team's maturity—so critical in volunteer organizations—came right out of Military Training 220 and 320. I've also been able to apply collaborative leadership techniques I learned at Squadron Officers School, process improvement from the Acquisition business, and even cockpit resource management principles from flight safety classes. Active duty gave me the opportunity to see, in a variety of situations, what worked and what didn't. But the larger point is that volunteer opportunities abound, and are great ways to honor the Core Value of "Service Before Self" while leveraging your leadership skills and knowledge.

27

INVESTING IN CHARACTER

by Mr. John R. Muse

John Muse
CS-36

*John Muse is an inspiring example of "giving back."
He's not only a highly successful and nationally recognized business entrepreneur, but a major donor
to character-based leadership development at the
Academy. Thanks to the generous contributions of
John and his wife Lyn, the Academy's National Character and Leadership Symposium (NCLS) program
has a robust endowment fund to support continuing
lectures and activities for future Academy classes.*

I recently turned 71 years old, am in good health, still active in business, and have become increasingly involved with my family foundation in philanthropy. I've lived the American dream and received more than my fair share of good fortune along the way—some due to hard work and persistence, but much due to good luck and fortunate timing in the private equity business in the 1990s. I recently retired from founding and running a large private equity firm and now operate as more of a "serial entrepreneur," controlling four private companies and sitting on two large company boards where I have a significant investment. I truly have a lot to be thankful for.

EARLY LESSONS IN CHARACTER

My mother and father grew up in a working-class neighborhood on the north side of Fort Worth, Texas. After the attack on Pearl Harbor, my father and five of his buddies left Texas A&M to enlist in the Marine Corps. When he completed basic training, he shipped out to the Pacific Theater and fought in the Solomon Islands, as well as in other island-hopping campaigns. After the war he stayed in the Marine Reserve and finished his education at Texas Christian University. My father's reserve unit was called up during the Korean War, so my early years were spent with my mom and grandparents looking after me in Fort Worth. My father stayed in the Marine Corps until I was five years old. I vaguely remember living in San Diego before returning to Texas, where my father started a career as a civil engineer with a large construction company. Most of my youth was spent in Tyler, Texas, a relatively small town of 60,000 people about 90 miles east of Dallas, where we lived a pretty normal white picket fence, middle-class life.

Character was always a point of emphasis in my family. Being a Marine, my father was a tough taskmaster who demanded high achievement and insisted we finish whatever we started. He had strong values of integrity and honesty. Like many in his generation, he was very short on compliments and didn't outwardly display much affection, but he taught us to treat everyone with respect, regardless of color, ethnicity or socioeconomic condition. If Dad was the salt, Mom was the sugar—very loving and nurturing to me and my brothers. She was a devout Presbyterian and was very involved in the church and associated volunteer activities.

I played football and baseball and did well academically, particularly in math and science. I was active in Boy Scouts, becoming an Eagle Scout at age 15. I was also active in our church and in the Fellowship of Christian Athletes and Young Life. Growing up in conservative Tyler and a traditional household, I was raised to be very patriotic. To this day I have a strong belief in "God and Country." I also believe that we live in a very special country based on two very important principles: absolute freedom and unlimited opportunity for every citizen to chase their own dream. Because of my patriotic beliefs, I always felt the pull to serve.

When I began looking at colleges, I wasn't interested in attending a large university where I'd just be a face in a crowd. Instead, I wanted to find a school where I could get a great education and still participate in sports. I was recruited to play football at both West Point and Annapolis but decided to look at other options. The football coaches at Air Force suggested I apply for an appointment at the relatively new Air Force Academy. I applied for admission through my congressman, Ray Roberts, and received an appointment my senior year of high school.

CONTINUING LESSONS IN CHARACTER

As with most doolies, I was shocked to go from being a high school "hot dog" to being "lower than whale poop in the deepest ocean." I approached BCT with grit and determination, just as my dad had taught me. Although I didn't make it as a football "walk-on," I discovered a new sport, lacrosse, which I enjoyed for four years. Because social life was not great for us in those years, I threw myself into classroom achievement, cadet leadership positions, and the lacrosse field. I was captain of the lacrosse team and squadron commander my first-class year. I was on the Superintendent's List half of my third-class year and all of my second and first-class years.

While I came to the Academy with strong values, the leadership challenges were at a level I'd never experienced before. In fact, what distinguishes all the military academies is the opportunity to experience "hands on" leadership. As a result, we were able to learn from leadership positions at a very young age. For instance, one of my most gratifying leadership experiences was being an element leader during Second BCT. The other element leaders and I were on the ground with 12 basic cadets, teaching subjects like night navigation and other tactical skills. Activities like the Confidence Course gave us the chance to test our basic cadets' physical and mental toughness. I found it much more productive to inspire my doolies to win competitions, rather than to yell at them for their shortcomings. My experience as an element leader also taught me that at its most basic level, leadership is about modeling good character, striving for excellence, and building the grit and determination required to get through challenging situations. Later, as a squadron commander, I learned how to manage everyone, from doolies to my own classmates. There were times when I had to get on my own classmates for poor grades or bad behavior, but I made it my mission to model the best behavior I could, rely on an inner core of character and integrity, and always try to do the right thing.

I ended up graduating from the Academy in the top 10 percent of the class and, as a result, was fortunate enough to be selected to attend the University of California Los Angeles (UCLA) under a cooperative program with our Engineering Management major. As a result, I was able to complete UCLA's two-year program in one year.

AIR FORCE SERVICE AND TRANSITION
TO CIVILIAN LIFE

I had several good assignments in the Los Angeles area as a junior officer. My first assignment after graduate school was with the B-1 program office general contractor, North American Rockwell. I was assigned to program control, where I was responsible for budget approval, change orders, and adherence to cost and schedule milestones. Unfortunately, I frequently observed bad business practices, such as wasteful spending and failure to control change orders submitted by engineers. I also had some bad experiences with civilian performance reports, in that I couldn't get rid of the poor performers or reward the outstanding ones. After the B-1 program was canceled in 1977, I was able to secure a post with the Space and Missile Systems Organization (SAMSO), helping manage our global weather satellites for all four branches of the armed forces and NASA. This was a well-functioning program, and I enjoyed my role in cost and schedule control. At the end of my stint with SAMSO I had a couple of good assignment options, including the program office in Brussels for the F-15 joint venture with our allies, but had decided a career in the Air Force was not for me. The phase point for major had been pushed out by two years, and I was uncomfortable with the thought that one bad boss could ruin my career. I also realized that I wanted independence and to be in control of my own destiny. Furthermore, my experience in graduate school was fantastic and I was enamored with the thought of starting my own business one day.

In the late '70s, the "hot" career path for MBAs was management consulting, as the stock market was in the doldrums and investment banking was not hiring. After leaving the Air Force I interviewed for both McKinsey and Boston Consulting Group, the top two firms in consulting, and made it deep into the process for both. However, in the end I was told that they had not hired anyone to date that had not come out of Stanford or Harvard Business School. Fortunately, I was able to secure a job in investment banking at the regional firm Bateman Eichler, Hill Richards in Los Angeles. Just as I did at the Academy, I worked my tail off and went the extra mile on every assignment. I threw myself into every due diligence exercise in researching companies that we were contemplating financing. As a result, I was promoted and received bonuses for the next three years.

In late 1979 we were collaborating on a number of deals in the energy sector with Schneider Bernet in Dallas, and they were looking for someone to head their corporate finance effort. Although I was still fairly young and inexperienced, they offered me the job with a modest salary but a 50% share of the profits of my unit as a bonus pool. This was the kind of entrepreneurial opportunity that I was looking for. I had a great run with them for four years. In 1984 I was recruited by Prudential Bache to head their southwestern region. Prudential Bache was a large, national firm with extensive research and capital markets capabilities that I hadn't had access to with regional firms. During my five years with Prudential Bache, I did a number of financings and sale assignments for investment firms, including a new firm named Hicks and Haas. I was the banker for them in three consequential deals and developed a close relationship with one of the principals, Tom Hicks. Tom decided to build his own institution and raise an investment fund, so he approached me to be his partner. We were able to secure backing from a Prudential, GE Capital, and S.G. Warburg in London, and with that we were off to the races. From our founding in 1989, we grew into one of the largest private equity firms over the next ten years, and one of the few that was not based in New York. By the late '90s, we were expanding rapidly; we launched a fund in Latin America and then extended our business model into Europe by raising a separate $1.5 billion fund and recruiting a group of European professionals and entrepreneurial managers to run it.

Tom Hicks retired from the firm in 2003. We went back to the basics, shut our New York and Buenos Aires offices, and refocused on the industry sectors we knew best. We ultimately split into three firms, one in Europe and two in the U.S. I rebranded one of the U.S. teams into Kainos Capital with a focus in food and beverage, where I had spent most of my career and where our firm had achieved our best, most consistent returns. In 2016 I stepped out of the day-to-day functions and became chairman of the board. I appointed a well-deserved managing partner to replace me. I retired from my post in 2018 and now have a family office that manages my investments and the four businesses we own for our own account.

THE ROLE OF CHARACTER IN BUSINESS

Character is gold in the business community. While that may run counter to the way many view the business world, my experience has been that character-based leadership is essential in building long-term gains. For instance, we once recruited a guy who had done a couple of high-profile turnarounds for large businesses. He had a gold-plated resume, but we quickly discovered that he was willing to cut corners because he was in such a hurry to show results. He prioritized quick gains over long-term, fundamental success. Despite his on-paper pedigree, we ended up having to let him go. Looking back, what was missing in our hiring process was the ability to measure character—precisely what this guy was lacking.

One of my early mentors was a guy named Norman E. Brinker. Norman was the guy who virtually invented fast casual dining, such as Steak and Ale, and Bennigan's. One day I told Norman about the guy we had just let go. And he said, "I tell you what I do. I don't hire a store manager or a senior executive without having done a psychometric analysis. I use this analysis to look for integrity, because that will tell us whether we can believe everything they say. And if they say they're gonna do something, they'll do it." What Norman was after was a measure of character-based leadership skills, such as integrity, the ability to inspire and lead by example, solve problems, and learn and grow. Of course, psychometric analysis won't necessarily tell you who has necessary experience in a particular career field, but it's a great window into some of the leadership traits critical to long-term success. In fact, there's a cottage industry of people these days that do this at the C-suite level, putting candidates through a rigorous battery of written questions, oral questions, and then interviews. In my view, this is a highly profitable approach.

Strong leadership in the business world—as in the military—means that you genuinely care about your people, and you need to demonstrate that wherever and whenever possible. For instance, our Lucchese [boot] factory in El Paso, Texas was particularly hard-hit during the COVID shutdown in 2020. About eighty percent of our workforce consisted of hard-working Hispanic artisans. Like many other businesses, COVID forced us to suspend our operations, furlough some people, and offer early retirement to others. But we made a determined effort to retain our nucleus of employees during this difficult period and, when we were finally in a position to return to full strength, we not only brought back our most talented artisans, but did so with a salary increase. We also invested in technology to make their jobs less monotonous and physically demanding. In the end, both initiatives paid off with higher productivity. Looking back, the business fell off a cliff for a while; however, through proactive investment and our workers' faith, persistence, and hard work, we came out stronger in the end. From a business leadership perspective, the central lesson is that success doesn't ultimately come from the C-Suite—it comes from the people who are doing the job. If you take care of your people, it pays off every time.

INVESTING IN CHARACTER

I've been very fortunate to have had a part in some great wins over my 40+ years in business, but by far the greatest wins are ones in which we've been able to change the trajectory of a human being's life and make it much better. That's the most rewarding thing that we can do.

My wife Lyn and I have always felt a responsibility to give back, and about 20 years ago we decided to establish a new scholarship program with Dallas County Community College. Along with that, we discovered a real need for mentoring. As we interviewed all our Muse scholars, we found that when they started looking for a job, they didn't know how to put a resume together. They didn't know how to write a letter or get a referral. That's when we started helping them move beyond the classroom and successfully conduct themselves in job interviews. As it turned out, it's been one of the most rewarding things we've ever done.

More recently, Lyn and I decided to focus our charitable activities on closing the opportunity gap in education and training for young people who come from challenging socioeconomic backgrounds, kids who don't have access to quality education and training. More recently, we've significantly increased the size of our Muse Foundation and are now trying to address other opportunity gaps in poor neighborhoods: affordable housing, safety/security, access to healthy food and healthcare. We're finding this to be an even bigger challenge than addressing the opportunity gap in education. Our guiding principle in each philanthropic endeavor is to give a hand up, as opposed to a hand out. We've found that when executed properly, these initiatives can become self-sustaining over time.

NATIONAL CHARACTER AND LEADERSHIP SYMPOSIUM

After our 30th reunion, the Association of Graduates development team asked the Class of 1973 if we would be interested in funding a statue or building project. Our class officers discussed the idea, but decided they'd prefer to see more of a living legacy. As an alternative, our class treasurer at the time, William "Trapper" Carpenter, proposed NCLS as a nascent program that, with additional funding, could grow its mission of character and leadership development, thereby touching every cadet.

In 2006, I began to take a greater interest in the Academy and its mission and returned to Colorado Springs to attend the Graduate Leadership Conference, organized by the AOG. I met and listened to a number of Academy leaders and graduates who wanted to help the Academy improve its programs. The earlier focus of our class leadership—character building—was right in line with my passion.

To help our class leadership generate wider interest among our classmates, I offered a $250,000 matching grant for NCLS. Quite a few of our classmates responded to the call and, as a result, our class was able to match our gift. My wife Lyn and I are particularly proud of that, as it kickstarted a class-wide movement that culminated in our class being recognized as the Flagship Sponsor of NCLS. Two additional fundraisers later, over 230 of our classmates have endowed the NCLS program in perpetuity.

As of this writing we, "The Class of Character," are the largest single underwriter of the two-day annual symposium that brings in both national and Air Force leaders. Our gifts touch every cadet, which in turn impacts not only our Air and Space Forces, but our society as well.

28

CHARACTER IN THE COURTROOM

by Judge (Ret.) Kirk S. Samelson

Kirk Samelson
CS-35

Following his career as an Air Force judge advocate, Kirk Samelson was appointed by Governor Bill Owens to serve as a district judge in Colorado's Fourth Judicial District, and later as chief judge. He credits our Core Values for playing a formative role in his career, as well as providing an important framework for making difficult decisions.

When I was in sixth grade, my family took a vacation to Colorado. While we were there, we visited the Air Force Academy, which at that time was still pretty new. I decided I wanted to attend the Academy because it was a great education, I wanted to fly, I wanted to ski, and coming from the Midwest, I wanted to live near the mountains. I wrote to the Academy ski coach asking if I could be on the ski team, thinking that would help me get an appointment. I naively discounted the fact that I hadn't ever raced, and that skiing on a man-made hill in Illinois was much different than skiing in Colorado. Fortunately, my appointment didn't depend on my skiing ability, and I was accepted into the Class of 1973.

I'd always been intrigued with the idea of going to law school and, through the course of my four years at the Academy, I decided I'd make that my goal, rather than flying. I majored in Political Science and International Affairs, but ended up taking almost all the law courses available at the Academy. The instructors were terrific, and I was attracted to both the problem-solving challenges and the opportunity to serve others. What particularly intrigued me was making sound decisions in very complex situations: how can you help your client and, at the same time, ensure you're doing the right thing? As we approached graduation, I was given a waiver for pilot training; however, in 1973 it wasn't possible to be both a pilot and a lawyer in the Air Force, so I had to make a choice between the two. I chose law.

After graduation I served as a special agent in the Office of Special Investigations (OSI). I thought the experience would be useful as a lawyer, and I couldn't afford law school right out of the Academy. OSI was interesting. Once on a protective detail, I had to rent a tuxedo two sizes too big to fit a shoulder holster and brick radio (this was well before cell phones) underneath. No one tested the radios, so after 30 minutes the batteries ran out. Luckily no one we were protecting was threatened. Another time, after a drug bust, I took a large bag of marijuana home before going to the office to lock it up. When I turned my back, my golden retriever tried to get into the bag. I pictured having to tell my boss the dog ate it. It probably would not have been a good career move.

In 1974 Congress enacted the Funded Legal Education Program, which allowed up to 25 active-duty USAF officers to be selected for law school. Best of all, under this program tuition and fees were paid and the selectees received full pay and allowances during their time at school. I was fortunate enough to be selected, so after two years in OSI I went to law school at the University of Denver. After law school, I spent a year-and-a-half at Lowry AFB in the legal office, working primarily as a prosecutor. As a new lawyer, most of the cases I prosecuted were relatively minor crimes. The Air Force gave me the opportunity to work on my trial skills and to interact with commanders. Following that, I was reassigned to the Academy and spent four years as an instructor in the Law Department. That was an amazing assignment, working with great lawyers in the department and teaching law to cadets. Most of us in the law department were the same age and rank and had little kids. It was a great bunch of people and the families all got along well. Some of us still get together, 40 years later. The assignment also opened up the opportunity down the road to teach under the Fulbright Program in New Zealand, Germany and the Czech Republic.

After four years on the Academy faculty, I decided to leave active duty and join the Air Force Reserve. It was a difficult decision, as I'd loved my time in the active-duty Air Force and really enjoyed the people I'd served with. But there were additional factors to consider. From a professional standpoint, I was very interested in water law, which was an area I really couldn't practice in the Air Force. On the family side of the equation, my wife and I had four kids, the fifth was on her way (soon to be followed by number six), and we thought it was important for the family to be in one place. I joined the Air Force Reserve in January of 1984 and worked in the legal offices at Peterson AFB and the Academy while practicing law until my retirement from the Air Force Reserve in 1995.

Looking back, the Academy was great preparation for my career as a lawyer. I was never under the illusion that I was the smartest or the most talented lawyer in the courtroom, but I was probably better prepared than most, largely due to the discipline from my Academy days. That turns out to be a critical factor in the courtroom, because if you can anticipate what's going to happen and what the opposing arguments are going to be, you'll be in a better position to deal with most situations that come up during a trial. Having a strong motivation to do the right thing—something that was also engrained in us at the Academy—shaped all aspects of my legal work. After active duty, I had several law positions, but decided to open my own firm in 1986.

TRANSITIONING TO THE BENCH

In 2000, my career took a different turn, as I was appointed a district judge in Colorado's Fourth Judicial District by then-Governor Bill Owens. Being a judge provided a different perspective on the law, and the public service aspect appealed to me. The primary goal of a judge is to do the right thing, to follow the law, and to be fair. The main pressure on a judge is to make legally correct decisions. In many cases, a jury would make the ultimate decision on the merits of a case, but a judge has a lot of influence in applying the law to a case, to assist the jury in making its decision. The U.S. has a great legal system—it's not perfect, but it is better than systems that I have seen in other countries.

Integrity is always critical in the courtroom, but I found that a judge's perspective is different than a lawyer's perspective. The judge needs to be fair to all parties, and not be an advocate for one side or the other and should adequately and clearly explain any decisions made. A judge sees very quickly which lawyers are prepared, reliable, and not out to play games. Unfortunately, a judge can't always take it for granted what some lawyers (a small minority) argue. He or she may be shading their interpretation of the law, misconstruing it, or attempting to apply it to facts that don't quite fit. That's where our Core Values come into play. From that perspective, "Integrity First" is a linchpin in the legal profession, just as it is in the Air Force.

JUDICIAL CHALLENGES

As you can imagine, making sound decisions in a case can be a challenge. While the correct decision in most cases is usually clear, occasionally there are complex cases in which two very good lawyers make sound opposing arguments that can be challenging. I remember reading motions filed by lawyers and thinking, "This is a really good argument," then reading the opposing side's response to that motion and thinking, "These are some really good contrary points." When two really good lawyers are making excellent opposing arguments, particularly when motions could be determinative of the outcome of the case, the decision can be difficult, especially where the law or the facts aren't clear cut. That's where the ability to analyze the law and apply it to the facts is critical.

Sometimes there are cases in which the judge must make a decision in conformance with a law the judge or the public doesn't agree with. While it's easy to become conflicted, as a judge, you're not supposed to use your own definition of "what's right"—you're obligated to apply what the law says is right. You have to put any emotion aside and apply the law the way the legislature has written it. While those decisions may be difficult, it's the legislature's role to change the law. I've also presided over criminal cases in which I was convinced the defendant was guilty, but the district attorney didn't prove it. Because the burden is on the government to prove guilt beyond a reasonable doubt, if the jury let that person off, that was the right thing to do—regardless of what the judge may personally believe.

Sometimes unexpected situations come up which remind you of the importance of your work and the effect your job has on people. I was in my chambers one day when my assistant told me that there was a man who wanted to see me. I didn't recognize his name but was usually willing to talk to anybody as long as it didn't involve a case. The gentleman came into my office and told me that I sent him to prison two years ago, and he had just gotten out. At that point I was a little concerned and wondered where he was headed. He said, "That sentence changed my life and I wondered whether you'd be willing to perform the wedding ceremony for my fiancée and me." There was no way I could say no to that.

On the lighter side, there are times where you wonder what is going on in someone's thought process. For instance, I tried one case in which a lawyer cited the lyrics of a Grateful Dead song as legal precedent in an argument. He was later disbarred for an unrelated reason. In a second case, a defendant was arrested for a traffic offense and was searched while being booked into jail. The deputy who searched him found a package of methamphetamine in his underwear. During his arraignment in court, he blurted out his defense—to his lawyer's dismay—that he wasn't guilty of possession because that wasn't his underwear. In a third case, a man was brought to court on a charge of robbing a Subway sandwich store. The 6'6", 250-pound defendant was caught wearing a beany hat he thought would be a good disguise. Needless to say, it wasn't hard to recognize him as the same employee who had been fired from that Subway the week before.

Sentencing can be a real challenge for a judge because, in most cases, there are both punishment and rehabilitation considerations, particularly with respect to drug-related charges and non-violent crimes. In fact, I'd say that most of the felony cases over which I presided involved drugs in one way or another. The majority of the defendants I saw facing felony charges were relatively young men who dropped out of school, had a drug problem, and came from a broken family. It was disheartening not to be able to stop that cycle. Those defendants never had the advantages and opportunities that we had as cadets. On the less serious cases, particularly those involving non-violent or victimless crimes, I usually didn't send that person to prison—I wanted to get help for the defendant. In cases like that I normally sentenced the person to probation or to community corrections, which is a halfway house. But many times, I'd see those defendants come back in front of me because they couldn't comply with the terms of probation. My experience with many of these cases was that it's difficult—and, in some cases, impossible—to break a drug-addiction cycle. That was particularly sad and frustrating to me, given my Academy experience and the attitude that the Academy fostered—that we could pretty much do anything we set our minds to do.

CHIEF JUDGE RESPONSIBILITIES

From 2007 to 2012, I served as the chief judge for the Fourth Judicial District. While I kept the majority of my judicial workload, my additional responsibilities as chief judge were to oversee and manage operations within the district. My leadership responsibilities included supervising about 250 employees and 45 judges and magistrates. Because district and county judges are appointed by the governor, if a chief judge sees the need for changes due to performance issues, options are somewhat limited. The chief judge cannot fire another judge. All judges need to be completely independent in their decisions so, by necessity, the chief judge has no authority to tell district judges what to do or how to decide a case. It is completely appropriate for judges to exercise their authority independently. Occasionally however, judges may make decisions that appear biased. For instance, there can be a tendency for a new judge with a prosecution or defense background to lean in one specific direction— or even completely in the opposite direction to show they were being fair as a judge. In instances like that, a chief judge has to depend on influence, rather than "command authority," to ensure fair and consistent rulings.

The teamwork I learned at the Academy was important in managing a judicial district. There were four judges who were responsible for each of the major divisions that we handled in our district: criminal, civil, domestic, and juvenile. My approach was to pick good people to run the different divisions, rely on them to make the day-to-day decisions, and to keep me informed as to what was going on. But I also expected them to consult with me on the big decisions so that I would be part of that process and the ultimate decision maker, of course taking their advice into account. Communication works both ways, so I also met with the judges on a regular basis to keep them informed and to discuss trends and concerns.

Maintaining strong judicial ethics was always a point of emphasis with me. One of the most essential requirements is to avoid any appearance of impropriety—to not only do the right thing in all situations but avoid any word or deed that could cast doubt on the impartiality of our decisions or erode faith in our judicial system. If you make a decision that is adverse to one side, you need to be able to explain the decision in such a way that it makes logical sense. In the end, all parties may not agree with your decision, but at least they understand how you arrived at your conclusion.

I've learned a great deal in my career as an OSI agent and JAG in the Air Force, a civilian lawyer, a judge, a professor, and now in semi-retirement as an arbitrator and mediator. Our Core Values have not only played a formative role in my career but have also provided an important framework for making difficult decisions. Looking back on my Academy experience and my decision to go into the law, my advice to new graduates would be to follow your passion and understand that your passion may change and send you on a different career path. Find a career path you feel good about, one that provides value. Then put all your effort and energy into it. When I think about my Academy experience, I realize that the outstanding education, deep friendships, and our Core Values gave me the ability to further my education and take advantage of some amazing opportunities.

29

LEADERSHIP IN PUBLIC EDUCATION

by Major General (Ret.) John L. Barry

John Barry
CS-26

Maj. Gen. John Barry served in the Air Force for more than 30 years in a variety of command staff positions. He was a USAF "Top Gun" (Fighter Weapons School) graduate, combat veteran, White House Fellow, and military assistant to the Secretary of Defense. He commanded at the squadron level, twice at the group level, and twice at the wing level. John was a survivor of the 9/11 attack on the Pentagon, and his last Air Force assignment was as executive director for the Space Shuttle Columbia Accident Investigation. Following his Air Force retirement, he applied his leadership skills to public education, serving as superintendent of Aurora Public Schools. He reflected here on his career of public service.

It was 1:30 on the morning of July 20, 2012, when my phone rang at home, waking me from a deep sleep. I'd had many phone calls at strange hours in the military over a 30-year career, but this was highly unusual during the seven years I served as superintendent of a large urban school district. I snapped awake when our school district chief operating officer informed me that there had been a shooting at a local movie theater, and that authorities needed help in opening a high school as a place to take witnesses of the crime scene. As the reality began to sink in, I had flashbacks of being in the Pentagon on 9/11 and being in combat as a commander/fighter pilot flying over Iraq for 30 months. I was struck by the confluence of the crises I had experienced in the military and now in a city I called home, in my own country. I agreed to immediately assist by opening Gateway High School for whatever was needed.

As I struggled to get initial information, I realized that, based on my history in crisis situations, 80 percent of initial reports would be wrong. I knew this was going to be a long day and made plans to assemble our school district Incident Response Team (IRT)—a team that we had trained scores of times in emergency simulations and minor school incidents over six years.

As the phone calls started coming in, it was evident our IRT would be in a major support role for the first responders on the scene. Media outlets from the state and national levels were busily trying to report what was happening. I knew they were a valuable resource to assess initial situations in civilian events, something we were never guaranteed of in the military when fighting wars in other countries. The TV and internet were awash with floods of video and interviews as media reporters responded to the shooting and reported what they knew regarding the who, what, where, when and how—the questions you must start working on as soon as possible—while recognizing that the fog of a crisis will blanket the facts with great uncertainty.

While this was not a shooting in a school, the pending outcomes would resonate throughout the city and directly impact our opening of school in two weeks after the summer break. I knew immediately that this tragedy was developing into a calamity that would affect our Nation, the State of Colorado, and our school district. The issues of safety, security and recovery of our 40,000 students and more than 4,500 staff members would surely become a primary focus of our efforts for months to come.

Here was a convergence of realities and life experiences that I knew would have long-time impacts and consequences. It would compel me to examine the lessons learned in my careers as a retired major general in the United States Air Force, vice-president of an international corporation, and superintendent of the sixth largest school district in Colorado. I had other crisis experiences that had caused me to be introspective in the past. The theater shooting in Aurora became one more.

COLUMBIA INVESTIGATION

2003 promised to be a compelling year of celebration for the USAF, as it was the 100-year anniversary of the Wright Brothers' flight at Kitty Hawk. By that time, I had been a pilot for almost 32 years, and I was excited about the pending celebrations. As a major general in the USAF, I would be participating in several celebrations and giving speeches on how manned flight had transformed our world, our Nation, and our military services. Sadly, this excitement was all shattered on Feb 1, 2003, as the world witnessed the sudden and tragic loss of the Space Shuttle Columbia that killed all seven astronauts.

Because I had been a strategic planner for the USAF and had served as a White House Fellow in NASA during the Challenger Space Shuttle mishap in 1986, I was asked by Air Force Chief of Staff General John Jumper to serve on the investigation board for the Columbia mishap. The investigation was painful for the families of the seven crewmembers, as well as the public at large. Our board and contributing investigators worked tirelessly to develop credible findings and recommendations that were grounded in rigorous scientific and engineering principles. What the Columbia Accident Investigation Board concluded was that

NASA had two causes for this accident. One was technical: a piece of foam, weighing 1.2 pounds, broke away from the external tank and impacted the left leading edge of the orbiter wing, causing a breach that allowed super-heated air to penetrate the wing on re-entry, resulting in a break-up of Columbia. The second cause was organizational: NASA had allowed cultural traits and organizational practices to develop that were detrimental to the safety of the organization. As it turned out, the Columbia investigation was to be my last assignment on active duty in the USAF. It was a compelling challenge that took almost ten months to complete and ended with my serving as the executive director for the mishap investigation.

AIR FORCE RETIREMENT AND TRANSITION

After 30 years in the USAF, I had the honor and privilege to help defend the great nation of the United States of America, but now it was time to retire. Upon my retirement, I was asked to speak on the lessons learned regarding the Columbia Accident Investigation and, through that, continued to expand my understanding of how large organizations fail. I found myself serving more and more as a teacher of how complex organizations fail in complex ways.

While I was in this phase of giving talks and speeches, I accepted a position with SAP, a German international corporation for industrial software. While I was a bit of a novice in international business, I found the experience exciting and challenging as I served as the vice president for defense and security. For almost three years, I traveled the world (in one year, I traveled more than 246,000 miles) and was introduced to the compelling challenges of business development and solution management in countries in Europe and the Pacific. Working for SAP was insightful and extraordinary. I was impressed with the integrity of the company, and I felt fortunate for the opportunities it provided me in learning about the world of business. However, the travel was wearing on me and I knew there was something else I needed to do with my life.

I had always thought about doing something with education in my retirement years, largely because of the formative role it had played in my youth. I was raised in a one-bedroom apartment in the Bronx—a very different environment from that of most of my contemporaries. My family was somewhat dysfunctional, which put me at an even greater disadvantage. Under those circumstances, it's very easy to get off track. I was headed in a very bad direction in my early years and ended up getting into trouble a lot of the time. I was able to turn that around, primarily due to one high school teacher who helped me channel my energy into positive outcomes and focus on constructive goals. As I approached my sophomore year, I began to think about my future.

As you can imagine, the Air Force Academy wasn't well-known in the Bronx. In fact, the only reason I knew about it was because I was dating a girl in high school whose two brothers had gone to the Academy. I had a chance to talk to them when they came home on leave. Hearing them talk about Colorado and flying really fired my imagination and gave me the motivation I needed to redouble my efforts in my last two years of high school. To my amazement—and eternal gratitude—I received an appointment and entered the Academy with the Class of 1973. In light of my difficult beginnings, I feel I walked in with a deficit in character, but the Academy changed all that.

Because education had always been an important part of my adult life, I decided that when I retired from the Air Force, I'd want to do something in education. Serendipity arrived in my mailbox in the form of a letter inviting me to consider the Broad Superintendent Academy. After my retirement, I had been receiving notices from various sources on prospective follow-on careers, so I put it aside to look at some other time. Weeks later, while I was cleaning off my desk, I saw the letter again. I was curious now. The letter included an application for a Broad Superintendent Fellowship.

I had never heard of the program sponsor, Eli Broad, but I was intrigued by the opportunity. I learned that the Broad Superintendents

Academy, which was the basis of the Fellowship, was a rigorous 10-month executive management program designed to prepare CEOs and senior executives from business, non-profit, military, government, and educational backgrounds to lead urban public-school systems. It was structured in such a way that students were able to learn the ins-and-outs of public education while continuing in their current jobs. I also learned that Eli Broad was a billionaire philanthropist who was a leading advocate of educational reform. His basic approach was to get people who run large organizations to apply their business sense to running school districts. That made sense to me, as school districts are, in many cases, big businesses. For instance, in some cases, Colorado superintendents are running organizations that are comparable to some of the largest companies in the state.

As I researched his offer, I became more and more curious to understand what the art of the possible was with respect to leadership in public education. I realized that as head of a large school system, there were a lot of skill sets that I had from the USAF and SAP that would be transferable if I were ever to become a superintendent. I also began to see a lot of commonalities in my numerous experiences in command and the roles and responsibilities of running a school district. On a philosophical level, it was a chance for me to repay a debt I owed to the teacher who turned my life around. So, I applied for the fellowship and was accepted.

The program required us to meet once a month for about four days, each time in a different city. As I went through the fellowship, I was exposed to the worst part of education system in the United States. We traveled to large school districts across the country, from New York City to Los Angeles, and were able to see first-hand what the challenges were. But the more I saw, the more excited I became and the more convinced I was that my background could really help a school district. I also found that I had about 70 percent of the skillset required to be a superintendent (leadership, personnel management, strategic planning, etc.), while the Broad Fellowship would give me the remaining

30 percent (union relationships, pedagogy, educational politics, etc.). I also knew that I wasn't going to learn everything in a one-year fellowship but would learn enough to feel comfortable about applying for a superintendent's position.

LEADING THE AURORA SCHOOL DISTRICT

I graduated from the Broad Superintendent Academy in December 2004. After completing the fellowship, the Broad Academy doesn't assign graduates to a position, but makes them aware of available openings. While I continued to meet my obligations at SAP, I began to consider which school districts I could apply for as superintendent. In another case of serendipity, I learned that the Aurora superintendent position had just opened up. This was a great opportunity, since I had always wanted to return to Colorado. I was an Academy grad, my children had attended college in Colorado, and I had owned mountain property near Steamboat Springs since 1973. So to even be considered for a job in Colorado would be a true godsend.

I also learned that the Aurora Public School District, with 60 schools, would be a diverse challenge from the get-go, as 80 percent of the 42,000 students came from low-income households, 40 percent were English language learners, 52 percent were students of color, and student achievement had been rapidly declining. It was obvious that the Aurora community was a strong one and committed to improving opportunities for their children, but educational outcomes were not improving. Although I knew it would be difficult, given my background, it seemed that Aurora would be a good fit for me. My service in the military and in the business world was a great background, and made me realize that my values would help me prepare the next generation to lead this great Nation.

In 2006, I was fortunate enough to be included in a candidate pool for the next Aurora superintendent. Three other candidates applied for the position, all of whom were former superintendents. The selection process was arduous, with multiple interviews with community stakeholders, but it was fair. To my delight, I was selected to serve the students of Aurora starting in July 2006. I think the reason they took a chance on me was because they thought they needed to do something different. In addition, I could offer them some strategic planning and present different approaches than they were used to seeing.

As it turned out, I inherited a solid team. There were quite a few talented people on staff and I was able to hire additional good ones. It was due to these talented men and women that we were as successful as we were at helping kids understand the art of the possible, visualizing what they could become, and seeking the help they needed to achieve their dreams.

SORTING THROUGH THE PRIORITIES

There was a lot of work to be done. One of the key lessons I had learned as a board member and executive director of the team investigating the Columbia Space Shuttle accident was that complex systems fail in complex ways, and that they inevitably require complex solutions. Applying this logic to our school district, I realized that success could not be achieved through a single action—there was no "silver bullet." Rather, success would come from multiple initiatives that would allow students, parents, and staff to find the right path for them. I also believe that ownership equaled motivation, and that it would be critical to develop, encourage and support new definitions of what schools can be. An organization can be structured to advance and succeed, but it would take more than good intentions—it requires vision, open and honest conversations, and enlightened attitudes. While these were essential elements, we would also need good structural design work to integrate the elements and be responsive to the students and community the district served. Furthermore, there were no cookie-cutter solutions: in the end, each district would have find its own integrated strategy that matched its culture.

I also knew that success would depend on stakeholder engagement.

In every organization I had been a part of, I'd learned that everyone wants and needs to understand the big picture before becoming engaged and supportive. In a school district, I found that the first step was to make each stakeholder—the Board of Education, students, staff, parents, unions, and the business community—believe that real change was possible and to unite around a common vision and mission. Sustainable leadership requires engaging all stakeholders. The next step was encouraging and building capacity for leadership that extended from the superintendent and board to every teacher and classroom, as well as to parents and the community. One of the first things I did when I arrived in my new position was to go on a 90-day listening tour. I visited with all our major stakeholders and held open discussions to listen to their concerns and ideas. As we worked through the issues, I realized that, because there was no single reason why students were not succeeding in our district, no single solution could produce the results needed for a transformation. I told our stakeholders that we would be developing a strategic plan to present to them in six months.

It was a significant undertaking, but we created a multi-faceted, integrated strategic plan that transformed the entire school district with revolutionary ideas like offering choices of pathways in health, business, STEM, arts, and communications, even as early as middle school. Additionally, we were first in the nation to offer college courses in our high schools, taught by our high school teachers who were qualified as adjunct professors in our local Aurora Community College.

In terms of execution, one of the things we learned in the Air Force was to manage by walking around, to get out of the office and see what's happening on the ground level. In line with that philosophy, I gathered my leadership team, and we visited every single school in our district—60 in all. In fact, we ended up visiting each school as a leadership team every single semester for my entire tenure.

THE TRUANCY PROBLEM

I had been in my position a couple of weeks when I drove by one of the high schools and saw a lot of kids outside the building during normal school hours. I assumed that the principal had instituted an early release, so I decided to find out what was going on. I said to the principal, "No one told me there would be an early release today. How's that going?" To my surprise, he said, "Oh, no, we don't have an early release. Since truancy is a major problem, we decided to concentrate on those students that wanted to learn." Obviously, we had a significant truancy problem, since by law students in K-12 are required to be in school. In response, our team developed a multi-faceted program for dealing with truancy. It was a multi-faceted program, because I knew from experience that there wouldn't be a single "silver bullet." But our efforts succeeded in cutting the truancy rate by 35% that year and years after.

In addressing the truancy problem, our preferred option was to try to work with families to bring their student to school. The final option was to work with the authorities and the courts to ensure both parents and students clearly understood what their responsibilities were, but I considered that a last resort. So, my team and I started knocking on doors and saying to students, "Please come back. You've got to come back because you need this opportunity to learn. And I don't want to have to go through the truancy courts." I think this sent a clear message that we cared—that we wanted our students to come back for their own future well-being, not just because they were breaking the law. And sometimes that's all it took to get the family's support. But it never would have happened if we hadn't been willing to get out and about and visit families in their homes. Our visible presence in the community was a clear demonstration that we were determined to put the kids first. That hadn't always been the case, as adult issues often detracted from the real educational mission.

I found a lot of the values I saw in the school district aligned with what we were taught at the Academy. However, there were cases where kids were coming to us from environments that were even more challenging than my situation in the Bronx, so these values were unfamiliar to them. Our approach was to provide them with a clear understanding of what was expected. That gave them a benchmark and frame of reference to evaluate their behavior, as well as a clear picture of the road ahead.

I met with a number of problem kids during my tenure—kids who had really gotten off track. In those cases, I found it useful to talk about time horizons. I'd sit them down in my office, look in their eyes, and say, "I hear you're on a downward trend here. Now, whether you turn that around is up to you, but consider this: where are you going to be in 10 years? Where are you going to be in 20 years? How are you going to take care of your mother or your future family? If you have kids someday, what values are you going to teach them?" It didn't always resonate, but often I saw that spark of recognition in their eyes. Some students would have a time horizon of tomorrow or next week. When's the next football game? When's the next party? And I'd talk about the need to widen their time horizon, to consider where they were going to be in the future. Some kids would look at me square on and say, "I'm going to be dead before I am 21," or "Well, I'm probably going to be in jail." I'd ask, "Do you really want to go down that road?" And they'd say, "Well, no, but you know, that's just what's going to happen." So I tried to give them an understanding of the art of the possible. Often, I'd see a little spark in their eyes, and that's what I zeroed in on. Other times I'd just see a blank look, an indication they were not listening to anything I was saying and I was not making a connection. And frankly, those are the kids that I ended up supporting the recommendation for an expulsion. But, if I saw just a spark, then we'd build on that and see if we could bring the student back to the reality of the situation. There were some tough decisions that had to be made but, in the end, there were values we had to uphold.

Based on my experience in the military, the business world, and in public education, I've found that leadership is the cornerstone of any successful transformation. Genuine leadership is not about racing ahead and hoping that others are following. The more effective approach is to lead by inspiring, rather than commanding. But, as I look back, those insights started with the Academy. In fact, any success I've had in my varied careers can be traced in one way or another back to my time on the Terrazzo, in Fairchild Hall, or on the athletic fields. The Core Values we were raised with—integrity, service, and excellence—have not only served as guiding principles, but as a moral compass to help guide me through the most difficult of times. In the end, that's an enduring lesson for all of us to learn.

30

REMEMBER YOUR ROOTS

by Captain (Ret.) William L. Thompson, Esq.

"T" Thompson
CS-29

As with several of our classmates, William "T" Thompson attended pilot training, was an instructor pilot, and then left active duty for the airlines after completing his initial commitment. But that's where his path diverged from the familiar. He completed his law degree, established a law practice, founded the Summit Group conglomerate, sat on various corporate and charitable boards, and served as commissioner of the Massachusetts Aeronautics Commission for 20 years—all while flying with Delta Air Lines. The Air Force Core Values have been his guiding principles throughout his multi-faceted career. In 2008, he returned to the Academy as the president and CEO of the Association of Graduates, applying his business acumen to lead the organization through a period of unprecedented growth and service to the Academy and its graduate community. His story exemplifies lifelong dedication to the Air Force, the Academy, and our Core Values.

I didn't grow up expecting to go into the military, but the war in Vietnam was a decisive factor. Many kids I knew were being drafted, so I assumed I would probably end up being drafted as well and serving in Vietnam in one role or another. I knew the difference between the enlisted corps and the officer corps, so I decided I wanted to serve as an officer if I went. That got me thinking about my options after high school graduation.

My high school record was pretty strong. I had done well academically and was an All-American honorable mention in football, so I ended up getting many college catalogs in the mail, including one from each of the service academies. I wasn't particularly interested in either the Army or the Navy, so I eliminated both West Point and Annapolis as possibilities. The Merchant Marine Academy didn't sound particularly interesting either, but the Coast Guard Academy might offer me a chance to fly, so I kept that as a possibility.

But the fifth catalog I received had me scratching my head. Growing up in South Carolina, I had heard of both West Point and Annapolis; however, I didn't even realize there was an Air Force Academy. But, when I looked through the catalog, everything seemed interesting—the flying, as well as the mountains and the picturesque setting, were particularly attractive. But realizing I had to go through a political process to get an appointment, I had my doubts. My senator was Strom Thurmond, a strong segregationist who voted against any civil rights legislation that crossed his desk. And no African American had ever been appointed to the Air Force Academy from South Carolina, so I figured my chances were not good. But, I thought, "Why not give it a try? What do I have to lose?" So I applied. To my surprise—and delight—I ended up getting a nomination to the Air Force Academy.

TWO SERVICE ACADEMIES

In addition to the Air Force Academy appointment, I was also accepted at the Coast Guard Academy, which flew me up for a visit. Further complicating the picture, about the same time I received a scholarship to the Citadel. So I had three good options, but it set up one of the most challenging decisions in my young life. My parents made it clear that it was my decision, but my dad asked me what I really wanted to do. I told him I wanted to fly. He pointed out that, while the Coast Guard had a flight program, only ten percent of graduates got to fly; however, virtually all Air Force Academy graduates who were medically qualified went on to pilot training. He also pointed out that, while my Air Force commitment may seem like a lifetime, that time would pass quickly, and other career opportunities would come along. I had three days to decide my future. For the first time in my life, I put emotion aside and made a business decision. And that decision was to go into the Air Force Academy—one I never regretted.

As it turned out, my dad was right, and my time in the Air Force passed quickly. In what seemed like a flash, I graduated from the Academy, attended pilot training at Moody AFB, Georgia, and was stationed at Mather AFB, California as a T-37 instructor pilot. Because I wanted to keep my career options open after fulfilling my Air Force commitment, during my tour at Mather, I began to think about what I might do after the Air Force.

Law School

Flying for the airlines seemed like the most logical alternative, so that's where I put my focus. I also got to know a senior advisor in Sacramento politics who had extensive business interests in California. One day we were discussing my future plans, and he gave me some great advice: don't totally rely on the airlines—always have a business on the side. That made a great deal of sense, because I knew I'd need a fallback if I couldn't get an airline job. Coincidently, I had read a recent article in *Fortune* magazine that stated that a third of all Fortune 500 CEOs had law degrees. I realized that a law degree would give me many more options, so I decided to apply to law school and focus on business and tax law. I was fortunate to be accepted into the University of the Pacific's McGeorge School of Law, and spent the next three years flying during the day and going to school at night.

Law school was challenging, but was the first educational program that I truly enjoyed, primarily because I could see a clear connection between what I was studying and practical uses for the education. The fact is that everything we do in this country is, in one way or another, based on law, and most of what we hold dear is implemented through the tax code. A law degree would offer great insight into how the system works, not to mention providing a great back-up career and side business while flying for the airlines. As an airline pilot, I knew that I'd be surrounded by well-paid contemporaries in need of tax advice. Shortly after separating from the Air Force, I was fortunate to be hired by Delta Air Lines. Just as my friend in Sacramento had advised, having a law degree turned out to be a very compatible and worthwhile side business. After a few years of providing tax and investment advice to my fellow pilots, I became involved in numerous other business opportunities outside the airlines.

LIVING THE CORE VALUES

Throughout my business dealings, I kept returning to the values instilled during our time at the Academy and reinforced on active duty. For instance, while I was still providing financial and tax planning services, I realized that many of my clients had an insurance shortfall. I didn't have an insurance background, so I decided to go out and find someone who could help me fill that gap and improve overall service. An insurance guy I knew from serving on a corporate board seemed like a logical candidate, so I reached out to him to see if there was an opportunity for us to collaborate. After some back-and-forth, I started using his services to integrate insurance into my bigger financial planning picture. I quickly ran into problems. My stated business goal was to save my clients money through prudent tax and investment advice—that was my brand.

Unfortunately, I discovered that my insurance partner didn't share the same goal, which was a real problem for me. He recommended expensive high-end solutions to our clients, where less expensive insurance products would be just as beneficial. We were making more money because of the products he used, but I couldn't accept the current practice from an integrity standpoint. I brought my concerns to him, but we could not agree to use lower-cost products. Therefore, I ended the relationship.

Looking back, it was probably more of an ethical issue than an integrity one, but in my experience, it's sometimes hard to separate ethics from integrity. Integrity was always first with me in all my business dealings. There were deals that I avoided because of potential integrity issues. In questionable situations, I walked away with no hesitation. In fact, in all my years since leaving the Air Force, I've found that the Air Force Core Values and business—at least, the kind of business I want to be associated with—are very compatible.

THE VALUE OF DIVERSITY

I've also found that diversity has been a significant factor in the business world, either through its presence or absence. And just because I'm black doesn't mean I don't have something to learn about diversity. For instance, when I lived in Boston, I belonged to a group that got together each Sunday to play basketball. Unlike some parts of Boston, our group was very diverse, both in race and business profession. While most were black guys, there were a couple of white guys. One of my friends was a superintendent of one of the school districts in the well-to-do suburbs north of Boston. He said to me, "'T', I need to get you into some of my schools because you'd be a great role model for the kids." My response was, "I go to Boston often to talk with kids from the inner city about personal growth and achievement. Your school district is very affluent, so I don't know what I have to teach them." His response was a diversity eye-opener for me: "You need to be talking to white kids, too, so they get a different perspective on who black people are. I want these white kids to see there are black people out there doing things other than playing NBA basketball or making rap music. They can be and are highly successful in a wide variety of professions." I had never looked at diversity from that point of view—I'd been focused on going into the inner city and trying to be a role model for black kids who were struggling. It never occurred to me that there was a diversity lesson that needed to be taught in an affluent white suburb of Boston. His comment opened my mind to the full meaning of diversity.

LEADING THE ASSOCIATION OF GRADUATES

Years later, I got an unexpected opportunity to come back to the Academy and reconnect with my roots. A grad friend told me that the AOG was looking for a new CEO and suggested I apply. I said, "Well, that's interesting, but I'm living in Atlanta, serving on some boards, and I'm not looking for another job." His response was brutally honest: "You owe it to the Academy to get involved and give back because that institution has been the foundation for your career success."

That got me thinking. I decided to reach out to the acting CEO and get some insight into what was going on. I also called the CEO at West Point and the interim CEO at the Naval Academy to compare notes about their organizations. Frankly, I was embarrassed at how far we were behind them in every metric. In many points of comparison, we've often used the excuse that we're the newer service academy, but the reality is that we have just as many living graduates as they have. Next, I spent quite a bit of time reviewing the AOG website and minutes from every past board meeting. I wanted to learn as much as I could about the organization, its goals, and its performance. Based on my research, I concluded that a lot needed to be done to improve AOG support to both the Academy and the graduate community.

I decided to throw my hat in the ring and submitted my resume on the last day of the application period. It was primarily due to an innate competitive drive to improve organizational performance, because

I didn't need or want a job. Had I not been selected for the position I wouldn't have minded—it would certainly have made things easier.

I got a call from the search committee chairman, who asked me if I'd be willing to fly out to Colorado for an interview. The first question they asked me was, "Well, tell us, "T", why do you want this job? And my response was, "To be honest, I don't know that I want this job." Everybody was taken aback and asked me to elaborate. I said, "Well, basically, this is a dysfunctional organization. You've got some serious issues that need attention. I don't want the job, but if I'm going to take it, then we're going to get it fixed." I began going through my list of AOG challenges, starting with the lack of a transparent system of governance and declining revenues. I also pointed to the lack of a grassroots infrastructure for graduates: West Point had 120 local chapters, the Naval Academy had 100, but we had only 31 and been stuck at 31 for the last six years. I asked them, "How can graduates be connected to each other and the institution when you don't even have a grassroots infrastructure to give them the opportunity?"

I was asked what the most pressing problem was, in my opinion. My response was, "If I were to take this job, the first thing you're going to have to do is put a system of governance in place. Let me run the organization; give me the big picture of where you want to go. And if I don't get you there, fire me and hire somebody else." The interview was scheduled for 45 minutes, but it ended up being an hour and a half. And I remember the final question: "Is that governance system a deal-breaker for you?" And my response was, "Absolutely." Then I got up and left.

That night I got together with a classmate who asked me how the interview had gone. I said, "Well, it was an interesting conversation. It went twice as long as it was supposed to, but I'm sure I'm not going to get the job because I was very straight with them—I told them how dysfunctional they are." We had a good laugh, and I went back to Atlanta. One week later, they called and told me I was the unanimous choice for the job.

A GREAT RUN

As it turned out, the next nine years were some of the most rewarding years of my professional life. We established a solid governance system that clarified the CEO and board's roles. We significantly increased assets from $35 million to $60 million, expanded the number of local chapters to 87, and made substantial efforts to bring younger grads into the AOG. That was an issue that would frequently come up at board meetings—the need for more diversity on the board. Yet there are some realities that we must deal with here, because when you talk about expanding graduate involvement in the AOG, you need to look at diversity and inclusion from a bit of a different angle.

The AOG has traditionally been dominated by the older grads, kind of the "old guard." But the reality is that a 2023 grad looks at things through a very different lens than a 1973 grad does, and that's something that the AOG needs to be aware of. Frankly, it's a phase of life issue. The AOG tends to be an older person organization because people have had their kids, are steady in their careers, or are just retiring. They have the time to get involved. But younger grads have different priorities at that stage in their lives, which is entirely understandable. We certainly want to allow older grads to be involved. And we should honor them for the great things they're doing for our Air Force. But just because older grads are more active doesn't mean our younger grads aren't contributing.

Of course, diversity and inclusion encompass far more than age. I remember discussing with our *Checkpoints* [AOG alumni magazine] editor about that not long after I took over as CEO. I said, "You know, we have female, African American, Hispanic, and Asian cadets. Why is it that there's not one picture of anyone other than white male cadets when I look through this magazine?" I don't think anyone had ever asked a question like that before. Our *Checkpoints* staff of predominately white males were back in the communications department putting together what they are, which had become ingrained in their subconscious thinking. But, once I pointed that out, everything became diverse in terms of presentation because they knew "T" Thompson was going to look at it. It wasn't that our staff was purposely trying not to be diverse—it's that they were doing things the way they'd always been done. All it took was someone bringing it to their attention and raising their level of consciousness for things to change. That's a powerful lesson.

OUR OBLIGATION

When you consider Academy graduates as a group, we're a tiny and privileged segment of society. And, when you break it down and start looking at minority members of that privileged group, it gets even more exclusive. But, regardless of your demographic, having been given this fantastic opportunity creates a responsibility for us all to be role models and actively give back to society, in one form or another.

PART VII

UPON REFLECTION

Age provides two things: the ability to step back and reflect on decisions made and paths taken—or not taken—and history, which provides a rich context with which to evaluate past events. Both are critical elements in developing perspective. The 50 years that have passed since our graduation have provided us with a unique vantage point to consider a variety of "could-a, would-a, should-a" issues.

In response to the question, "Looking back, what are some of the seminal lessons and experiences you'd like to pass along," our classmates offer a variety of answers. Here is a sample.

MIKE EDWARDS

Someone asked me recently whether I was happy with what I was doing. That really got me to thinking.

Of course, there will always be little regrets along the way but, when I considered the big picture, my answer to that question was, 'Absolutely.' I

Mike Edwards
CS-13

have felt blessed my entire life, because the things I've chosen to do have put food on the table, and what others might call 'work' have been exactly what I love to do.

I've been so fortunate to be able to do what I've done in my career. But in all honesty, I think that's largely a function of attitude—looking at situations in a positive light, rather than in a negative light. In fact, I've always told people I'm a 'glass half-full' guy. In my experience, having a positive attitude enables you to look back on your life and appreciate how things have worked out to make you who you are. That's when you realize how truly blessed you've been. So, from my perspective, attitude is everything.

I remember 'bitch sessions' at the Academy on Friday nights. We'd go to the snack bar [now "Hap's Place"] in Arnold Hall. I quickly became disillusioned with those sessions because they seemed pointless to me. They weren't constructive. In reality, there was never a time that I wanted to leave the Academy—not once. From the time we reported in, I thought 'What an amazing place and what an amazing opportunity,' and that never changed for me. Of course, I had tough times like everyone else, but no matter what was going on, I never really wanted to leave. So I got tired of the sessions. I'd go to the snack bar with my friends, but once the bitch session started, I'd just go back to my room and relax. One of my friends ended up leaving the Academy, mainly because he was there because that's what his parents wanted, not for himself. It was tough to watch him leave, but I also understood that wasn't what he really wanted out of life.

One of the things I've told my kids over the years is to find their passion and follow it wherever it leads. Do what you believe in, and don't look back. This great country of ours offers tremendous opportunity. If you work at it and keep a positive attitude, you can be whatever you want to be.[130]

HERB HARRISON

People always say to me that I always seem to have a good attitude, and I'd like to think that's true. The way I look at it, I don't have the right to have anything less. Every morning I wake up thinking that I have a chance to do it all over again. Whatever I may have gotten wrong yesterday, I can get right today. Any mistakes I made yesterday just made me stronger for what I have to do tomorrow, and maybe I'll get it right this time.

Herb Harrison
CS-25

Obviously, there are bad things that happen that are beyond our control. In those situations, I know it's easy to feel sorry for yourself. I can't—and won't—let those things define me or stop me from moving ahead. That's where maintaining a positive attitude comes in. If you take the right attitude about any obstacle you run into, you'll figure out a way to be successful.

When I'm talking to homeless veterans, my message is the same: 'Yeah, you're down at the moment. But let's figure out how to make your future better. Let's get you some benefits. Let's get you down to the VA. This is a new

130 | Interview with Howard M. Edwards, November 30, 2021.

beginning. What's happened may slow you down, but it doesn't keep you from moving ahead. It may change your path, but you can still move forward.'[131]

"T" THOMPSON

"T" Thompson
CS-29

Looking back, I learned a critical lesson at the Academy that has stayed with me over the years: figure out what you want and then aggressively pursue it. In my experience, there's a natural tendency for people to stand back rather than go after something they want. Call it timidity or apprehension, but the reluctance to step forward stops people from achieving their full potential. I learned that early in my doolie year.

I had a successful high school football career but, when I went to the Academy, I thought I'd need to put football aside to concentrate on academics. Still, I never lost my desire to play. One day I was headed back to the squadron from the Cadet Gym. There was an open field to the right of the gym in those days, and I saw the first team varsity offense running plays in shoulder pads and shorts. I had never seen such speed and precision before. I thought, 'Wow, this is football on a whole other level than what I'm used to.' That gave me the football bug again, and right then and there, I decided to put aside any doubts and go out for the team. With enough effort, maybe I could play football and handle the academic program. But first, I needed to get my foot in the door.

131 | Interview with Herbert A. Harrison, January 4, 2022.

The next day, I went down to the Field House and talked to the freshman head coach, Jim Bowman, who was also the top recruiter for Head Coach Ben Martin. I gathered my courage, walked into his office, and told him, 'Coach, I want to come out for the football team.' He just looked at me and replied, 'Well, we've got 90 recruited athletes this year. Why don't you play intramural football, and we'll have an open day for those folks who want to come out. We'll give you a look then.' I said, 'Well, to be honest, if I do that, I think I'll just be another face in the crowd. I know I'm better than that.' I'm sure he thought I was just another cocky kid, rather than someone who seriously wanted to play football. But to my relief, he passed me an application and asked me to go ahead and complete it. The form asked me a series of questions, like 'What position did you play? Who was your coach? Did you have any post-season honors?'

Once I finished filling out the form, I slid it back across his desk. He picked it up, looked at it, and started laughing, saying, 'You know, we've got an Honor Code here, and we take it very seriously.' Well, I had no idea what he was talking about. I knew we had an Honor Code but thought, 'What's that got to do with me?' My sheet summarized my post-season honors, to include All-State and All-American Honorable Mention, but he must have thought I was just making all this up to ensure he'd give me a look.

I left his office and went back up to the squadron. By the time I got there, the CQ handed me a message, telling me to report to the Field House immediately. My instant reaction was, 'I was just there; what's going on?' Anyway,

I walked back to Coach Bowman's office, and he said, 'I can't believe it—I've got a walk-on All-American. We were only able to recruit one other All-American. Go see Smitty (the equipment manager) and tell him to give you a locker.' And just like that, I became a recruited athlete.

The lesson for me was not to be afraid to go after what you want. Most people don't go after the big things in life, often because they're afraid of failure. Over the years, it's been my experience that, when you ask for something, even though the odds may be against you, you'll get it 85% of the time. Then if you work hard and don't give up, you'll prosper.[132]

BOB MUNSON

Bob Munson
CS-34

Looking back, I can offer two big lessons I learned in my career. The first was that sometimes the best opportunities turned out to be the ones I didn't want. For instance, my last choice of pilot training location, Craig AFB outside of Selma, Alabama, turned out to be a better experience than many of my classmates at, say, the much sought-after Williams AFB outside of Phoenix. As another example, after becoming a pilot-physician, I was competitive for astronaut training, which was my original career goal. But had I applied and been accepted, I would have languished in Houston for a decade awaiting that one trip, instead of getting a number of great experiences, including flying with the Royal Air Force. Finally, toward the

132 | Interview with William L. Thompson, December 2, 2021.

end of my career I wanted to attend a gastroenterology fellowship (which would have led to a lucrative post-retirement practice), but the Air Force needed me in a four-year Acquisitions tour. What? A pilot-physician going into a third career field? Who wants that? It turned out to be incredible experience.

The second important lesson I learned was to never turn down a training opportunity. Many officers avoid the Air University schools, often because they prefer to stay operational. Bad choice. The Maxwell AFB courses open your leadership eyes, help you learn from others in different career fields, and create career opportunities. Furthermore, just 'filling the square' through distance learning is no substitute for in-person attendance. As another example, in the medical field, my hubris told me I didn't need to do a residency in Aerospace Medicine. As an experienced pilot-physician, I was already training residents at the School of Aerospace Medicine, and I felt that going through that residency myself would detract from more important work. As it turned out, that decision limited my assignment options and career paths. So don't fall into the trap of thinking that your current job is too important to leave for a school slot. In my experience, it isn't.

In hindsight, had I paid attention I would have learned both of those lessons at the Academy. Ironically, the Air Force Academy was my last choice of colleges. But it was the best choice I could have made—I just didn't realize it. And, once there, I didn't take advantage of the many training opportunities the Academy offered because I didn't think I would need the experience. As it turned out, I did.[133]

JOE KAHOE

Joe Kahoe
CS-07

I've often wondered, 'What if I had to do it again?' With the benefit of 50 years of maturity, I know I'd be way different—more open to guidance on leadership, character development, and the Honor Code. If I had it to do over again, I'd soak it up, try to learn and grow from it, rather than being so resistant.

Ironically, 30 years later, I had a chance for a do-over of sorts. My son went to the Prep School and the Academy, so I had a chance to relive the whole experience through his eyes. During those five years, there wasn't a day that went by where I wasn't in direct contact with him, either through email or instant messaging. And, when he got a cell phone his junior year, we talked every day. So, I was able to mentor him, guide him, motivate him, and talk him off the ledge when the kind of things happened that typically spin up a 17, 18, and 19 year old kid.[134]

RON SCOTT

I grew up in poor, tough neighborhoods. Even though my father completed high school through the GED program while deployed to the Korean Conflict, he and my mother

133 | Interview with Robert A. Munson, January 7, 2022.
134 | Interview with Joseph J. Kahoe, March 27, 2020.

wanted their sons to go to college and pursue a higher quality of life. An appointment to the Air Force Academy was an affordable option. Although I had no interest in a military career, I figured I would serve the five-year commitment and then continue with 'normal' life. Much to my surprise, the Academy opened my eyes to a completely dif-ferent culture—one based on honor, responsibility, and serving a greater cause. Performance was a way of demonstrating worthiness to be part of a worthy cohort.

Ron Scott
CS-34

The Academy instilled a set of virtues that served as a moral compass when confronted with questionable behav-ior. My very first assignment involved corruption and a duty to address it on a scale not typical for a brand-new second lieutenant. I learned very early that with a sound moral compass and the courage to act, doing the right thing was valued and appreciated by superiors, peers, and subordinates—it reinforced a culture of Integrity First, Service before Self, and Excellence in All We Do. These experiences further motivated me to remain in the Air Force and to dedicate myself to serving its important mis-sion. Other assignments brought other challenges requir-ing moral decision making, such as firing incompetent officers and preferring court-martial charges. Yet, these experiences paled in comparison to the joys of mentoring talented people—officers, NCOs, and civilians—in sup-port of our mission and how it directly relates to support-ing and defending the Constitution of the United States against all enemies foreign and domestic.[135]

135 | Interview with Ronald J. Scott, January 30, 2022.

JOHN MUSE

John Muse
CS-36

As a businessman, when people ask me, 'What's your formula for success?' I say three things. First, at the most basic level, take care of your people, because your people are the ones who will make the business succeed. You can have all the right ingredients at the strategic level, but superb execution only comes from the people doing the work.

Second, find good people who you know will take care of your customers. If you get the right people in the right positions, your customer won't even consider doing business with anyone else. As a result, you'll keep your clients forever.

Finally, remember that relationships really matter, in that you can't accomplish anything of great significance on your own. With respect to building relationships, as an Academy graduate you've got instant credibility, in that you've gone to a school that everyone knows is highly selective and very rigorous. But, even more important, you've gone to a school that places a high value on character. For that reason, you'll be looked at as someone who is reliable, who's going to say what you do and do what you say. That's the fundamental basis for strong relationships, the kind that can make great things happen.[136]

136 | Interview with John R. Muse, July 5, 2022.

ROCKY AVVENTO

I've lived and continued to live a blessed life and have used three guiding principles that I collectively call 'ACT' to find my purpose in life and stay on track. ACT stands for: Action, Community and Transformation.

Rocky Avvento
CS-02

First, be a person of action. Be proactive: take charge. Don't let the day dictate its terms. Make things happen, rather than waiting for them to happen, and be willing to challenge your comfort zone. This is a major first step in finding your true calling. I was willing to take on the hard things in life. Had I not done that, I'd never have gone to the Prep School, graduated from the Academy, and accepted a challenging assignment working on and operating the National Space Transportation system—the Space Shuttle.

Next, be a person who uses the power of community. Show respect for others every day and become a part of your community. Start each day with a simple smile and kind words, support the people around you, and be willing to accept help when you need it. I couldn't have succeeded in the Air Force and beyond had I not been willing to accept the help of others and given help in return. For instance, it gave me great joy to have inspired a young NCO in my unit to go on to college and earn an appointment to Officer Training School.

Finally, commit to your daily transformation: self-improvement of the mind, body and spirit. Fill your mind with new facts and ideas. Maintain a solid foundation of health and energy. Make yourself a person God would be proud of. Let the Air Force Core Value of 'Service Before Self' be your foundation. During my AF career, I was challenged in all three aspects of that transformation. On permanent changes of station and other deployments, I worked hard to be a better officer and family person. I believe such focus helped me achieve the success that I've enjoyed.

In my experience, practicing these ACT principles every day has the power to change your life, and will help you to find the unique purpose God has assigned to you. Joy, success, and happiness will follow.[137]

BOB SUMMERS

Bob Summers
CS-02

Being charged to lead others is a noble and exciting endeavor. As members of the United States Air Force, we decided to serve our country because it gave us an opportunity to answer the call to a higher moral and ethical purpose. As military officers, we are obligated to display professionalism and an image that reflects our Nation's military capabilities. This needs to be evident to our citizens and our enemies.

As you start your service career, remember that your actions will define who you are to others. No one is perfect. When you make a mistake, recognize and correct

137 | Avvento, Gennaro J. *Success Is a Grilled Cheese Sandwich.* Amazon Book Baby, January 6, 2020.

your error, admit your mistake, and get back to your core values.

As a follower, I learned that it was important to be a strong team player and support the leader you're working for. Look out for your boss. Know and understand his or her point of view. If you're confused, ask questions and get some clarification. Support your leader's point of view by being visibly loyal or, if you see a problem, don't just point it out but rather take the next step and bring your leader a solution.

As a leader, I always held one foundational principle at the forefront: believe in your people. Take care of them, and they'll take care of the mission and the organization. As you assume higher positions, it's important to remember that leadership is a covenant between the leader and each individual in the organization. Therefore, it's important that you take care of your people. My belief is that everyone wants to succeed and, more important, everyone wants to be on a winning team. This belief, in turn, drives my priorities and behaviors in helping the team accomplish the mission.[138]

138 | Written on behalf of Brigadier General Robert P. Summers by his family, on July 28, 2022. During his 28-year Air Force career, Bob served in a variety of federal departments and agencies and was often charged with turning around struggling organizations. He was passionate about the topic of leadership and was known for jotting down his thoughts for future publication. Bob passed away before he was able to write his book, but the thoughts presented here reflect some of his fundamental beliefs.

KIRK SAMELSON

Kirk Samelson
CS-35

In retrospect, there are many things I took away from the Academy and my time after graduation. These are the ones that are most important to me.

If you have a goal, don't give up. Keep fighting for it. You may not achieve it right away, but if you were able to graduate from the Academy, you can accomplish almost anything you set your mind to.

Keep in touch with your classmates and other grads. You are part of a group with shared experiences and accomplishments. No matter where you go, there will be another grad there, happy to help, offer advice, and be a friend. I've run into grads that I hadn't seen for years, and we were able to pick up where we left off. There is something to be said for the 'Long Blue Line.'

Take advantage of as many experiences as you can. The Academy and the Air Force offer opportunities that you can seldom find other places. Don't sit on the sidelines. Be a participant.

And don't forget your family. They are the most important part of life.[139]

"O" MITCHELL

As I look back on my career, I wouldn't change anything. The Academy was good to me. There have been both hard

139 | Interview with Kirk S. Samelson, July 26, 2022.

times and good times, but I've been richly blessed. I tell people, 'I've been able to do things that many people only dream about doing.' I've been able to participate in athletics at a high level in both football and basketball. I've also been able to participate at a high level academically. I've been able to do well financially and share my good fortune with family members. I've been able to help younger individuals understand the beauty of things.

"O" Mitchell
CS-22

Of course, success always comes at a price. But, in my experience, if you're willing to work hard, and listen to people around you that are willing to help, you're going to do well.

I would tell freshmen who are coming to the Academy now that if you don't succeed in life, it's because you don't want to, because the Academy will give you all the help and nourishment you need to be successful. They educate us. They expose us to all different things. If you don't use what you've been given and use those advantages to succeed, it's your own fault.[140]

GARY ANDERSON

Looking back, I realize I have made my share of mistakes in life. Even at the Academy, I could have looked back at my high school years and known that, if I had paid closer attention or put more effort into learning what I should have been learning, the Academy, at least academically,

---

would have been easier. I think if we are honest with our-selves, we all can see things in life we should have done differently. With 50 years of perspective, it's easy to say, 'If

I could have put more effort into doing certain things, I'd be better at whatever I'm doing today.' But the key is to learn from the mistakes (and successes) of the past and adjust our behavior and actions today, so we constantly become a better version of ourselves.

Gary Anderson
CS-34

Most people seem to take years to develop a level of maturity and reflection that helps them avoid some of life's mistakes or to truly learn from them and carry those lessons forward. Some people never do figure it out. I guess you could chalk that up to human frailty. On the other hand, there's a certain level of maturity that some peo-ple seem to achieve long before their peers. As an exam-ple, when we were doolies in 34th Squadron at the Acad-emy and someone had asked, 'Someday, one of your 34th Squadron classmates is going to be chief of staff of the Air Force, who do you think it will be?' there would have been several possibilities. But the short list definitely would have included Nort Schwartz. Even at that point in his life, most of us recognized that he had an unusual level of maturity, focus, and commitment.

Nort is obviously an exceptional person, but the larger message is that, whether personally or professionally, com-mit yourself to the moment. We will always make mis-takes, but our goal should be to learn from them and to 'press on.'[141]

141 | Interview with Gary L. Anderson, May 2, 2022.

CHRIS TARAVELLA

Looking back on the last 50 years since USAFA graduation, I offer the following three take-aways that apply to me and may resonate with others: Never give up, do your best, and don't look back.

Chris Taravella
CS-21

First, never give up. Right next to my USAFA 1973 graduation diploma I have framed in my office a 20 November 1968 letter from the USAFA associate director of admissions. The letter was written in response to my congressman's appointment to USAFA, and states: 'The Director of Physical Standards has reviewed the results of the medical examination and has determined that you are disqualified medically for admission to the Air Force Academy because of excessive refractive error. A medical waiver for this disqualification cannot be granted.' And, in my current office, right next to my Chrysler Corporation picture of Lee Iacocca (Chrysler's former CEO and chairman of the board), I have a framed letter from a Chrysler associate general counsel, dated 12 November 1984. The letter was written in response to my application to work for Chrysler Corporation after leaving active duty in the Air Force, and states: 'Unfortunately, there are no positions currently available for attorneys with your experience.' It would have been easy to give up, and I thought about it. But, in both cases, I refused to take 'no' for an answer and continued to doggedly press ahead. As a result, I was accepted at the Academy. I had a 21-year Air Force career: 12 years on active-duty and nine years in the Air Force Reserve. And then I served as the general counsel for Chrysler Financial Corporation. So don't let the odds deter you. In the end, statistics only describe a central tendency. There are exceptions to just about every rule: be the exception. Don't settle for the average.

Second, always do your best. Toward that end, always give everything your best effort. Notwithstanding the cynical mantra that 'If the minimum weren't good enough, it wouldn't be the minimum,' you'll find it most rewarding to do the best you can at whatever you do. If you don't give everything your best effort and you subsequently fail, you'll never know whether your failure was due to an inherent limitation or because you didn't try hard enough. There will be times when you do your best and still fall short. But falling short doesn't necessarily mean you 'failed.' Are there lessons to be learned? Pick yourself back up, learn from the experience, and move on. Climbing back into the saddle may be difficult but, in my experience, it will ultimately pay handsome dividends.

Finally, don't look back. I've noticed that many people tend to focus on the past. In my view, that's a mistake. Looking back may cause regrets, and let's face it—you can't change what's already happened. That isn't to say we shouldn't learn from past experience, but when it's time to move on, it's time to move on. The more constructive approach is to learn from your mistakes, but don't dwell on the past. Living in the here and now is the key to happiness.[142]

---

142 | Interview with Christopher A. Taravella, May 26, 2022.

DON RIGHTMYER

Don Rightmyer
CS-02

My USAF career didn't turn out as I had expected.

When I arrived at the Academy in June 1969 my plan was to graduate, become a USAF pilot, and ultimately a NASA astronaut. During my second-class year, I found I wasn't qualified to fly at all because my eyesight had somehow gone from 20/20 to non-flying qualified. When I went to Cadet Personnel my first-class year to confirm what I thought was going to be an intelligence school slot, I was told the vision requirements for being a navigator had just changed and I could be a navigator, so I jumped on the opportunity to go to navigator training.

Following navigator training and checkout in the F-4, I had flying assignments in Korea, England, and West Germany. Once again though, my career took an unexpected turn. In the spring of 1978, I lost the vision in my right eye for a single day and was grounded from flight duty for the next five years. During my non-flying years, I served in wing intelligence and in the vice wing commander's office at Hahn Air Base, in the Office of Air Force History in Washington, D.C., and finally on the USAF Soviet Awareness Team at Bolling AFB. In 1985, MPC had me reevaluated for any vision problems—there were none— and I was returned to flying status and flew F-111s at Mountain Home AFB, Idaho. Later I edited and published TAC Attack magazine for four years at Langley AFB, VA, served in the NATO Southern Region at the 16th Air Force

War Support Center, and finished up my career at HQ USAFE editing USAFE's Air Scoop safety periodical.

One thing I did during my USAF career was to pursue every professional military education opportunity I could, to include Squadron Officers School (SOS), Air Command and Staff College, Air War College, and Naval War College by correspondence; and SOS in residence in the summer of 1978. Looking back, did my U.S. Air Force career and all my assignments go according to my plan? Not even close, but I had an interesting and challenging career, made significant contributions to the operational mission of the USAF, and was able to travel around the world.

Understand that the career plans you have as a new USAFA graduate may not match the 'real world' you encounter. My recommendation is to do your best wherever you are and always be ready to step up to unexpected challenges. In my experience, those unexpected challenges will teach you more about the ins and outs of the Air Force than you can ever imagine and, in the end, will lead to a rewarding career.[143]

PAUL TAYLOR

Like many of my classmates, I graduated from the Academy as an idealistic and somewhat naïve lieutenant. I quickly learned you can't take anything for granted— nothing in life is guaranteed. But 50 years of perspective taught me that life's toughest challenges can be overcome with faith, determination, and hard work.

143 | Interview with Donald W. Rightmyer, June 13, 2022.

I graduated from UPT at Williams AFB and was selected to return to Williams as a T-37 IP. While in pilot instructor training I had a serious motorcycle accident that resulted in critical injuries and grounding for nearly a year. I managed to return to flying status after a long recovery, but a freak sports injury four months later resulted in another six weeks of non-flying duties. My return to flying status seemed to be in jeopardy as I was medically grounded by the flight surgeon pending a full physical at Brooks AFB, and my chain of command was indifferent to my plight. As my flying career seemed increasingly doubtful, I decided to apply for law school. Unfortunately, I had to deal with administrative roadblocks put up by unsupportive commanders. But I kept at it, was accepted, and attended law school at Arizona State University. I served as a judge advocate for 13 years on active duty and another 16 in the Air Force Reserve. I retired in 2001 as a colonel.

Paul Taylor
CS-32

Looking back at the physical challenges, medical complications, administrative roadblocks, and lack of support from what seemed to be a capricious and unsympathetic system, my experiences taught me some hard-earned lessons. First, much as we'd like it to be otherwise, no system is perfect and there are injustices in the world. But all is not lost— the challenges you'll face can be overcome through dogged determination and perseverance. Second, there are good leaders and not-so-good leaders, and you need to recognize what makes the difference. Resolve to be one of the good ones who work hard to support their people. Third, character matters, and your character will really show in times of difficulty. In the end, that character is what will pull you out of the toughest situations. And lastly, never give up, even when things are at their most bleak. With perseverance, hard work, and strong character, you can turn things around.[144]

JOHN MANN

John Mann
CS-25

My Air Force career of nearly 25 years was a bit different from most of my peers. I avoided many of the assignments considered 'essential' for a successful career. Instead, I pursued jobs/assignments that supported critical Air Force missions and to which I thought I could make a valuable contribution. In my view, if I did a good job and served well, the career would take care of itself.

Two formative experiences defined that approach toward my career. The first occurred in the fall of my doolie year. My vision had begun to get fuzzy, and I had gone to the Cadet Clinic for help. But, instead of help, I was simply told I was no longer pilot qualified and would never fly; case closed. When I questioned that, the USAFA chief flight surgeon told me I'd never fly and that, if I ever did manage to get to pilot training, I'd never be any good. I left thinking, 'Okay, I'm on my own. Now, how do I fix this?' Thanks to an upper classman, I connected with a civilian optometrist who prescribed hard contacts that would correct my vision to 20/20. I wore them religiously for nearly three years, and they worked. I managed to pass the eye

144 | Interview with Paul W. Taylor, July 31, 2022.

exams and, upon graduation, was off to UPT. But I had learned a valuable lesson: don't leave things to chance. Take responsibility for your own future.

The second formative experience happened near the end of UPT, as we were sitting around debating the merits of an assignment to this or that aircraft. The vice wing commander stopped by and told us we were using the wrong criteria, that the aircraft was less important than the mission. He recommended we prioritize the mission we wanted first, and then pursue the aircraft that best supported that mission. He told us that, throughout our careers, it would be the job that we would find most rewarding and advised us to pursue the job that best matched our aspirations. Even though I was a headstrong lieutenant, I paid attention, and I'm so glad I did. I went on to fly the F-4D/E, the F-15, and several models of the MiG-21 and MiG-23 in squadrons around the world. Along the way, I served in many important Air Force organizations.

So the lesson I learned was to take responsibility for my career—no one was going to do that for me. As it turned out, that would often require negotiating skills. For example, when I was a first lieutenant flying the F-4E in Korea, I called the personnel center to talk to my 'career manager' about my next assignment. He told me I was due to leave the F-4 and fly the O-2. The O-2 was obsolete and had no mission. I countered by asking him what the crummiest, most hard-to-fill F-4 job there was. He replied, 'Holloman AFB,' to which I replied I was the strongest possible volunteer to go to Holloman. Ten days later, I had orders to Holloman—it was a win-win.

It often seemed I was on my own. Nearly every commander I had advised me that I needed to fill this or that square to manage my career, and that they would not support the path I wanted to pursue. Several predicted that, if I pursued a particular assignment, it would ruin my career. The career managers at the personnel centers often said the same things. But I stuck to my guns and experienced tremendous job satisfaction in every assignment I pursued. Further, the career-ending predictions turned out to be incorrect, as I was promoted early to both lieutenant colonel and colonel.

My bottom-line advice would be to avoid being a career 'square filler.' Don't be afraid to let your idea of mission and service guide your aspirations. Always do your absolute best. Establish a great reputation. Let that combination define your Air Force or Space Force career, and you'll do well.[145]

CHARLIE FELTON

I honestly thought I had my life figured out before I stepped on the plane to Colorado Springs. After all, my father was a 1941 Annapolis grad who saw his first action at Pearl Harbor, and my grandfather was a 1917 West Point grad who commanded the 11th Armor Division for the D-Day landing at Normandy and fought under Gen. Patton on

---

145 | Interview with John C. Mann, July 25, 2022.

the march to Berlin. Both were career officers, and I was proud to be following in their footsteps.

After graduation, I went to UPT and was assigned to B-52s. It wasn't my first choice, or my second, or even my third. But, as my father and grandfather told me, there are no bad assignments—they're all what you make of them. So I studied and worked hard, and my efforts paid off. I was assigned to high-visibility test crews, won Crew of the Year, won bomb competitions, and was assigned to standardization/evaluation as a young first lieutenant. I had solid OERs and applied for the first class of the new Uniformed Services University of the Health Sciences (med school). After my interview, I was told I was conditionally accepted and could expect orders within a few months. Everything was going my way—or so I thought.

Charlie Felton
CS-10

After the bombing in Vietnam ended, Strategic Air Command (SAC) found itself overstaffed with air crews, and squadron commanders had to ground several pilots. Since I seemed to be headed for med school, my commander asked me to give up my pilot slot and take a temporary staff assignment until my orders arrived, which I agreed to do. But it was during that assignment that my fortunes changed. The letter from med school came, but it was not orders—I was informed the congressional appropriation for the new med school had been indefinitely postponed. Suddenly, I was in trouble: I was grounded and sidelined in a go-nowhere staff job, writing lesson plans, while my contemporaries were becoming instructor pilots, working on master's degrees, and going to professional schools. As I saw it, I had been derailed from the fast track and was rapidly falling behind.

I truly believed I was screwed. Wanting desperately to salvage my career, I took my situation all the way up to the SAC director of operations. He agreed my planned career path was shot, and suggested I get an airline job and finish my career through the Air Force Reserve or Air National Guard. That meeting left me angry and disillusioned. A few weeks later, I left the Air Force.

I did get hired by a major airline. But, in another twist of fate, the airline industry fell on hard times, and I was furloughed before my new-hire class convened. So, there I was, with a wife, two kids, a new mortgage, two car payments, and no job. I had encountered tough times at USAFA, but nothing like this. On the other hand, USAFA taught me that, when faced with a tough problem, you gather your resources, make a plan, and execute. You always move forward and stick with the plan. Resilience and persistence will ultimately pay off.

So I met with job recruiters, mailed dozens of resumes, and went to every job fair I could find. Remarkably, I was hired by a Department of Defense contractor to learn nuclear engineering and train U.S. Navy personnel how to operate nuclear submarine propulsion systems. That job led to a training management position with a large nuclear utility. Ironically, the resume credential that helped me land that job came from that 'go-nowhere' staff position that I believed had ended my Air Force career.

The instructional systems development course I completed while grounded was considered leading edge, and as a result, was in high demand in the private sector. The next thing I knew, I was managing the development of new simulator training programs and consulting with training organizations across the nuclear industry.

I was also able to find a non-flying Air Force Reserve position. While none of it was as fulfilling or enjoyable as my time on active duty, it did qualify me for retirement benefits. And, after 20 years in nuclear energy, I left the industry and spent the last 20 years flying for a world-renowned private jet company.

Looking back, I'd say the moral of this story is there are no certainties in life. Despite your best efforts, forces outside your control can take your life in directions you never anticipated. Looking back, I lost sight of my long-term goals when things went sideways. I was so upset about losing my cockpit slot and the chance for med school that I became more concerned with recovering what I thought I had lost, rather than regrouping and going after other opportunities. As it turned out, the pilot overage situation resolved itself in a couple of years. Had I just kept moving forward, I would have put myself back on track with minimal impact to my career. Instead, I let myself become a victim. I became disgruntled, angry, and made an impulsive decision to leave active duty—a choice I've regretted for decades.

My advice is this: never lose sight of your long-term goals, no matter what life throws at you. Almost everyone I know has had a 'less than desirable' assignment in their career, but how you choose to deal with it is what matters. Always look for opportunities to expand your professional knowledge and skills, and you'll find new paths that you never even considered.[146]

MIKE MOSIER

Mike Mosier
CS-34

When I consider 'coulda, woulda, shoulda' issues, my conclusion is that I should have taken my career more seriously in the first few years. For instance, while I loved flying, I was more focused on regaining a 'normal' social life in pilot training, rather than studying for academic exams. As a result, I got my last choice of assignments. You'd think that would have been a wake-up call, but it really didn't change my immature behavior. But after a few years of aimlessly drifting along, I realized that if I was going to stay in the Air Force I'd have to take my responsibilities seriously. Fortunately, it wasn't too late, and things worked out in the long run. Still, I regret having been one of the proverbial 'late bloomers,' because it was an unnecessary distraction from more important issues I should have dealt with and contributions I could have made.

Along those lines, it's always easy to wonder, 'What would have happened if I had gone left instead of right?' While that kind of intellectual exercise may be interesting, in my experience it's a waste of time, as you can't change the past—you can only learn from it. But with the right attitude, things always seem to work out for the best. For instance, after being selected for Senior Service School, we were all required to fill out a 'dream sheet,' listing our top war college choices. I put National War College first. I figured that would be everyone's number one choice, as it was considered the premier institution for up-and-comers. Without really thinking about it, I instinctively put the NATO Defence College second, primarily because I had served at the US Embassy in Germany and had an interest in European affairs. But, like the National War College, relatively few were selected to attend the more obscure NATO Defence College, just based on numbers. In fact, only six Americans from all services were selected for each class. So, from that standpoint I figured it was probably a 'throwaway' selection. My next choice was Air War College—the most likely assignment—followed by Naval War College and then Army War College. Given the odds, I fully expected to be sent to Air War College, so I sat back and waited for my orders.

Imagine my (and my wife's) shock when I got orders to report to Rome, Italy rather than Montgomery, Alabama. Wow. The logistics alone were a real challenge, from pulling kids out of the middle of the school year and finding a new school in Rome, to locating appropriate housing in an 'unsupported' location. But that assignment led to three years at U.S. European Command Headquarters in Stuttgart, Germany, and another three years as the Joint Chiefs of Staff representative to the U.S. Mission to the Organization for Security and Cooperation in Europe, in Vienna, Austria. During that critical six years, I was privileged to have a front row seat to the drawdown and reconfiguration of U.S. forces in Europe, the immediate aftermath of the war in Bosnia, the struggles of the former Soviet states, NATO Enlargement, arms control negotiations with the newly created Russian Federation, and a fascinating trip to Serbia and Kosovo on the eve of war. Furthermore, my family had some life-changing travel opportunities. So, while my war college selection may not have been particularly well-considered, it all worked out for the best.

For me, the takeaway is first, to work hard from day one, because it builds expertise and opens up future options. Second, plan ahead to the extent you can, but realize that in our business, life is rarely predictable. Finally, keep a positive attitude and view the unexpected as an opportunity, rather than as a derailment. Buckle up—it'll be a great ride!

ORVILLE WRIGHT

Orville Wright
CS-39

As you take this leadership journey, there are three things worth keeping in the front of your mind. First, in every organization you'll serve in, both in and out of the military, there are always people who will stand out for things like outstanding subject area expertise, intellectual or physical ability, or even personality traits. But, even among these standout performers, there are varying levels of character. In the end, character is the ultimate measure and that's what you'll be judged by. Furthermore, in my experience, character doesn't tend to change—the people who were good people at 18 are still good people at 71.

Second, remember that you always need to hold yourself accountable, particularly to the institution you represent. Whether you go to France, the UK, Australia, or Japan, you'll find that other military academies want to look a lot like the Air Force Academy. For that reason, you'll be looked at as an exemplar among military professionals worldwide. That doesn't mean you're better than anybody else—only that you should always strive to live up to the highest standards of our Academy.

Finally, be thankful that you graduated from an institution that continues to provide strong and principled leadership across the organizational spectrum, not only in our military, but throughout industry, education, nonprofits, charitable foundations, and entrepreneurial ventures as well. I challenge each and every one of you to maintain that great legacy of leadership as a member of the Long Blue Line.[147]

KEES RIETSEMA

Reflecting back over the years, we all can identify time/places where we might have made different leadership decisions. Sometimes it was within the context of organizational leadership; at other times, it was within the context of self-leadership. None of us is perfect. At times our thinking was

Kees Rietsema
CS-14

147 | Interview with Bruce A. Wright, July 1, 2022.

flawed; at other times, not so much. That said, we all will continue to make leadership decisions, professionally and personally, as we march into the sunset. These decisions will be guided by our experiences as well as the values we hold dear, many of which were birthed and developed as part of our Academy lives.

If we're really honest with ourselves, most of us can also identify how we have literally changed our perspectives over time. As you've read, we were 'raised' at an Academy that reflected the tenor of the times, when 'men were men' and strength was perceived to be about strong and forceful direction. Fifty years ago, as we sat in Arnold Hall and listened to Robin Olds, I venture to say that few of us questioned his fervor, his commitment, his talents as a combat aviator, and his ability to 'lead.' Nevertheless, times have changed, and we have changed...along with the nature of society and how organizations are led. So-called traditional, 'top-down' leadership is not passe (there are certainly times and places for it!), but it has been joined by other ways of thinking about how to lead organizations. Concepts like complexity, diversity, servant leadership, empathy, transformative leadership and others have provided us with additional tools. I know they have become part of the discussions at USAFA and, as one who has studied leadership for most of my adult life, I endorse that completely. I recall the words of Lt. Gen. Bob Kelley (now deceased) who once told me that we 'are all trainable'—words to live by!

On the other hand, we also see that there are some threads of leadership that have not changed; rather, they have become even more salient over the past few years. The importance of concepts like fundamental values, organizational culture, personal accountability and responsibility, humility, listening to others, and teamwork have not changed. In fact, they represent the touchstones of organizational success. While our weapons systems and tools have advanced with technology, the human software that operates them and leads organizational members remains the same.

It is in this spirit that we have collected and offered the stories of our lives (Academy experiences as well as beyond) to you for your consideration and, at times, your entertainment. We know you will all be successful in your own ways, and we hope that, as you peruse these pages, you will find bits and pieces of our lives that will help inform you as you assume the reins of our Air and Space Forces.[148]

148 | Interview with Kees W. Rietsema, July 17, 2022.

CONCLUSION

As we approached graduation, we excitedly talked about the future that lay ahead. In late-night sessions with our roommates and buddies, we often compared notes about the heroes we wanted to become. Although the war in Southeast Asia was winding down, we assumed that combat would be in our future, and we were determined to follow in the footsteps of those who surrounded us. But a point generally lost on us was that heroics are often demonstrated on a day-to-day basis, under less dramatic circumstances: acting honorably and consistently doing the right thing, regardless of the pressures or consequences; putting organizational success ahead of individual recognition or personal advancement; and doing your job as best you can under the most trying of circumstances. In the end, those are the same Core Values we recognize today: Integrity First, Service before Self, and Excellence in All We Do.

We had been taught the fundamentals during our time on the Terrazzo, in the classrooms, and on the athletic fields, but the more difficult challenge of consistently applying these values in the "real world" lay ahead. Unfortunately, our ability to learn from those who preceded us was limited. Other than the occasional "war story" told by motivating instructors at the end of a class, most of us had few opportunities to benefit from personal insights or introspective conversations with exemplars at the Academy. Furthermore, there were no "legacy classes" to offer advice. So we started our careers with high hopes, and no clear idea of what lay ahead. To that extent, we were making it up as we went along: talking with classmates who were on the same path and getting advice where we could, doing our best to serve in whatever position we found ourselves, and ultimately relying on the fundamental lessons we had learned during our time as cadets.

Our early years were ones of transition and adaptation, from the black-and-white idealism of the Academy to the gray tones of the "Real Air Force." One of our early hard-earned lessons was that core values, regardless of how deeply engrained they may be, won't always keep us from making mistakes—life is inherently messy and, in the end, we're all human. But the values we learned at the Academy provided us with a compass to find our way in difficult times, helped us recover when we made the inevitable mistakes, and paved the way on our journey to becoming leaders of character during an era of fundamental change. And given that change is a dominant feature of today's society, strong, principled, and stabilizing leadership will continue to be as essential as ever to assure the continued success of our foundational institutions. For those who aspire to become leaders of character, this will be your charge.

So, to the Class of '23: the Academy has prepared you well for a life of service, and now it's your turn. We pass you the sword to defend our great Nation with this advice: follow your passion, always do your best, and let the Air Force Core Values be your guide as you take your place in the Long Blue Line.

APPENDIX A

TAKING RESPONSIBILITY: A MESSAGE TO CADETS IN RETROSPECT

by Brigadier General (Ret.) Malham Wakin

Note from our class president: The importance of honor and character at the Academy had no better benefactor or mentor than Brig. Gen. Mal Wakin. He was there at the beginning and guided its development for nearly 60 years. The Class of 1973's honorary member induction script following this essay gives a more in-depth explanation of his tremendous contributions, as well as why we recognize Gen Wakin as an honorary member of our class.

BGen Mal Wakin
Head, Department of
Philosphy and Fine Arts

L adies and gentlemen, I come to address you as one who experienced fully the agonizing and disrupting throes of the Academy's first and perhaps most unsettling cheating episode in 1965 and numerous other outbreaks of bad character behavior through the late sixties and seventies. I was also caught up in the frustrating failures evidenced in our 1984 cheating problems, which were so disturbing that we suspended the honor system for six months while we had cadets and officers study the issues before we reestablished a system that was voted on and overwhelmingly approved by the Cadet Wing.

In this paper, I want to pursue with you in a very serious way the theme of "Taking Responsibility" for our character training program at an institution where we frequently are reminded of our mission to develop officers of character.

First of all, we may legitimately ask, "Why all this fuss about incidents involving bad behavior?" The first and most obvious answer to that question is that bad behavior is the outward evidence of bad character. Now, good people sometimes do bad things as an aberration, but they can recover. Consistently doing bad things is a clear indication of bad character. Mom and Dad and the commandant and the superintendent can all tell us what they think good behavior is. Only you, each individual, can be responsible for the development of your own character. Knowledge alone is not enough. Knowledge is necessary, but it is not sufficient. It takes moral courage to do the right thing all the time and no one can give that kind of courage.

Good leaders set good examples and that helps. Are you helping your peers and your fellow cadets in the lower classes? Is that not one of your clear responsibilities as a potential officer leader? Aren't the citizens of this country providing you an education and paying you to do that? When you fail in this responsibility, have you done something morally wrong? When you set a bad example, have you abrogated an important duty?

What are the qualities or attributes of character that are especially connected with the reason you are here at the Academy? That's easy! You know what they are. You can't be a good officer leader if you lack integrity and that includes your whole character—your truthfulness, your honesty, your reliability, your trustworthiness, your sense of responsibility, and so forth. Ralph Waldo Emerson told us: "Who you are speaks so loudly I can't hear what you are saying." George Washington said: "I hope I shall always possess firmness and virtue enough to maintain the most enviable of titles, the character of an honest man."[149]

But, in addition to integrity, which is crucial in our profession (unlike corporations like Enron, in our profession, when we lie, our people die), we absolutely require loyalty, and obedience, and courage, and selflessness, or we can't do the basic job of the military profession. Those are the qualities of character necessary for the military profession. We have to have them. And we have to instill them in our subordinates because, if they don't have them, no military enterprise will ever succeed. Are you exhibiting loyalty to the Honor Code or to your institution or your profession when you ignore bad behavior? Are you exhibiting courage and selflessness when you engage in binge drinking?

There is no mysterious secret about acquiring good character. People of common sense from Aristotle to George Washington to your Mom and Dad have always known how that happens. We must practice those good character traits ourselves until they become habits. The resulting behavior is obvious—if we practice doing bad things, we become bad people. If we practice doing the right things, we become good people. Are there daily opportunities at the Air Force Academy to practice doing the right things?

Ask Lance Sijan where he acquired the courage and perseverance to crawl through the infested jungle, with a broken leg and no food or

149 | Ralph Waldo Emerson, *The Works of Ralph Waldo Emerson*, vol. 8 (Letters and Social Aims) [1909]. Retrieved on February 2, 2020 from https://oll.libertyfund.org/titles/emerson-theworks-of-ralph-waldo-emerson-vol-8-lettersand-social-aims

water, evading the enemy for over 40 days and later, while dying, over-powered a guard and escaped again. Ask Sijan where he acquired the loyalty and selflessness to wave away the rescue helicopter while his rescuer was already coming down the ladder, but he knew the enemy was all around them.

Where did Karl Richter cement the courage, loyalty, and selflessness that led him to volunteer for his 198th mission over North Vietnam from which he did not return?

Some of us at the Academy are clearly acting like persons of bad character.

We are practicing doing the wrong things, and we are not practicing doing those actions that develop our integrity, our obedience, our loyalty, our courage, and our selflessness. Surely, it is a good thing to step back from the furious pace of cadet life and ask ourselves if we ought to be doing something about this state of affairs that involves bad behavior. Does each one of us have some responsibility for developing good character in ourselves and others here at the Academy? Do you have some responsibility for setting the right example for your fellow cadets?

When one becomes a member of a public service profession, one takes on the responsibility of manifesting and protecting the standards of conduct of that profession. Your Honor Code is an example of how you pledge to act as a professional person. It does not tell the whole story of good character, but it certainly is an important part of that story. Codes of conduct, written or unwritten, are a crucial part of every profession. If a heart surgeon, who is part of a surgical team, notices that one of her colleagues is losing many more patients than any other member of the surgical team, should she be concerned? If, when assisting that surgeon, she realizes that his technique is not up to the current professional standards and that he has a strong smell of alcohol on his breath during surgery, should she do something about her colleague? Should she help him bury his mistakes or should she accept responsibility for upholding the standards of their profession? Take some time now, today, to seriously evaluate your own attitude toward this issue. Please take note of those seemingly small everyday behaviors that really are building your character and avoid the bad ones and practice doing the right thing. When the critical time comes, perhaps in combat, those good habits or those bad ones that you have practiced will determine how you behave. The citizens of this Republic are counting on you to become the leader of good character, who in a crisis will not hesitate to do the right thing on their behalf.

And that takes me back to the reason I began this conversation with references to previous episodes at the Academy that prompted us to take timeouts to review our approach to character building. Sometimes we fail to recognize that, as members of the Academy, we are not really private citizens. We have chosen and have been selected to serve our fellow citizens in a very special and very public way. When we act, we act on behalf of those citizens and always as representatives of their Academy and their Air Force. This is not a bad thing. If we were mere mercenaries, it would be a bad thing. But we are not paid outsiders. Like our policemen, and firemen, and teachers, and doctors, and judges, and ministers, we exist because there is now and probably always will be a need to defend our society as importantly as there is a need for domestic protection, and education, and justice, and health care. More visibly than the other professions, we are entrusted with a huge share of the national budget and such powerful weapons that with them we could tomorrow destroy all of humanity. Our citizens have the right to be assured that, when we use that military instrument on their behalf, we have the appropriate character to make critical decisions in all moral circumstances. They have entrusted their children to our commands and have given us complete authority over their lives. In the character crises of 1965 and 1984 at this Academy, people, including those highly placed in our government, began to question the need for an Air Force Academy if there were some doubt that it could fulfill the mission of developing leaders of character for our nation. Every member of the Academy community carries the reputation of the institution on his or her shoulders every day. From time to time, the behavior of some of our people has raised those nagging questions about the character component of good leadership. I am asking each member of the Academy family to resolve to take responsibility for the development of your own good character and to provide a good example for all of our cadets.

I'd like to conclude these reflections with some remarks by General Matthew Ridgway concerning events in WWII when the outcome for the free world was hanging in the balance. He said:

> *During a critical phase of the Battle of the Bulge, when I commanded the 18th Airborne Corps, another corps commander just entering the fight next to me remarked: 'I'm glad to have you on my flank. It's character that counts.' I had long known him, and I knew what he meant. I replied: 'That goes for me, too.' There was no amplification. None was necessary. Each knew the other would stick, however great the pressure; would extend help before it was needed if he could; and would tell the truth, seek no self-glory, and everlastingly keep his word. Such feeling breeds confidence and success.* [150]

Today, I ask you to ask of yourself, are you doing the kinds of things you must every day to make yourself into the kind of person about whom anyone would say: "I'm glad to have you on my flank!" "I'm glad to have you as my wingman." Surely, you know, it really is character that counts!

150 | General Matthew Ridgeway, "Leadership," Military Review, October 1966, p. 41. Retrieved on February 2, 2020, from http://cgsc.contentdm.oclc.org/cdm/singleitem/collection/p124201coll1/id/634/rec/2

At our 45th Reunion, Gen. Wakin was inducted as an honorary member of the Class of 1973. Here is the induction script:

Only two individuals have been inducted as an honorary member of an Air Force Academy graduating class: President Dwight D. Eisenhower by the Class of 1959 and President John F. Kennedy by the Class of 1963. Tonight, we induct the third honorary member in Academy history and the first for the Illustrious Class of 1973. In arriving at criteria for such a distinction, we settled upon an individual steeped in integrity who has made significant contributions to the Academy, our Air Force, and our Nation. Ladies and gentlemen, that individual is Brig. Gen. Malham M. Wakin.

Mal Wakin is emeritus professor of Philosophy at the United States Air Force Academy. He taught at the Air Force Academy from 1959 to 2016. He served as professor and head of the Department of Philosophy, chairman of the Humanities Division, assistant dean, associate dean, head of the Department of Philosophy and Fine Arts, head of the Political Science and Philosophy Department, and chair and member of numerous academic committees.

Gen. Wakin served on active duty with the Air Force from 1953 to 1995, including early tours as an Air Rescue navigator and a combat tour in Vietnam in 1968. He holds a number of military decorations, including the Distinguished Service Medal, and three Legions of Merit.

Gen. Wakin authored or edited five books, the most recent being Integrity First, Reflections of a Military Philosopher. He also published many articles in scholarly journals. He was featured as one of twelve "great professors" in People Magazine, Oct. 13, 1975, and was the subject of a feature article in the Nov. 19, 1984, issue of Newsweek. He helped found and then chaired the Joint Services Conference on Professional Ethics from 1979 to 1993. He served as ethics advisor to the U.S. Olympic Committee for 13 years. Gen. Wakin, during the seventies, eighties, and nineties, averaged 40 outside lectures a year in the United States, Europe, and Canada. He was the Air Force representative on the Department of Defense Medical

Ethics Committee for several years and served on a number of community medical ethics committees.

Gen. Wakin earned a B.A. from Notre Dame, an M.A. from State University New York in Albany, and a Ph.D. from the University of Southern California. He has also been awarded three honorary degrees.

In closing, here is an abstract from an academic journal article published in 1995 that singles out Gen. Wakin's extraordinary contributions to honor and character:

> *Prof. Manuel M. Davenport, in a tribute to Col. Mal Wakin entitled 'Ethics and Leadership,' examines Col. Wakin's views and qualities of leadership, comparing them with those of Albert Schweitzer, whom Prof. Davenport met in 1960. He claims that Wakin's and Schweitzer's views of leadership are quite similar. Wakin's concepts of competence and integrity parallel Schweitzer's technical expertise and moral authority. Both provide examples of transformational leadership. Schweitzer's Reverence for Life shares aspects of Wakin's discussions of Natural Law theory, and both men exemplify strong leadership. Prof. Davenport holds that, by emulating Wakin and Schweitzer, we will become better leaders as well as better persons.*

APPENDIX B

THE HONOR CODE AND THE CLASS OF 1973

by Colonel (Ret.) John Stefonik

We will not lie, steal or cheat, nor tolerate among us anyone who does."

Simple enough, it would seem. How many of us who arrived at the Air Force Academy in June of 1969 gave it much thought—within a week there was not much thinking but lots of "yes, Sir, no, Sir"? However, always in the background, seeping through the cracks in the Terrazzo, covering AFA like an east-driven dense fog

John Stefonik
CS-20

backing up against the Front Range of the Rocky Mountains, mentioned occasionally by upperclassmen, spoken of in only about 12 hours of instruction—it was there, with us; and, like it or not, we were subject to the Honor Code's iron commandments.

The Code language when we entered the Academy in June 1969 was the same as the Code voted upon and adopted by the Class of 1959 in 1955 on a one-year trial basis. The evolved language of the Code was taken word for word from West Point, which did not have a formal Code until 1921, when Douglas McArthur was Superintendent. As implemented, it said "A Cadet is fundamentally honest, and therefore taken at his word." Early on (West Point was established in 1802), West Point had a "vigilance system" to deal with wayward cadets. When the Code moved west, AFA added several regulations concerning its implementation and enforcement.

From 1969 to 1973 and beyond, the Air Force Academy had an Honor Committee composed of honor representatives elected from each squadron. Each "Honor Rep" was given supplemental training. If an Honor Code violation was alleged, an investigation was commenced and, if there was deemed to be sufficient basis, an Honor Board was convened to determine "guilt or innocence" (the "guilt or innocence" language was later changed to "violation"). A cadet found "guilty" of a Code infraction was asked to resign, and most did. "Discretion" was possible but rarely used, and the cadet could be retained at the Academy; however, a fully developed, graduated response to Honor deviations was not available until many years later. In fact, prior to 1961, guilty meant disenrollment—period.

SOURCES OF AUTHORITY FOR THE HONOR CODE

Why an Honor Code? Doesn't the military have a sufficient disciplinary system? Well, a modern Uniform Code of Military Justice ("UCMJ") did not make its appearance until May of 1951.

Before the UCMJ, there were the Articles of War for the Army, and the Articles for the Government of the Navy. As said above, West Point came into existence in 1802, the Naval Academy in 1845; and, although it was maintained all along that the military justice system set the bare minimum of acceptable conduct, something more was required of Academy cadets and military officers.[151]

Hence, an Honor Code, or Concept, was agreed upon by and among

151 | *Fictionalized name.

cadets and enforced by cadets. Therefore, agreement among cadets is the basic source of the honor system, as opposed to the Code of Conduct imposed by military regulations and a commander's lawful orders flowing from the U.S. Constitution and federal statutes.

'73'S EXPERIENCE WITH THE HONOR CODE

In 1972—our second-class year—there was a serious honor incident at the Air Force Academy. In fact, what later became known as the 1972 honor scandal only involved members of the Class of 1973. The *1972 Polaris* described how the scandal unfolded, the scope of the infractions, and the attitude within the cadet wing at the time.

> *During the week of 9-15 January [1972], Cadet Smith* was dismissed for violating the Honor Code by cheating. Prior to his hearing, the evidence in the case was stolen. Approximately 10:30 PM on Wednesday 19 January 1972, ten members of the Honor Committee and the cadet wing commander were questioning two cadets suspected of stealing a pair of ski boots, cadets Ronson* and Brown*. During this questioning, Ronson* divulged the names of the two cadets who had stolen the evidence in Smith's* cheating case the previous week. Cadet Ronson* also admitted that he had been involved in cheating with others in the 40th Squadron, implicating several second classmen. The Honor Committee realized that more assistance would be required to properly conduct the investigation, so they assembled the squadron commanders and the first-class honor representatives from squadrons 1-23, those in Vandenberg Hall. These cadets went to 40th Squadron in the new dorm and asked those cadets who had been implicated to come to Wing Staff for an important meeting. The cadets were not informed as to*

the purpose of that meeting. There, they were questioned in the squadron assembly rooms across from Wing Staff. During this phase of the investigation, Cadet Jacobs* of 40th Squadron implicated the entire second class of 33rd Squadron. Jacobs* also admitted to the use of drugs and implicated several other cadets in drug abuse. At approximately 5:00 AM Thursday morning, the Honor Committee and their assistants went to 33rd Squadron and escorted the second classmen to the Wing Staff area for questioning. Shortly before breakfast, the members of the Academy wrestling team were implicated. The individuals were called in. Some were detained for more thorough questioning; others were released after it was determined that they were not involved. At approximately 7:00 AM Thursday morning, all squadron commanders and first-class honor representatives were called to a briefing, the purpose of which was to inform them of the activities of the previous night and enlist their aid in conducting the investigation. Most of these individuals served as messengers or were placed in the assembly rooms to ensure that the cadets being questioned did not talk to one another.

As rumors had been received by the press and it was undetermined whether more cadets would be implicated Thursday afternoon, privileges were cancelled, and the telephones were restricted to official calls only. Commenting on the reasoning behind these two moves, Cadet Col. Charles M. Hardman, the Cadet Wing Commander, stated, 'The reason I restricted privileges was that at that particular time the names of individuals were accumulating rapidly. 33rd Squadron second classmen were suddenly implicated very early Thursday morning. Shortly before breakfast, the wrestling team was implicated. By noon, 15 more had been implicated and another 10 that afternoon. So the reason we cancelled privileges was that throughout that time individuals' names were coming up, and we needed to have ready access to those individuals for immediate questioning. With respect to the phones, we didn't want to leak to the press until we knew exactly what was happening. We did get a leak that morning that perhaps did more than anything to prompt the phone restriction. A cadet called a local paper and reported that there was a 'mass honor scandal involving up to 400 cadets.' We felt it was necessary to limit that type of false information as quickly as possible until we had the opportunity to organize a press conference to let the news services know exactly what was happening. We didn't want to blow this up into a national issue before we even had the opportunity to discover for ourselves how large the thing was, how the investigation would proceed, and how many cadets were involved.'

There had been some query as to whether any undue pressure was brought to bear on any of the cadets during the investigation. In reference to this subject, both Cadet Hardman and Cadet First Class Gary R. Adriance, vice-chairman of the Honor Committee, who were present throughout the investigation, stated that at no time were any of the cadets being questioned physically touched. There were one or two individuals, however, who underwent rather severe interrogation; these few individuals experienced what could be likened to a 'doolie year special inspection' in that they stood at a position of attention, responding to all questions with the use of 'sir,' and

*received strong verbal attack. It was pointed out, how-
ever, that if these interrogations lasted more than a few
minutes, the cadets being questioned were allowed to sit
down. When consulted on this matter of undue pressure,
Col. Irving of the Law Department stated the legal basis
concerning the matter of undue pressure. Among several
reasons was because of the particular environment, that
is, cadets questioning cadets, none of the methods used in
questioning could be considered as "undue" pressure. This
was due to the fact that all cadets have experienced the
fourth-class system in which they were required to stand
at the position of attention at all times, responded to all
questions with the use of 'sir,' and received strong verbal
attack frequently. In other words, because this type of pressure was a part of each cadet's experience for ten months,
it could not be considered extreme or undue.[152]*

*Forty honor hearings were conducted during the period
20-21 January 1972. One 'not guilty' and 39 'guilty' decisions were returned by the Honor Committee. Of the
39 cadets found guilty, 12 violated only the toleration
clause. The investigation disclosed that 11 cadets were
using drugs, 9 of whom were also involved in cheating.
The 39 cadets found guilty of violating the Cadet Honor
Code and the other two cadets who had been using drugs
were allowed to resign; no formal court-martial proceedings were instigated.[153]*

*What implications are to be derived from this cheating
incident? Does it mean the Honor Code is ineffective and*

152 | Ibid, pp. 34-35.
153 | Ibid, p. 35.

disregarded by cadets? Hardly! Any Honor investigation is the very proof that the Honor Code is supported by the vast majority of the cadet wing in that it is the cadets themselves who initiate, conduct, and resolve any investigation concerned with the honorable or ethical standards of their peers. We should be much more concerned if honor investigations never came to light. Upon acceptance into the wing, each cadet accepts with his shoulder boards the responsibility of supporting the Honor Code. It is hoped that the Code will influence cadets to live honorably so they will graduate as officers with the highest standards of individual honor and integrity. The Cadet Wing expects each cadet to make the Cadet Honor Code a part of his personal code throughout his life.[154]

The honor scandal of 1972 was a shock to the institutional system and ultimately resulted in administrative reforms. But, on an individual level, it was a cautionary tale of the dangers of temptation, human frailty, and failing to live up to the high standards of personal conduct we had pledged to support. To that extent, it was a formative experience in our journey of becoming leaders of character.

While the Code appears "black and white," the administration of the Code is not without challenges—court cases have modified the Academy administration of the Honor Code over the years; a book by graduate attorney Mike Rose, *A Prayer for Relief*, has had an enormous impact on the Academy's view of "due process" as set forth in the U.S. Constitution and the process due a cadet facing expulsion for honor; Frederic Malmstrom published several informative articles in *Checkpoints* containing important analysis and insight into the Code as it has developed, and the analysis of the history of the Honor Code continues in a very recent

154 | Ibid, p. 36.

Checkpoints article.[155] Very simply, the Honor Code is a "Work in Progress." Academic research has suggested that Honor systems in general are inherently unstable and require constant monitoring and supervision—presumably by the officers assigned to the Academy.

While our class's experience was not unique, it has profound implications, even today.

155 | Randolph, Stephen P. "A Condensed History of the USAFA Honor Code and System." *Checkpoints AOG USAFA Alumni Magazine,* March 2022, pp. 34-41.

APPENDIX C

A SHORT HISTORY OF THE UNITED STATES AIR FORCE ACADEMY

Excerpt from the National Park Service[156]

Born in the first decade of the Cold War, the United States Air Force Academy provided the new military service with a trained and educated officer corps at a time when national policy placed unprecedented emphasis on air power. Its campus, set in magnificent natural surroundings at the foot of the Rampart Range in Colorado, ranks among the finest examples of modern movement architecture commissioned by Federal agencies during the post-World War II era.

The United States reorganized its military under the National Security Act of 1947, establishing the Air Force as an independent service equal to the Army and Navy. In 1954, the Federal government authorized the creation of the United States Air Force Academy (USAFA) to serve as the primary undergraduate educational institution of that new

156 | Retrieved on March 31, 2020 from https://www.nps.gov/articles/united-states-air-force-academy.htm

service, and it continues to serve as an important military educational institution today. It joined the other two major U.S. academies—the United States Military Academy at West Point, New York, and the United States Naval Academy at Annapolis, Maryland—as the nation's undergraduate military schools.

Following World War II, the United States entered into a 45-year confrontation with the Soviet Union known as the Cold War. Although it was the newest service, the Air Force emerged as the nation's primary military arm, resulting in a major expansion of its ranks. The new service required an influx of officers, leading to the establishment of the USAFA. In the face of technological advances, including a burgeoning nuclear arsenal, the new service academy educated those officers for the increasingly complex demands of military leadership. In addition, it helped to define the Air Force's identity as distinct from the Army and Navy.

Built between 1958 and 1968, the campus was designed by Skidmore, Owings and Merrill (SOM), and broke from the traditions of West Point and Annapolis with its architectural vocabulary to become "the first U.S. national shrine to be designed in the modern style," according to *Architectural Forum* magazine. Its buildings stirred a national debate in Congress, professional journals and the popular media during the early years of the Cold War. In a survey of federally built architecture, Lois Craig declared, "Perhaps no architectural debate over government buildings in the 1950s equaled the discussion about the design of the new U.S. Air Force Academy." The responses encapsulate many of the significant issues debated about architecture in the postwar era.

In particular, the Cadet Chapel is an exceptional example of postwar modern movement architecture. In the 1950s, while the United States engaged in the Cold War, American civil religion stood in contrast with "godless Communism." Historian Sydney Ahlstrom remarked of the decade, "There seemed to be a consensus that personal religious faith was an essential element in proper patriotic commitment." President

Dwight Eisenhower summarized the non-sectarian attitude, stating, "Our government makes no sense unless it is founded on a deeply felt religious faith—and I don't care what it is." The Academy carefully embraced three major beliefs with distinct worship spaces in the chapel for Catholics, Protestants, and Jews, expanding in recent years to include Muslim, Buddhist and other faiths.

APPENDIX D

"BRING ME MEN" NEWS ARTICLE BY ROCKY MOUNTAIN NEWS, JUNE 1964

One of the most visible differences between the Air Force Academy of 1973 and the Academy of 2023 is enshrined in silver letters on the wide arch above the Ramp, which leads from the Terrazzo down to the wide parade field below. Today, the message enshrined above the Ramp is a solemn reminder to the Cadet Wing of the Air and Space Force Core Values: Integrity First, Service Before Self, and Excellence in All We Do. However, from 1964 until 2003 the Academy's aspirations were expressed in the opening line from a 1894 poem written by Sam Walter Foss, entitled "Bring Me Men." The following article from the Rocky Mountain News, published in June 1964, explains the origins.

Glistening in large aluminum letters against granite of Battle Ramp arch at the U.S. Air Force Academy are the words: "Bring me men…"

The Academy's 2,700 cadets walk beneath the arch frequently to the central cadet area buildings. They meet friends and parents at the arch. They march beneath it to the parade ground.

"Bring me men…" is a phrase from a poem, *The Coming American*, written by Sam Walter Foss, a poet, journalist, and librarian. He read the poem at a Fourth of July celebration at Woodstock, Conn., in 1894.

Three-fourths of the 164-line poem consists of a somewhat light-hearted, but stirring, exhortation to the audience to summon moral strengths for the patriotic tasks ahead. "Our Great Faith, from the hills to the sea, has sent forth this call to the years yet to be," one line reads. Then the poem's three most famous stanzas follow and through them, with the austerity of drum rolls, are repeated the words: "Bring me men . . ."

Researching in the Academy library last year, hunting a phrase to place on the Battle Ramp to inspire cadets, Col. Ralph J. Hallenbeck, chief of staff, chose the phrase from Foss's poem.

Miss Mary L. Foss, of Somerville, Mass., daughter of the poet, when notified of the selection, said the choice "represents "the finest tribute that could be paid to my father." Foss died in 1911.

Col. Hallenbeck, who has brought three men to the Academy—sons Don, Ted and Rudy—hopes the phrase, placed on the arch in June 1964, will become one of the traditions at the Academy, and that the meaning will "grow on the cadets, their friends, and their visitors."

THE COMING AMERICAN

Bring me men to match my mountains,
Bring me men to match my plains,
Men with empires in their purpose,
And new eras in their brains.
Bring me men to match my prairies,
Men to match my inland seas,
Men whose thought shall pave a highway

Up to ampler destinies.
Pioneers to clear Thought's marshlands,
And to cleanse old Error's fen;
Bring me men to match my mountains—
Bring me men!

Bring me men to match my forests,
Strong to fight the storm and blast,
Branching toward the skyey future,
Rooted in the fertile past.
Bring me men to match my valleys,
Tolerant of sun and snow,
Men within whose fruitful purpose
Time's consummate blooms shall grow.
Men to tame the tigerish instincts
Of the lair and cave and den,
Cleanse the dragon slime of Nature—
Bring me men!

Bring me men to match my rivers,
Continent cleavers, flowing free,
Drawn by the eternal madness
To be mingled with the sea,
Men of oceanic impulse,
Men whose moral currents sweep
Toward the wide-unfolding ocean
Of an undiscovered deep.
Men who feel the strong pulsation
Of the Central Sea, and then
Time their currents to its earth throb—
Bring me men!

ACKNOWLEDGMENTS

At the risk of stating the obvious, there'd be no book without the willingness of our classmates to commit their experiences and hard-earned lessons to paper. Forty-eight of these outstanding public servants have contributed to *Becoming Leaders of Character* and, as the one privileged to bring their experiences and words of wisdom to light, I'm humbled beyond words.

The tyranny of time and space have limited the scope of this book. That's a sad omission, because so many other members of our class quietly work in the background to make their organizations, communities, and families strong and vibrant, and are truly exemplars of character-based leadership. I only wish we could have brought their contributions to light as well.

Any attempt to thank all the people who have brought *Becoming Leaders of Character* to life would inevitably fall short, as so many classmates have taken the time to wade through numerous drafts and provide helpful comments. Two in particular—my first roommate and ever-patient "thought partner" Bob Munson, as well as my high school buddy and classmate Steve Lorenz—offered critical insights and sound advice throughout the writing process. Many other classmates also provided valuable feedback along the way. Herb Harrison is a great example: I asked for his help while he was doing missionary work in

Tanzania. Herb downloaded the draft manuscript to his laptop through a sketchy internet system, read the entire manuscript, and compiled extensive notes during an exhausting 47-hour flight back to the U.S. I also owe a tremendous debt of gratitude to classmates John Stefonik, A.J. Ranft, Mike Arnett, Bob Allen, John Mann, and Don Rightmyer for their reviews and suggestions along the way, as well as to Felicia Recker from the Association of Graduates for her support. We're also indebted to Alliance Press—and to editor extraordinaire Janet Musick in particular—for expert guidance, endless patience, and unflagging support in bringing this book to fruition.

Every worthwhile cause requires a great champion, and ours has been the class president, Dr. Ron Scott. His initial inspiration and unflagging enthusiasm have made *Becoming Leaders of Character* a reality. Here's how Ron views the importance of this project, in his own words:

> *As we prepared to participate in the Legacy Program, we recognized the significance of being alive and able to connect with those who followed us 50 years later. This preparation also prompted great interest in doing something that would be truly memorable. This led to the idea for a book—a snapshot of one class's experiences as they related to character development and its challenges during their 'lived experiences.' This is the very essence of what is meant by the expression, 'The Long Blue Line.'*
>
> *In developing the manuscript, we sought a wide range of experiences, from military leadership and business endeavors, and other professions such as law and medicine. The common denominator for all was honor and the Air Force Core Values of Integrity First, Service Before Self, and Excellence in All We Do. This is our story—a snapshot of only one of the many classes to experience the Academy*

and its gateway to a lifetime of experiences grounded in honorable character.

Ron unselfishly dedicated a great deal of his time to schedule and help conduct the numerous interviews that form the basis of our story. His suggested storytelling methodology was the key to bringing what would otherwise be a series of biographies to life.

Last but certainly not least, my wife Sandra has been my rock throughout this whole journey. She has demonstrated endless patience over the past two plus years as I struggled to do justice to my classmates' experiences and weave them into a complete and cohesive narrative. I can't recount the number of times I turned to her and said, "Hey, take a look at this and tell me what you think." I know I can speak for my classmates when I say we're all stronger with our life's partner by our side, and I'm eternally grateful for mine.

Michael L. Mosier
Colorado Springs, Colorado.

Made in the USA
Las Vegas, NV
14 June 2023